The Borders, Citizenship and Imn

BLACKSTONE'S GUIDE TO

The Borders, Citizenship and Immigration Act 2009

Ian Macdonald QC, Laurie Fransman QC, Adrian Berry, Alison Harvey, Hina Majid, and Ronan Toal

OXFORD UNIVERSITY PRESS

OXFORD
UNIVERSITY PRESS

Great Clarendon Street, Oxford OX2 6DP

Oxford University Press is a department of the University of Oxford. It furthers the University's objective of excellence in research, scholarship, and education by publishing worldwide in

Oxford New York

Auckland Cape Town Dar es Salaam Hong Kong Karachi Kuala Lumpur Madrid Melbourne Mexico City Nairobi New Delhi Shanghai Taipei Toronto

With offices in

Argentina Austria Brazil Chile Czech Republic France Greece Guatemala Hungary Italy Japan Poland Portugal Singapore South Korea Switzerland Thailand Turkey Ukraine Vietnam

Oxford is a registered trade mark of Oxford University Press in the UK and in certain other countries

Published in the United States by Oxford University Press Inc., New York

First published 2010

British Library Cataloguing in Publication Data
Data available

Library of Congress Cataloging in-Publication Data

Blackstone's guide to the Borders, Citizenship and Immigration Act 2009/Ian Macdonald ... [et al.].
p. cm.
ISBN 978-0-19-957957-0 (acid-free paper)
1. Customs administration—Law and legislation—Great Britain.
2. Citizenship—Great Britain.
3. Emigration and immigration law—Great Britain.
4. Great Britain. Borders, Citizenship and Immigration Act 2009.
I. Macdonald, Ian A.
KD5689.B58 2010
342.4108'2—dc22
2009040539

Typeset by Glyph International, Bangalore, India
Printed in Great Britain
on acid-free paper by the
MPG Books Group, Bodmin and King's Lynn

ISBN 978-0-19-957957-0

1 3 5 7 9 10 8 6 4 2

Acknowledgements

Thanks are due to Steve Symonds, Legal Officer, ILPA, for his work on the Bill, to Tania Poscotis at Garden Court Chambers for her help in compiling the materials for this book, and to Faye Judges and Roxanne Selby at OUP for their patience, help, and encouragement.

The Nationality Instructions

In the Guide references are made to the UK Border Agency's Nationality Instructions. These may be found at: www.bia.homeoffice.gov.uk/policyandlaw/guidance/nationalityinstructions/ References to the Nationality Instructions in the Guide are to Volume 1 of the Instructions unless otherwise indicated.

Contents—Summary

Contents—Detailed

Table of Cases

Table of Legislation

Table of Statutes

Statutory Instruments

European Legislation

Regulations

Directives

Treaties, Conventions and Agreements

1
INTRODUCTION

A. THE BORDERS, CITIZENSHIP AND IMMIGRATION ACT 2009

The Borders, Citizenship and Immigration Act 2009 (BCIA 2009) received Royal Assent on 21 July 2009. It is comprised of four Parts. Part 1 concerns border functions, including customs functions, the designation of a Director of Border Revenue, provisions on the use and disclosure of information, and powers of investigation, detention, inspection, and oversight. Part 1 came into force on the day the BCIA 2009 was passed.[1] 1.01

Part 2 of the BCIA 2009 concerns citizenship[2] including the acquisition of British citizenship by naturalisation, the acquisition of British citizenship by the children of members of the armed forces, and the acquisition of British citizenship by registration by minors, British Nationals (Overseas), and descendants in the female line. The provisions of Part 2 come into force on such day as the Secretary of State may by order appoint.[3] The Government intends to commence the provisions that apply to naturalisation no earlier than July 2011 and the other remaining provisions in January 2010. 1.02

Part 3 of the BCIA 2009 concerns immigration including restrictions on studies, fingerprinting, and detention at ports in Scotland. The provisions on the restriction on studies came into force on the day the BCIA 2009 was passed.[4] The other provisions come into force on such day as the Secretary of State may by order appoint.[5] 1.03

---

1 BCIA 2009, s 58(1).
2 Citizenship is the title of Part 2 and in this context probably means nationality.
3 BCIA 2009, s 58(2).
4 Ibid, s 58(3)(a).
5 Ibid, s 58(3)(b).

1.04 Part 4 of the BCIA 2009 concerns miscellaneous matters including the transfer of some applications for judicial review from the High Court to the recently created Upper Tribunal, the trafficking of people for exploitation, and the duty regarding the welfare of children. The provisions in respect of judicial review come into force on such day as the Lord Chancellor may by order appoint[6] and likewise in respect of the provisions on trafficking people for exploitation and the duty regarding the welfare of children on such day as the Secretary of State may by order appoint.[7]

B. AN INTERIM BILL

1.05 On 6 June 2007 the Government announced that it intended to consolidate and 'simplify' all immigration legislation since the Immigration Act 1971 into a single Act.[8] On 20 February 2008 the Prime Minister made a speech[9] launching the Green Paper consultation *The Path to Citizenship: Next Steps in Reforming the Immigration System*,[10] which also gave details of the 'simplification' project.

1.06 Thereafter, a draft (Partial) Immigration and Citizenship Bill (the draft (Partial) Bill) was published in July 2008 together with Explanatory Notes, proposals for a full 'simplification' of immigration law,[11] and other drafts documents.[12] The original intention was that a full Bill on this would be introduced in the parliamentary session 2008–09.[13] This did not happen. The project timetable had slipped and a full Bill simply was not ready.[14] This did not surprise anyone, and had been predicted by many in their response to the first consultation on 'simplification'.[15] Instead the Government prioritized certain matters and proceeded with them first[16] in what is now the BCIA 2009.

1.07 Only certain provisions of BCIA 2009, Part 2 (Citizenship) and s 25 (short-term holding facilities), build on clauses first put forward in the draft (Partial) Bill. All the rest is new. Both the Joint Committee on Human Rights and the Home Affairs Committee had called for evidence on the draft (Partial) Bill. Thereafter, both

---

6 Ibid, s 58(4)(a).

7 Ibid, s 58(4)(b).

8 *Simplifying Immigration Law: An Initial Consultation* UK Border Agency (6 June 2007). *Simplifying Immigration Law: Responses to the Initial Consultation Paper* (6 December 2007).

9 Available at <http://www.number10.gov.uk/Page14624>.

10 UK Border Agency (20 February 2008).

11 *Making Change Stick: an Introduction to the Immigration and Citizenship Bill* Home Office (14 July 2008).

12 *Draft Illustrative Impact Assessment* UK Border Agency 25 June 2008); *Draft Illustrative Rules on Protection* UK Border Agency (August 2008).

13 UK Border Agency, National Asylum Stakeholder Forum, 22 May 2008, Minutes at 6.2.

14 See *The Government's Draft Legislative Programme: Summary of Consultation*, Cm 7561 (December 2008).

15 See for example ILPA Response to Consultation on Simplifying Immigration Law, August 2007, para 14, available at <http://www.ilpa.org.uk/Responses/SimplificationConsultation.pdf>.

16 HL Deb 11 February 2009 vol 707 c1128, per Lord West of Spithead, Parliamentary Under-Secretary of State, Home Office; see also c1202, per Viscount Bridgeman (Conservative).

Committees published their reports on the Borders, Citizenship and Immigration Bill.[17] Reports on the Bill were also published by the House of Lords Constitution Committee[18] and the House of Lords Delegated Powers and Regulatory Reform Committee.[19]

The current Government does not intend to include British nationality law in the postponed 'simplification' Bill[20] (see para **1.10** below) but instead has sought in the 2009 Act to make important but piecemeal changes to the British Nationality Act 1981 (BNA 1981),[21] entrenching the latter's position as the governing statute on the subject. 1.08

The Government has given an assurance that the naturalisation provisions of BCIA 2009, Part 2, will not come into force before July 2011.[22] In addition, the BCIA 2009 has made transitional provision so that (i) those who have applied for naturalisation before the date of commencement apply under the current provisions, and (ii) those who have indefinite leave to remain on the date of commencement, or have applied for indefinite leave to remain before the date of commencement (and have been granted the same after the date of commencement), have two years from the date of commencement (ie until July 2013) to apply for naturalisation under the current provisions.[23] 1.09

The current Government intention is to produce a full draft 'simplification' Bill in October 2009, but without, as was originally envisaged, drafts of all proposed secondary legislation and rules.[24] It remains unclear whether this will be subject to formal pre-legislative scrutiny in what time remains before the next general election.[25] All the main political parties have expressed their exasperation with the current legislative framework of immigration legislation[26] but the future of a 'simplification' Bill, let alone a timescale for its passage, is uncertain. 1.10

---

[17] See JCHR Legislative Scrutiny: Borders, Citizenship and Immigration Bill 9th Report (2008–09) HL Paper 62 HC 375 (24 March 2009); Home Affairs Committee Borders, Citizenship and Immigration Bill [HL] 5th Report (2008–09) HC 425 (21 April 2009).

[18] Select Committee on the Constitution Part 1 of the Borders, Citizenship and Immigration Bill 5th Report (2008–09) HL Paper 41 (26 February 2009); Select Committee on the Constitution Part 3 of the Borders, Citizenship and Immigration Bill 7th Report (2008–09) HL Paper 54 (26 February 2009).

[19] Delegated Powers and Regulatory Reform Committee 3rd Report (2008–09) HL Paper 29 (5 February 2009).

[20] Communication to the Immigration Law Practitioners' Association (ILPA) from Peter Wrench, UK Border Agency, head of the 'simplification' project at Simplification Bill meeting (26 June 2009).

[21] eg BCIA 2009, ss 47–49.

[22] HC Deb 14 July 2009 vol 496 c244, per Phil Woolas MP, Minister of State, Home Office.

[23] BCIA 2009, s 58(9).

[24] Communication to the Immigration Law Practitioners' Association from Peter Wrench, UK Border Agency, head of the 'simplification' project (26 June 2009).

[25] See Leader of the House of Commons, Draft Legislative Programme 2009/10 available at <http://www.commonsleader.gov.uk/output/Page2835.asp>.

[26] HL Deb 11 February 2009 vol 707 c1128, c1133 per Lord West of Spithead, Parliamentary Under-Secretary of State, Home Office; HC Deb 14 July 2009 vol 496 c256, per Chris Huhne MP, Liberal Democrat Home Affairs Spokesman.

1.11 If immigration legislation is consolidated and simplified then all save the nationality provisions in Part 2 of the BCIA 2009 will be rolled up, modified, and then incorporated into the new 'simplification' Bill.

1.12 It is possible that there will be another separate piece of immigration legislation before the next general election. One reason for this would be to re-introduce proposals to bring in border controls at frontiers within the Common Travel Area, see para **1.40** below.

1.13 All debates on the Borders, Citizenship and Immigration Bill that became the BCIA 2009 and all related parliamentary papers can be found on the Parliament website.[27] Impact assessments can be found on the UK Border Agency website.[28]

1.14 As is now increasingly common, the debates on the Borders, Citizenship and Immigration Bill were developed through letters from Ministers to peers and MPs, explanatory documents placed in the House of Lords Library and the House of Commons Library, and even PowerPoint presentations by UK Border Agency officials. Interventions by peers during the debates[29] led to some of those letters being made publicly available, if difficult to locate.[30]

1.15 Whether it was necessary or desirable to add another storey to the rickety, sprawling edifice that is immigration legislation was the subject of debate.[31] Of the 59 sections in the BCIA 2009, 39 are freestanding and 20 amend existing provisions. Some 12 Acts, spanning the period 1971 to 2007 are amended. To define its provisions, the BCIA 2009 makes reference to 28 other Acts, dating back to 1933, four statutory instruments, one EC Directive, and four EC Regulations. In addition, it refers to some of these more than once. In the words of Lord Hylton:

> The Government may say that it is only interim and will be consolidated, but that does not make it easier for us to understand and consider now.[32]

---

27 <http://services.parliament.uk/bills/2008-09/borderscitizenshipandimmigration.html>; see also the House of Commons Library Research Paper 09/47 (22 May 2009).

28 <http://www.ukba.homeoffice.gov.uk/sitecontent/documents/policyandlaw/legislation/bci-act/>. At the time of writing six impact assessments have been produced, all dated 15 January 2009: Impact Assessment of the Earned Citizenship Proposals (updated June 2009); Impact Assessments for Parts 3 and 4 of the Borders, Citizenship and Immigration Bill; Impact assessment of Legal Powers to Support the Creation of the UK Border Agency; Final Impact Assessment of the Common Travel Area; Equality Impact Assessment Report; and Impact Assessment of Migration Impacts Fund.

29 HL Deb 25 March 2009 vol 709 cc675–6.

30 <http://deposits.parliament.uk/>. The Immigration Law Practitioners' Association holds an archive of many of the letters.

31 eg HL Deb 11 February 2009 vol 707 c1133, cc1137–8, c1181, c1189, c1193, c1195, c1199, and cc1202–3.

32 HL Deb 11 February 2009 vol 707 c1193.

C. THE BROADER POLICY AGENDA: BACKGROUND AND FUTURE POLICY

1. A Single Frontier Force?

1.16 Much of Part 1 of the BCIA 2009 is the latest stage in a process that began with the Nationality, Immigration and Asylum Act 2002, when border security became a big issue following the destruction of the Twin Towers in New York on 9/11, and was developed in later Acts, particularly the UK Borders Act 2007. The latest changes were foreshadowed by the Prime Minister's announcement on 25 July 2007 of the Government's decision to merge the work of Customs (at borders), the Border and Immigration Agency, and UK Visas, and thus 'establish a unified border force'.[33] This was followed by the Cabinet Office's publication on 14 November 2007 of *Security in a Global Hub: Establishing the UK's new border arrangements*. Thereafter, an interim partnership agreement was drawn up and took effect on 1 April 2008.[34] On this date the UK Border Agency came into existence 'in interim form'[35] as a 'shadow' agency of the Home Office. On 1 April 2009 the Agency moved to full Executive Agency status.[36]

1.17 There remained the question of a legislative framework if immigration officers and officials of the Secretary of State for the Home Department including staff transferred from Her Majesty's Revenue and Customs,[37] were to exercise powers previously exercised by officers of Her Majesty's Revenue and Customs. Neither the draft (Partial) Bill nor the accompanying documents (see para **1.06** above) which described what would be covered once that Bill was enacted, had made any reference whatsoever to such a legislative framework or the need for it, but much of BCIA 2009, Part 1 is taken up with providing just such a framework.

1.18 The implications of BCIA 2009, Part 1, for migrants and British nationals passing through UK ports are likely to result from the increased range of powers that a single official at the border will enjoy[38] and from new information sharing powers.[39] To get a glimpse of what these powers could entail in the future, they should be read in conjunction with Parts 1 and 2 of the draft (Partial) Bill.

---

[33] HC Deb 25 July 2007 vol 463 c842.

[34] Partnership Agreement between the commissioners of HM Revenue and Customs and the Home Office on interim arrangements and frontier delivery requirements for the UK Border Agency in 2008–09, Home Office and HMRC, in force 1 April 2008.

[35] Ibid, para 1.

[36] *Framework Agreement* UK Border Agency April 2009.

[37] See HL Deb 11 February 2009 vol 707 c1129, per Lord West of Spithead, Parliamentary Under-Secretary of State, Home Office.

[38] BCIA 2009, ss 1–13.

[39] Ibid, ss 14–21.

1.19 Is the BCIA 2009, Part 1, the culmination of a process, or a staging post? In 2001 the Home Affairs Select Committee recommended as follows:

> 109. We recommend that existing border control agencies should be combined into a single frontier force on the basis of secondment and direct employment, but with clear lines of communication back to the parent agencies.[40]

1.20 Although their policies differ, both the Conservative Party and the Liberal Democrats favour the inclusion of the police in a unified force.[41] The Government has not said 'no' but rather 'not yet' or 'not yet persuaded' to this notion.[42] It is by no means certain that the draft simplification legislation will simply propose re-enactment of BCIA 2009, Part 1.

2. From Nationality to Citizenship

1.21 In the United Kingdom, the BNA 1981 makes provision for the acquisition and loss of British nationality through the establishment and regulation of British citizenship and other classes of British nationality, such as British overseas territories citizenship and British Overseas citizenship. The terms 'British nationality' and 'British national' are not defined in British nationality law and their exact extent is uncertain. At least in large part, British nationality is realized through classes of statutory citizenship: British *citizenship*, British overseas territories *citizenship* and so on. The terms nationality and citizenship have been used in British nationality law without material distinction. Moreover, British nationality lacks an instrumental connection to citizenship in its other sense (ie the domestic, as opposed to international, status to which civic and other rights and obligations attach). Such rights and obligations are not found in the BNA 1981 but elsewhere. They are distributed throughout statute law and common law and do not attach to mere possession of a class of British nationality.[43] Thus in the UK system, nationality has been used interchangeably with citizenship to describe the corpus of laws governing acquisition and loss of nationality. However, citizenship in the other sense is increasingly the focus of policy-making by the Government. Citizenship in this sense was described by Lord Goldsmith QC in his review as:

> . . . the package of rights and responsibilities which demonstrate the tie between a person and a country . . .[44]

[40] Home Affairs Select Committee Border Controls: Report and Proceedings of the Committee 1st Report (2000–01) HC 163-I (31 January 2001).

[41] See for example HL Deb 11 February 2009 vol 707 c1134, per Baroness Hanham (Conservative); HL Comm Deb 25 February 2009 vol 708 cc205–8 per Baroness Hanham (Conservative) and Lord Avebury (Liberal Democrat).

[42] See HL Comm Deb 25 February 2009 vol 708 c214, per Lord West of Spithead, Parliamentary Under-Secretary of State, Home Office but contrast HL Deb 11 February 2009 vol 707 c1207, per Lord West.

[43] See L Fransman, *British Nationality Law* (2nd edn, London: Butterworths, 1998), pp 3–5, para 1.1.

[44] *Citizenship: Our Common Bond* (11 March 2008) Lord Goldsmith QC, ch 4, para 5, p 72.

Fuelling confusion, when referring to nationality there has been a shift of emphasis in recent Government policy documents. They speak less of 'nationality' and more of 'citizenship'. This can be seen in the title to the new Act itself (cf the titles: the British Nationality Acts, the Nationality, Immigration and Asylum Act 2002, and the Immigration, Asylum and Nationality Act 2006). The shift can be traced at least as far back as *The Governance of Britain* Green Paper (July 2007),[45] which stated: 1.22

> . . . the right to citizenship in law comes from the rules on British nationality.[46]

The Green Paper made it clear that one of the main policy concerns was about social cohesion, and the link between cohesion and citizenship, a theme which had its antecedents in the Home Secretary's announcement of the Ministerial Group on Public Order and Community Cohesion[47] and the report of the Commission on Integration and Cohesion, *Our shared future*. [48] 1.23

In the Government's eyes the concept of becoming a citizen carries much wider connotations than mere naturalisation and nationality and the chapter on citizenship in *The Governance of Britain* Green Paper sets out very clearly what the Government has in mind: 1.24

> 185 . . . there is common ground between British citizens, and many cultural traits and traditions that we can all recognise as distinctively British. The Government believes that a clearer definition of citizenship would give people a better sense of their British identity in a globalised world. British citizenship—and the rights and responsibilities that accompany it—needs to be valued and meaningful, not only for recent arrivals looking to become British but also for young British people themselves.
>
> 186. The Government believes that everyone in the UK should be offered an easily understood set of rights and responsibilities when they receive citizenship.

Before the publication of *The Governance of Britain* Green Paper, the Prime Minister had asked the former Attorney General, Lord Goldsmith QC, to carry out a review of citizenship looking at both legal aspects and other issues, including civil participation and social responsibility.[49] The terms of reference of his Citizenship Review were, in particular: 1.25

- To clarify the legal rights and responsibilities associated with British citizenship, in addition to those enjoyed under the Human Rights Act, as a basis for defining what it means to be a citizen in Britain's open democratic society
- To consider the difference between the different categories of British nationality
- To examine the relationship between residence, citizenship and British national status and the incentives for long-term residents to become British citizens

---

[45] Cm 7170, Secretary of State for Justice and Lord Chancellor.

[46] Ibid, ch 4, para 180.

[47] HC Deb 10 July 2001 vol 371 cc663–4, per David Blunkett MP, Secretary of State for the Home Department.

[48] 14 June 2007.

[49] *Citizenship: Our Common Bond* (n 44 above), ch 4, para 193.

- To explore the role of citizens and residents in civic society, including voting, jury service and other forms of civic participation.

1.26 Thereafter, the *Path to Citizenship* Green Paper consultation purported to introduce the notion of 'earned citizenship' as if it were some new and exciting buzzword. In fact it was nothing of the kind. Acquiring British nationality is not, and has never been, a matter of entitlement. As far back as 1915 a failure to obey the law, to pay taxes, or to speak the English language to a sufficient level of fluency have been statutory reasons to refuse naturalisation,[50] while the requirement to have 'sufficient knowledge about life in the United Kingdom' has been around since 2002.[51]

1.27 A comparison of Government publications from 2007 to the present permits identification of different emphases at different times in the Government's presentation of the earned citizenship proposals.

1.28 In the words of Ann Dummett:

> The tone of the Goldsmith's review proposals is calm, reasonable, even liberal in places. The tone of the Green Paper is quite different: wordy, pretentious and bossy . . . But . . . [b]oth papers appear to take for granted a simple contradiction: we want people to become British citizens, but we intend to make acquisition more difficult than before.[52]

1.29 There was also another text running through the Government's *Path to Citizenship* Green Paper consultation (see also para **1.37**):

> We are entitled to expect migrants who aim to settle permanently in this country to act responsibly and to abide by our laws.[53]

1.30 The Government chose to publish the *Path to Citizenship: Next Steps in Reforming the Immigration System* Green Paper in February 2008, just before the publication of Lord Goldsmith QC's review in *Citizenship: Our Common Bond* on 11 March 2008. Bar the passing remark 'We have carefully studied the Lord Goldsmith QC's report into citizenship',[54] there was no separate comment on Lord Goldsmith QC's proposals for nationality law nor any separate response to his review.

1.31 The very first of Lord Goldsmith's recommendations in his review was that:

> The residual categories of citizenship—with the exception of British Overseas Territories Citizenship and British Nationals (Overseas) status—should be abolished allowing people who would qualify for those categories with access to full British citizenship. Though this change will only affect relatively small numbers of people, it is important to address the history involved in the residual categories as part of renewing our common bond of citizenship; . . .[55]

[50] British Nationality and Status of Aliens Act 1914, s 2.

[51] Nationality, Immigration and Asylum Act 2002, s 1, amending BNA 1981, s 41 and Sch 1.

[52] A Dummett, 'Changes to Citizenship' [2008] JIANL 22(3) 213.

[53] *The Path to Citizenship: Next Steps in Reforming the Immigration System*, February 2008, para 160, p 28.

[54] *The Path to Citizenship: Next Steps in Reforming the Immigration System* Government Response to Consultation, July 2008, p 6.

[55] *Citizenship: Our Common Bond* (February 2008), p 6.

Lord Goldsmith identified that having categories of British nationality which carried with them no right of abode in the United Kingdom provided a shaky foundation on which to build citizenship as a package of rights and responsibilities. In other countries a right of abode and freedom of movement are an integral part of the notion of 'citizenship' or indeed 'nationality' and, as Lord Goldsmith noted, are recognized in international law, inter alia, in Article 12 of the International Covenant on Civil and Political Rights[56] and Article 3 of Protocol 4[57] to the Convention for the Protection of Human Rights and Fundamental Freedoms (the Human Rights Convention). Lord Goldsmith's discussions of the citizenship settlement were set within the context of his first recommendation (see para **1.31** above). That position was entirely absent from the Government's Green Paper consultation *The Path to Citizenship*. 1.32

Whereas the current Nationality Instructions on naturalisation take as their starting point the choice of the migrant to seek British citizenship, captured in the phrase that applicants 'have genuinely thrown in their lot with this country',[58] the new proposals in *The Path to Citizenship* Green Paper consultation and the BCIA 2009 leave a migrant with little alternative but to seek British citizenship or face insecurity and restrictions on their entitlement to social security and housing assistance (see para 5.204). If the desire of migrants to throw in their lot with this country is replaced by an ultimatum that you acquire citizenship or risk losing out on important social advantages, how can becoming a citizen be said to promote social cohesion? 1.33

By 3 August 2009 when, subsequent to the passage of the BCIA 2009, the UK Border Agency published the consultation paper *Earning the Right to Stay: a New Points Test for Citizenship* (the Points Test Paper) that tension remained visible but less so than before. By then, perhaps in part as a response to recession, there was a much greater emphasis on not allowing people to progress as far as citizenship. The Ministerial preface to the document continues to appeal to 'encouraging cohesion', but also highlights the Government's intention to: 1.34

> . . . challenge what has been perceived as an automatic right to move from temporary residence to permanent settlement . . .[59]

The 2005 notion of 'low skilled' migration as temporary and 'highly skilled' migration as permanent,[60] which had persisted in *The Path to Citizenship* Green Paper 1.35

[56] New York, 16 December 1966; UNTS vol 999, p 171 and vol 1057, p 407, ratified by the UK on 20 May 1976.

[57] Strasbourg, 16 September 1963 CETS No 046, signed by the UK on 16 September 1963 but not ratified.

[58] Nationality Instructions, Chapter 18, para 18.1.7.

[59] At p 4.

[60] *Selective Admission: Making Migration Work for Britain,* Immigration and Nationality Directorate, Home Office, July 2005 at para 1.10.

consultation[61] has been superseded by the notion that it is preferable that all migration for work is temporary.

1.36 During the passage of the Borders, Citizenship and Immigration Bill through Parliament the notion of 'earned citizenship' was largely welcomed and deemed acceptable. Discussion focused on migration for work and of those seeking international protection; the effect on those who have migrated on the basis of family relationships received little attention. Concerns about the new system were articulated as concerns about bureaucracy, perverse consequences, practical difficulties, and unfairness to individuals.

1.37 In August 2009, Alan Johnson MP, the Home Secretary, introduced the new Points Test Paper consultation with the warning that 'bad behaviour will be penalised'[62] and Phil Woolas MP, Minister of State, Home Office, added his own gloss to those comments by acknowledging that behaviour that would not amount to a crime could be penalized. The notion was already there in February 2008 in the Green Paper *The Path to Citizenship*, with the reference to 'act responsibly and abide by our laws'[63] but had been given less prominence. A journalist asked whether the Minister might effectively be saying to a migrant that once you have British citizenship 'you can demonstrate as much as you like, but until then, don't?' and he replied 'In essence, yes'.[64] Only then did a wider audience start to review comments made during the passage of the BCIA 2009 such as '. . . earned citizenship encourages people with the right values to become citizens'[65] and to voice the concerns which Ann Dummett had identified:

> . . . The suggestions about naturalisation, and the rights and duties of citizens, are dependent upon a temporary political situation and a mood which puts obedience to state authorities at the centre of the law. The basis is unsound.[66]

1.38 The next chapter in the citizenship debate is unlikely to be about nationality law but rather to circle around proposals for a 'Bill of Rights and Responsibilities' as set out in the Green Paper *Rights and Responsibilities: Developing our Constitutional Framework*,[67] which itself refers back to the Green Paper *The Governance of Britain*[68] and the Green Paper *The Path to Citizenship*.[69]

1.39 Drawing the threads of the proposals, policy initiatives, and legislation together, there is a tendency (i) to refer to nationality as citizenship, and (ii) for citizenship in

---

61 See also *A Path to Citizenship: Next Steps in Reforming our Immigration System*, UK Border Agency February 2008, 3.1, para 100, p 19.

62 'This system is a winner on points' Alan Johnson MP, Secretary of State for the Home Department, *News of the World*, 2 August 2009.

63 *The Path to Citizenship: Next Steps in Reforming the Immigration System*, February 2008, para 60, p 28.

64 Phil Woolas MP, Minister of State, Home Office, interviewed on The Today Programme, BBC Radio 4, 3 August 2009.

65 *Hansard* HL Deb 11 February 2009 vol 707 c1208.

66 A Dummett, 'Changes to Citizenship' (n 52 above), p 217.

67 Ministry of Justice 23 March 2009, Cm 7577.

68 para 5.1.

69 para 2.62.

that sense also to serve as citizenship in the other sense—the primary status to which civic and other rights and obligations attach. Thereafter, the policy appears to be to put pressure on the population of long-term settled foreign national residents either to become British citizens (if they are 'good citizens' in the Government's view) or to leave. This is a hard line policy, given that access to British citizenship is at the same time being made harder and longer. On the other hand, residual groups of historical origin are being brought bit by bit within the fold of British citizenship—the BCIA 2009 continues this trend by extending British citizenship to British Nationals (Overseas) without any other citizenship or nationality and those, of any age, who would be British citizens by descent but for their mother's incapacity to transmit British nationality under earlier laws.

D. THE EFFECT OF PARLIAMENTARY SCRUTINY

1. The Common Travel Area

The Borders, Citizenship and Immigration Bill as presented to Parliament[70] made provision to introduce provisions for border controls within the Common Travel Area (CTA).[71] The CTA comprises the United Kingdom, the Republic of Ireland, the Channel Islands, and the Isle of Man. The proposals for the introduction of immigration control followed a UK Border Agency consultation.[72] The Government was defeated in the House of Lords on this proposal, and for the provision originally contained in the Borders, Citizenship and Immigration Bill an amendment was substituted to strengthen the protection of free movement within the CTA.[73] 1.40

The Government reinstated the original provision in the Public Bill Committee[74] but at the House of Commons Report Stage, Phil Woolas MP, Minister of State, Home Office, accepted the Opposition amendment to remove the Government's clause from the Bill, while not retaining the provision inserted in the House of Lords.[75] 1.41

As far as one can ascertain from the Minister's comments at the time, it was pressure of time in a very busy legislative session and the prospect of a subsequent parliamentary session that would be truncated by a general election, prompting a desire to see the Bill pass before the summer recess, that led the Government to decide to 1.42

[70] HL Bill 15, Clause 46.

[71] Immigration Act 1971, ss 1(3) and 11(4); see also the Immigration (Control of Entry through Republic of Ireland) Order 1972, SI 1972/1610 and the Immigration Rules HC 395 of 1993–94 as amended, para 15.

[72] *Strengthening the Common Travel Area*: consultation paper (24 July 2008), Partial impact assessment of common travel area (24 July 2008), *Strengthening the Common Travel Area*: Government response to the public consultation (15 January 2009), and Final impact assessment of common travel area reform (15 January 2009).

[73] HL Bill 36, clause 51 (2008–09).

[74] HC Bill 115, clause 50 (2008–09).

[75] HC Deb 14 July 2009, vol 496 cc238–9.

take this course of action. He recognized that the Government had not persuaded Parliament of the need for the provision but stated 'We are committed to the policy'.[76] This was reiterated when the Bill returned to the House of Lords and Lord Brett, Government Whip, Government Spokesman for the Home Office, stated:

> . . . the Government still believe that the CTA amendments are needed. Pursuing such amendments would require new proposals to be brought forward to Parliament at a later date, but no decision has been taken as to when or in what form such proposals will be made. There will be no new immigration checks at the land border at this stage.[77]

2. New and Amended Provisions of the BCIA 2009 Arising During the Passage of the Bill after Parliamentary Pressure

1.43 There are four key provisions that were amended or inserted during the course of the passage of the BCIA 2009 as a result of parliamentary pressure on the Government:

(a) the limitation imposed on the provision for the transfer of certain judicial review applications to the Upper Tribunal (see para **8.51**);[78]
(b) the insertion of a provision for registration as a British citizen for British Nationals (Overseas) without other citizenship (see para **6.37**);[79]
(c) the modifications made to provisions for the registration as a British citizen by minors (see para **6.28**);[80] and
(d) the provision introducing amendments to the offence of trafficking people for exploitation (see para **9.03**).[81]

3. On-going Campaigns

1.44 As will be seen from the above, Parliament had considerable influence on the shape of the BCIA 2009. During the passage of the Bill a range of other amendments were proposed, among them changes to British nationality law,[82] most notably in relation to the people of the Chagos Islands, part of the British Indian Ocean Territory, who were removed and thereafter excluded from the islands by the British Government.[83]

---

76 Ibid, c239.
77 HL Deb 20 July 2009 vol 712 c1395.
78 BCIA 2009, s 53.
79 Ibid, s 44.
80 Ibid, s 43.
81 Ibid, s 54.
82 HL Comm Deb 4 March 2009 vol 708 c734ff.
83 See *R (on the application of Bancoult) v Secretary of State for Foreign and Commonwealth Affairs* [2008] UKHL 61.

Further amendments proposed sought to make provision in British nationality law for those born to parents not married to each other and for stateless children. In particular, it is time to accommodate those stateless children with a parent or parents who are dual British citizens/British Overseas citizens (BOCs)—these children, who are ethnic Asians in East Africa, are perennially refused discretionary registration as British citizens under BNA 1981, s 3(1), and as BOCs under s 27(1). In addition, amendments were advanced to make provision to alter the position of children under immigration control, most notably relating to the detention of children under Immigration Act powers.[84] None of these succeeded but, as illustrated by the examples which did succeed (see para **1.43** above), it is likely that Parliament will be asked to consider these questions again in subsequent debates on immigration legislation. 1.45

One of the most likely questions to return is the question of the provision made in British nationality law for the Chagos Islanders in exile, where the amendment,[85] which was proposed and was unsuccessful during the passage of the Bill, sought to take forward a recommendation made by the House of Commons Foreign Affairs Committee in its July 2008 report *Overseas Territories*.[86] The Committee's primary recommendation was support for the return of the Chagos Islanders to the British Indian Ocean Territory[87] but it also recommended that British overseas territories citizenship should be extended to third generation descendants of exiled Chagos Islanders.[88] 1.46

[84] HL Comm Deb 10 March 2009 vol 708 c1137.

[85] HL Comm Deb 4 March 2009 vol c734–9.

[86] Foreign Affairs Committee *Overseas Territories* 7th Report (2007–08) HC 147 vols I and II. The Government has entered a formal response to the report, Cm 7473.

[87] Ibid, para 69.

[88] Ibid, para 74.

2
INTRODUCTION TO PART 1 AND CUSTOMS FUNCTIONS

A. INTRODUCTION

1. Outline of Part 1 of the BCIA 2009

2.01 Part 1 of the Borders, Citizenship and Immigration Act 2009 (BCIA 2009) creates the legal framework for customs functions performed at the border by Her Majesty's Revenue and Customs[1] (HMRC) to be performed concurrently by the Secretary of State and officials designated by him or her so as to create a unified border force within the UK Borders Agency (UKBA). It is thus concerned with the redistribution of existing functions rather than the creation of new powers. Its most innovative feature is the conferral of already existing powers on single individuals or bodies that were previously held separately. So, for example, the Secretary of State receives customs powers that previously belonged to the HMRC and one individual will be able to be both an immigration officer and a customs official. It came into force upon the BCIA 2009 being passed.[2]

2.02 Part 1 carries out this distribution of functions and powers, first, by identifying the persons who are to be responsible for carrying out customs functions and delineating the functions to be performed by them. Section 1 is concerned with the customs functions to be performed by the Secretary of State; s 3 gives the Secretary of State a power to designate immigration officers and any other officials in his department to carry out 'general customs functions' (ie those not concerned with

[1] The Commissioners and the officers of the Revenue and Customs may together be referred to as Her Majesty's Revenue and Customs (Commissioners for Revenue and Customs Act 2005, s 4(1)).

[2] BCIA 2009, s 58(1).

revenue and tax); s 6 requires the Secretary of State to designate a Director of Border Revenue whose responsibility for 'customs revenue matters' is set out in s 7 and who is given a power to designate immigration officers and other officials in the Secretary of State's department as 'customs revenue officials'.

Powers in relation to customs matters are given to these persons by requiring legislation that gives powers to the Commissioners and officers of HMRC to be read as applying to these persons (ss 1(4), 3(7), 7(5), and 11(4)) and by conferring enormous legislative powers on the Secretary of State and the Treasury, including powers enabling him or her to amend primary legislation (ss 2, 8, 35, and 36). 2.03

The BCIA 2009 also confers powers on these persons to share and disclose information, subject to constraints and penalties for wrongful disclosure (ss 14–21). 2.04

Police-like powers of investigation and detention are conferred on customs officials within the UKBA concerned with the investigation of customs related offences (ss 22–25) and provision is made for the Director of Revenue and Customs Prosecutions to institute and conduct prosecutions. 2.05

The Commissioners for HMRC are empowered to make schemes for the transfer to the UKBA of property, rights, and liabilities so that officials of the UKBA can step into the shoes of the HMRC in relation to private law matters (s 26). 2.06

There is provision for HMRC and the UKBA to share their facilities and services (s 37). 2.07

Provision is made for existing oversight mechanisms to operate in respect of the UKBA by the Chief Inspector of the UK Border Agency (s 28), HM Inspectors of Constabulary (s 29), and the Independent Police Complaints Commission (s 30). 2.08

Arrangements are made for the payment of revenue to the HMRC (s 32) or into the Consolidated Fund (s 33). 2.09

The Secretary of State's duty to issue a code of practice to ensure that children are kept safe from harm by those carrying out immigration functions is extended to those who carry out customs functions (s 34). 2.10

2. The Origins of Part 1 of the BCIA 2009

This part of the legislation originated in two parliamentary statements on national security made by the Prime Minister and a Report of the Cabinet Secretary, commissioned by the Prime Minister. 2.11

In the first of the parliamentary statements, made in the light of the attempted terrorist bombings in London and Glasgow on 29 and 30 June 2007, the Prime Minister referred to the borders as 'the second line of defence' against terrorism, as well as against crime and illegal immigration. He announced that 'to strengthen the powers and surveillance capability of our border guards and security officers we will now integrate the vital work of the Border and Immigration Agency, Customs and UK visas overseas and at the main points of entry to the UK, and we will 2.12

establish a unified border force'.[3] He also announced that the Cabinet Secretary had been asked to report on 'the stages ahead in implementation' of that objective.

2.13 The Cabinet Secretary reported[4] on 14 November 2007. The report said:

> [T]he objectives are clear: the facilitation of legitimate travel and trade; security from the threats and pressures of crime, whether illegal migration, terrorism or attacks on the tax base; and protection of the border itself, our international transport networks and the people using them and working on them.[5]

The report

> . . . highlighted the benefits that could be achieved through increased integration of work at the border. These include: exploiting commonality of process; better management of the flow of people and goods at the frontier; improved relationships with partners; more flexible distribution of resources at a national level and the effective and efficient deployment of resources on site.[6]

It elaborated:

> 65. This is a substantial change in the machinery of government. Together, the new organisation will number around 25,000 people. By bringing border resources together under the Home Office, their effectiveness in participating in ensuring security will be improved.
>
> 66. The change should improve the ability to act early through: more integrated use of the visa regime, ensuring that it takes account of the full range of risks and has a feedback loop incorporating the experience of work on arrival and inside the UK; combining the efforts of visa Risk Assessment Units and HMRC and BIA overseas work to 'export the border', to learn from each other and have more impact as a result; and more efficient interface with key partners such as the SOCA liason officer network.
>
> 67. It should enable more effective targeting of movements—both identifying high risk movements for greater scrutiny, and expediting legitimate movements—through: the single approach to information use flowing from a single business plan. The Immigration, Asylum and Nationality Act and related secondary legislation will oblige information sharing between the organisations concerned. The organisational change will allow for coherent planning of how to use that information to best effect; removal over time, of duplication of staff effort examining the same movements in the same location and of unnecessary rework on arrival of checks done before arrival. The end-to-end control over passenger movements in particular should enable the development of improved watchlists as well as the development and roll out of trusted traveller schemes designed to allow legitimate travellers to pass quickly through controls; and establishing a clear link with programmes already underway and ensuring maximum benefits are derived from these, for example the enhanced data capability delivered

[3] HC Deb 27 July 2007 vol 463 cc842–3.

[4] *Security in a Global Hub: Establishing the UK's New Border Arrangements,* Cabinet Office (14 November 2007).

[5] Ibid, p 5, para 3.

[6] Ibid, p 62, para 5.11.

by the e-Borders programme, and the integrity of identity delivered by the biometric identity scheme.

68. It should enhance the ability to manage bottlenecks by: defining, through collective ministerial agreement, what checks should be permitted at pinch-points and what the permissible acceptable levels of delay are as a result of those checks, and monitoring performance; providing additional flexibility to respond to changing priorities, for example surges in low risk traffic or a peak of high risk arrivals; and providing a single overview of flows at a given entry route with a simpler and stronger relationship with delivery partners such as airport operators and the police.

69. It should improve breadth and depth of protection by: ensuring, through the border strategy, that the border challenges are seen and addressed as a whole including outside the main points of entry and exit; allowing, over time, more efficient use of resources—in particular the removal of overlaps referred to above, permitting staff to be deployed to enhance checks either in the same location or elsewhere; and training individuals to identify and respond to a wider range of risks and making deployment decisions so that wherever an officer is deployed, there is some coverage of the full range of risks.

70. It should deliver increased visibility of the UK border, improving confidence and enhancing deterrence. The single primary line will be the focal point for border activity on arrival, and UK border signage and instructions to passengers should be rolled out, combining immigration and customs messaging to all major passenger arrival points by June 2008.[7]

Among the recommendations made in the report was that 'the Government should legislate to establish a new organisation that takes on the work of BIA,[8] UK visas and the border control work of HMRC'.[9] It also recommended that 'the Government should legislate to permit the controlled designation of customs, immigration and police powers to officers of the new organisation'.[10] 2.14

On the day that the report was published, the Prime Minister made the second parliamentary statement on the subject of border control saying: 2.15

there will be one single primary checkpoint for both passport control and customs. The UK Border agency, which will have 25,000 staff in total, will now apply controls at points of entry and exit on people and goods, into and out of the UK, as well as working throughout the world. The new agency will enable us to transfer intelligence from UK operations overseas to those making visa decisions and to check biometrics taken from visa applications against criminal and counter-terrorism records. Further details of the new UK Border Agency, . . . are published in the Cabinet Office report issued today.[11]

Part 1 of the BCIA 2009 stems from the Prime Minister's announcement in July 2007 of the creation of 'a unified border force' and the Cabinet Secretary's Report, 2.16

[7] Ibid, p 16, para 65–70.
[8] Border and Immigration Agency.
[9] *Security in a Global Hub,* p 10, para 30.
[10] Ibid, p 12, para 42.
[11] HC Deb 14 November 2007 vol 467 c669.

Security in a Global Hub.[12] It provides 'the legislative framework for immigration officers and officials of the Secretary of State to exercise revenue and customs functions which have to date been exercised by Her Majesty's Revenue and Customs ("HMRC")'.[13] It enables the same individual to perform functions as both immigration officer and customs official.

B. CUSTOMS FUNCTIONS

1. Introduction

2.17 The first 13 sections of the BCIA 2009 provide for customs functions and customs revenue functions to be exercised by the Secretary of State, the Director of Border Revenue (an office newly created by the Act) and by officials designated by them. A 'function' is 'any power or duty, including a power or duty that is ancillary to another power or duty'.[14]

2. The Secretary of State

2.18 Section 1 of the BCIA 2009 provides for the Secretary of State to exercise, concurrently with the Commissioners for Her Majesty's Revenue and Customs, the functions of the Commissioners in relation to 'general customs matters'.[15]

(a) *Meaning of 'General Customs Matters'*

2.19 Unfortunately the BCIA 2009 does not define 'general customs matters' by identifying what the substantive content of 'general customs matters' is, other than that they are matters in relation to which the Commissioners and officers of Revenue and Customs have functions. The only matters that are specifically identified are the functions of the Commissioners and officers of Revenue and Customs that are not 'general customs matters' (as to which, see below). This failure to delineate the subject matter was much criticized during the passage of the legislation as giving the statute an opaque quality.[16] It was defended by the Government[17] on the basis that the powers and functions conferred on customs officers by centuries of legislation are so many and varied that they could not sensibly be set out in the Act. They include by way of examples: the power to seize a vessel used for the purpose of the

[12] HL Deb 11 February 2009 vol 707 c1129, per Lord West of Spithead, Parliamentary Under-Secretary of State, Home Office, introducing the Bill at the second reading in the House of Lords.

[13] BCIA 2009, Explanatory Notes, para 4.

[14] BCIA 2009, s 38.

[15] Ibid, s 1(1).

[16] For example HL Deb 25 March 2009, vol 709 c674, per Baroness Hanham (Conservative).

[17] HL Deb 25 March 2009, vol 709 cc674–6, per Lord West of Spithead, Parliamentary Under-Secretary of State, Home Office.

slave trade;[18] to take custody of any ship taken as a prize;[19] preventing the import of horses whose tails have been docked;[20] functions relating to ensuring ship safety, requiring production of ships' documents and detaining ships;[21] and functions conferred by the Chemical Weapons Act 1996, the Rabies Act 1974, the Explosives Act 1875, and the Salmon and Freshwater Fisheries Act 1975.

The definition of general customs matters specifically refers[22] to the functions of the officers, as well as the Commissioners, in order to make clear that functions conferred by legislation directly on the officers of Revenue and Customs, as opposed to being delegated to them by the Commissioners, fall within the definition.[23] Examples given by the Minister when seeking to amend the definition so as to refer to officers' functions were the ability of officers to detain goods being imported under the Consumer Protection Act 1987 to allow for their inspection by trading standards officers and the ability of officers to detain ships under the Public Health (Ships) Regulations 1979.[24] Such matters would appear to fall outwith the jurisdiction conferred on the Secretary of State, his or her jurisdiction being limited to the functions exercisable in relation to general customs matters by the Commissioners. 2.20

As mentioned above, the only specifically identified matters are those which, although related to functions of the Commissioners and officers of Revenue and Customs, are excluded from the definition of 'general customs matters'. They are:[25] a matter listed in Schedule 1 to the Commissioners for Revenue and Customs Act 2005,[26] (ie various matters, principally taxes, duties, and levies for which the Inland Revenue was responsible prior to the creation of 'Her Majesty's Revenue and Customs'); 'any tax, duty or levy' not mentioned in Schedule 1 to that Act;[27] the administration and oversight of the Office of the Paymaster General[28] and various matters relating to money laundering and terrorist financing.[29] 2.21

These exclusions are intended to give effect to the constitutional convention that decisions relating to individuals' tax liabilities, including customs duties and tax 2.22

[18] The Slave Trade Act 1873.

[19] The Naval Prize Act 1864.

[20] The Docking and Nicking of Horses Act 1949.

[21] The Merchant Shipping Act 1995.

[22] As a result of a Government amendment introduced at the Report Stage in the House of Lords.

[23] BCIA 2009, s 1(2).

[24] HL Deb 25 March 2009 vol 709 c672, per Lord West of Spithead, Parliamentary Under-Secretary of State, Home Office.

[25] BCIA 2009, s 1(2).

[26] Ibid, s 1(2)(a).

[27] Ibid, s 1(2)(b).

[28] Ibid, s 1(2)(c), ie those matters transferred to the Commissioners for Her Majesty's Revenue and Customs by Transfer of Functions (Office of Her Majesty's Paymaster General) Order 2006, SI 2006/607.

[29] BCIA 2009, s 1(2)(d) and (e) to the extent that they are the subject matter of Directive 2005/60/EC of the European Parliament and of the Council of 26 October 2005 on the prevention of the use of the financial system for the purpose of money laundering and terrorist financing and Regulation (EC) No 1781/2006 of the European Parliament and of the Council of 15 November 2006 on information on the payer accompanying transfers of funds.

administration generally are kept at arm's length from Ministers.[30] Further effect is given to that Convention by the creation of the Director of Border Revenue and customs revenue officials to whom the Directors functions may be delegated and who have responsibility for 'customs revenue matters' (as to which, see below).

2.23 Thus:

> the Secretary of State is left with the non-revenue customs, shipping and enforcement functions of HM Revenue and Customs. These are the functions that the Commissioners and customs officers exercise in relation to ports and airports, the movement of goods, preventing drug smuggling and the smuggling of prohibited and restricted goods, and the regulation of trade and shipping.[31]

The 'main headings' of 'general customs functions' would include:

> seizing criminal cash . . . preventing unsafe products being imported into the UK; maintaining sanctions on countries and arms embargos; reducing and deterring trade in endangered species of animals and plants; control of commercial vessels and ships coming into our ports; preventing the importation of offensive weapons such as knives, daggers and so on; preventing the importation of obscene or indecent material, particularly child pornography; preventing the introduction of pests and diseases harmful to animals and/or humans such as foot and mouth, bird flu and fowl plague; preventing the import and export of controlled drugs; and preventing chemical weapons, toxic weapons and so on from coming into the UK and being obtained by terrorist organisations.[32]

(b) *General Customs Functions*

2.24 The section also defines 'general customs functions' as being functions exercisable by the Secretary of State or by general customs officials in relation to 'general customs matters'[33] and functions conferred on them by ss 22–24 of the BCIA 2009, ie investigations and detention and functions under Community law that are exercisable by the Commissioners or officers of Revenue and Customs but are not excluded from the definition of 'general customs matters' set out above.[34]

(c) *Secretary of State's Power to Change the Definition of General Customs Matters*

2.25 The Secretary of State may, by statutory instrument, approved by both Houses of Parliament,[35] amend the definitions of 'general customs matters' and 'general customs functions'.[36] That power extends to modifying any enactment in consequence of any change to the definition of 'general customs matters' thus effected by the

---

[30] HL Deb 25 February 2009, vol 708 c218, per Lord West of Spithead, Parliamentary Under-Secretary of State, Home Office.

[31] HL Deb 25 March 2009 vol 709 cc673–4, per Lord West of Spithead, Parliamentary Under-Secretary of State, Home Office.

[32] PBC Deb 9 June 2009 1st sitting c12, per Phil Woolas MP, Minister of State, Home Office.

[33] BCIA 2009, s 1(8).

[34] Ibid.

[35] Ibid, s 37(1), (3), and (4)(a).

[36] Ibid, s 2(1).

Secretary of State, including legislation passed after this Act;[37] that power is also to be exercised by statutory instrument subject to the affirmative resolution procedure.[38] The Government explained these powers as being necessary to enable the definition of 'general customs matters' to be amended so that functions conferred on the Commissioners by future legislation could also be conferred on the Secretary of State.[39]

The Delegated Powers and Regulatory Reform Committee of the House of Lords was satisfied that these powers to modify future legislation, as opposed to leaving the legislator to include relevant provision, were not inappropriate. It reached that conclusion because 'although no examples are given, it seems not unlikely that there will be cases where the Treasury might prefer to allow HMRC to exercise new functions alone for a period, before deciding whether it is sensible or practicable to make those functions exercisable concurrently by the Secretary of State and the Director'.[40] It was also influenced by the fact that the power was subject to the affirmative resolution procedure. 2.26

These powers may not be used to bring tax and customs revenue matters within the ambit of 'general customs matters'[41] and the Secretary of State is required to consult with the Treasury before exercising them.[42] 2.27

(d) *Construction of Other Legislation Relating to General Customs Matters*

Primary and secondary legislation[43] made before the end of the parliamentary session in which the BCIA 2009 was passed and instruments and documents issued before the passing of the BCIA 2009[44] which refer to Commissioners for Her Majesty's Revenue and Customs or to Her Majesty's Revenue and Customs are to be construed as referring also to the Secretary of State for the purposes of the provision (s 1) conferring general customs functions on the Secretary of State and his or her officials.[45] However, only certain specified provisions of the Commissioners for Revenue and Customs Act 2005 are to be construed as including reference to the Secretary of State.[46] They include: s 5(2)(b) which vests in the Commissioners all of the functions which vested in the Commissioners of Customs and Excise prior to commencement of that section; s 9 which confers on the Commissioners power to 'do anything which they think—(a) necessary or expedient in connection with the 2.28

[37] Ibid, s 2(1)(d).
[38] Ibid, s 37(1), (4).
[39] HL Deb 25 February 2009 vol 708 c237, per Lord West of Spithead, Parliamentary Under-Secretary of State, Home Office.
[40] House of Lords Delegated Powers and Regulatory Reform Committee 3rd Report (2008–09) HL Paper 29 (5 February 2009).
[41] BCIA 2009, s 2(2).
[42] Ibid, s 2(3).
[43] ie 'enactments' as referred to in BCIA 2009, s 1(6)(a) and defined in s 38.
[44] BCIA 2009, s 1(6).
[45] Ibid, s 1(4).
[46] Ibid, s 1(7).

exercise of their functions, or (b) incidental or conducive to the exercise of their functions'; s 31 which creates an offence of obstructing an officer of Revenue and Customs or a person acting on behalf of or assisting such an officer; and s 33 giving a power of arrest to Revenue and Customs Officers in relation to the obstruction offence or assaulting an officer of the Revenue and Customs.

3. General Customs Officials

2.29 The Secretary of State may designate an immigration officer or any other official in his or her department as a general customs official.[47] In the first instance, this provision is intended to enable 4,500 existing Revenue and Customs officers to transfer to the new border force by means of their designation as general customs officials or revenue customs officials[48] (as to whom, see below). Private contractors, not being officials, could not be designated; an individual would not have to be an immigration officer in order to be designated.[49]

2.30 The Secretary of State's power to designate general customs officials, as well as to withdraw or vary the designation, must be exercised by notice in writing to the official.[50]

2.31 A designation may be permanent or for a specified period;[51] it may be limited, including as to the functions that the official is to exercise and the purpose for which they are exercisable.[52] Thus the terms of a designation can reflect a specialist role or function such as the exercise of general customs functions in relation to international post or dog handlers for which the full range of powers would not be needed.[53]

(a) *Training of Designated Customs Officials*

2.32 The Secretary of State may only designate an official if satisfied that he or she is capable of effectively carrying out the functions designated; has received adequate training in respect of those functions; and is otherwise a suitable person to exercise them.[54] In the House of Lords, Lord West of Spithead, Parliamentary Under-Secretary of State, Home Office, stated that 'for training to be deemed adequate, it must provide a designated customs official with all the instruction and skills appropriate and necessary to exercise the customs revenue function conferred upon

---

[47] Ibid s 3(1).

[48] HL Deb 25 February 2009 vol 708 c240, per Lord West of Spithead, Parliamentary Under-Secretary of State, Home Office.

[49] PBC Deb 9 June 2009 1st sitting cc20–1, per Phil Woolas MP, Minister of State, Home Office.

[50] BCIA 2009 s 4(4).

[51] Ibid, s 4(3)(a).

[52] Ibid, s 4(2).

[53] Phil Woolas, PBC Deb 9 June 2009 1st sitting c23, per Phil Woolas MP, Minister of State, Home Office.

[54] BCIA 2009, s 4(5).

them fully and properly'.[55] Such training would broadly mirror that currently given to officers of Revenue and Customs which entails 'guided learning for 2 weeks, a residential course of six weeks and training at a port or airport for four to six weeks, depending on the location and the skills required'. It is externally accredited by Edexcel. It would be 'needs-based' according to the role and customs function that the officer would be intended to exercise.[56]

(b) *Functions of General Customs Officials*

2.33 Subject to the Secretary of State's power to impose limitations on a designation as a general customs official, they have the same functions in relation to a general customs matter as an officer of Revenue and Customs would have and may exercise the general customs functions of the Secretary of State.[57] General customs officials must comply with the directions of the Secretary of State in the exercise of general customs functions.[58] Provision is made for legislation, documents, and instruments to be construed as if references to an officer of Revenue and Customs or to Her Majesty's Revenue and Customs included reference to a general customs official.[59] The provision applies to legislation, documents, and instruments that predate the passing of the BCIA 2009 and, unless the contrary is expressly stated, to enactments, instruments, and documents that postdate the BCIA 2009.[60] However, it applies only to specified provisions of the Commissioners for Revenue and Customs Act 2005, ie: s 2(4) (anything done by or in relation to one officer may be continued by or in relation to another), s 6 (officers to be vested with functions previously vested in customs officers); s 25(1) (an officer may conduct civil proceedings in a magistrates' court or in the sheriff court relating to a customs function); s 25A(1) (providing for certificates of debt); s 31 (creating an offence of obstructing an officer or person acting on his or her behalf or assisting the officer); s 32 (creating the offence of assaulting an officer); and s 33 (giving an authorized officer a power of arrest in respect of offences under ss 31 and 32).

[55] HL Deb 25 March 2009 vol 708 c687, Lord West of Spithead, Parliamentary Under-Secretary of State, Home Office; see also PBC Deb 9 June 2009 1st sitting cc14–16, per Phil Woolas MP, Minister of State, Home Office.

[56] HL Deb 25 March 2009 vol 709 cc687–8, per Lord West of Spithead, Parliamentary Under-Secretary of State, Home Office: 'Customs training covers a wide range of areas, including relevant legislation; customs regimes, such as the common agricultural policy; targeting for customs purposes; disclosure handling of material gathered during criminal investigation; questioning and note taking; how to arrest and caution; custody, charging and bail procedures; rules of evidence, interviewing, witness statements and giving evidence; customs allowances; dealing with EU and non-EU goods; calculation of duty and VAT; how to take payments, seize or detain goods and vehicles, and issue paperwork; prohibitions and restrictions; recognition of, and how to deal with controlled drugs and offensive weapons; searching persons, baggage and vehicles; personal safety training; and for officers working in Scotland, specific training in the workings of the Scottish legal system and the different regimes in place there.'

[57] BCIA 2009, s 3(2).

[58] Ibid, s 5.

[59] Ibid, s 3(5), (6), and (7).

[60] Ibid, s 3(7).

4. Director of Border Revenue

2.34 The Secretary of State by whom general customs functions are exercisable must designate an official in his or her department as the Director of Border Revenue (the Director); prior consent of the Treasury to the designation has to be obtained.[61]

(a) *Functions of the Director of Border Revenue*

2.35 The creation of that post was intended to give effect to the principle that revenue related powers should be exercised at arm's length from the Minister.[62] The functions of the Commissioners for Her Majesty's Revenue and Customs that are exercisable in relation to customs revenue matters are exercisable concurrently by the Director.[63] Customs revenue matters are defined as: agricultural levies;[64] anti-dumping duties;[65] countervailing duties;[66] customs duties;[67] duties of excise;[68] and value added tax relating to import or export of goods to or from the United Kingdom.[69]

2.36 The Director may not exercise the Commissioners' functions of making rules or regulations by statutory instrument or issuing notices, directions, or conditions applicable generally to particular classes of persons concerning value added tax.[70] However, the Treasury may, by statutory instrument subject to an affirmative resolution procedure,[71] amend the provision that stops the Director from performing any of those functions.[72] Concern was expressed by the Delegated Powers and Regulatory Reform Committee of the House of Lords about the potential for this provision to confer powers to make statutory instruments on the Director and to do so without

---

[61] Ibid, s 6.

[62] PBC Deb 9 June 2009 1st sitting c26, per Phil Woolas MP, Minister of State, Home Office, noting that presently the UK Government receives about £22 billion from tax revenue collected at the border each year.

[63] BCIA 2009, s 7(1).

[64] Ibid, s 7(2)(a); agricultural levies within the meaning of the European Communities Act 1972, s 6(8), ie levies charged in accordance with European Community arrangements.

[65] Within the meaning of Council Regulation EC 384/96 of 22 December 1995 on protection against dumped imports from countries not members of the EC. A dumped product is one whose export price is less than for the like product in the exporting country. BCIA 2009, s 7(2)(b).

[66] Within the meaning of Council Regulation EC 2026/97 of 6 October 1997 on protection against subsidised imports from countries not Member States of the EC. Article 1(1) states 'A countervailing duty may be imposed for the purpose of offsetting any subsidy granted, directly or indirectly, for the manufacture, production, export or transport of any product whose release for free circulation in the Community causes injury', BCIA 2009, s 7(2)(c).

[67] BCIA 2009, s 7(2)(d).

[68] Ibid, s 7(2)(e), other than amusement machine licence duty; bingo duty; gaming duty; general betting duty; pool betting duty; and remote gaming duty.

[69] Ibid, s 7(2)(f).

[70] Ibid, s 7(3).

[71] Ibid, s 37(4)(b).

[72] Ibid, s 8(b).

any indication of what accountability there would be to Parliament.[73] The Government acknowledged that such an amendment was possible but said it was 'highly unlikely to arise in practice, as HMRC currently has the policy (and thus the legislative) responsibility in relation to' the customs revenue matters listed in the statute.[74]

A 'customs revenue function' is a function that is exercisable by the Director or by customs revenue officials, a function conferred on them by ss 22–24 of the BCIA 2009 (relating to investigations and detention), or a function under Community law exercisable by the Director or customs revenue officials in relation to a customs revenue matter.[75] 2.37

The Treasury may, by order,[76] amend the definition of 'customs revenue matters' so as to add, modify or remove a matter and make consequential amendments to legislation whether passed before or after the BCIA 2009.[77] 2.38

(b) *Construction of Legislation Referring to the Commissioners*

Similar provision is made, as in relation to the Secretary of State and general customs officials, for legislation passed before the end of the session in which the BCIA 2009 was passed, and instruments and documents predating the BCIA 2009 to be construed as if references to functions of the Commissioners include a reference to the Director.[78] The provision does not apply (as the similar provision relating to general customs officials does) to legislation, instruments, and documents postdating the BCIA 2009. It applies only to specified provisions of the Commissioners for Revenue and Customs Act 2005 which are: s 5(1)(b) and (2)(b) (vesting in the Commissioners the functions performed by the Commissioners of Customs and Excise);[79] s 9 ('the Commissioners may do anything which they think—(a) necessary or expedient in connection with the exercise of their functions, or (b) incidental or conducive to the exercise of their functions');[80] parts of s 24 (relating to documentary evidence);[81] s 25(1), (1A), (5), and (6) (enabling an officer of Revenue and Customs or a person authorized by the Commissioners to conduct civil proceedings in a magistrates' or sheriff court and proceedings in the county court for an amount payable to the Commissioners);[82] s 26 (enabling the Commissioners to pay a reward to a person for a service relating to a function of the Commissioners or an officer of 2.39

[73] House of Lords Delegated Powers and Regulatory Reform Committee 3rd Report (2008–09) HL Paper 29, para 10 (5 February 2009).

[74] Letter from Lord West of Spithead, Parliamentary Under-Secretary of State, Home Office, appended to the House of Lords Delegated Powers and Regulatory Reform Committee 4th Report (2008–09) HL Paper 48 (5 March 2009).

[75] BCIA 2009, s 7(9).

[76] ie statutory instrument; see BCIA 2009, s 37(1).

[77] BCIA 2009, s 8.

[78] Ibid, s 7(5), (6), and (7).

[79] Ibid, s 7(8)(a).

[80] Ibid, s 7(8)(b).

[81] Ibid, s 7(8)(c).

[82] Ibid, s 7(8)(e).

Revenue and Customs);[83] s 31 (creating the offence of obstructing an officer of Revenue and Customs or a person acting on behalf of the Commissioners or an officer or assisting an officer);[84] and s 33 (the power of arrest for the obstruction offence or for assaulting an officer of Revenue and Customs).[85]

(c) *Delegation of Functions*

2.40 The Director may make arrangements to delegate a function of the Director.[86] Doing so does not prevent either the Director or a customs revenue official from exercising the function.[87] It is not apparent from the BCIA 2009 to whom such functions may be delegated: at the Committee Stage of the Bill in the House of Commons it was said for the Government that 'it is right that the director should also be able to delegate her functions to others including those in the UK Border Agency'.[88] If the Director delegates a function, he or she must monitor the exercise of the function by the delegate and the delegate must comply with the directions of the Director for exercising the function.[89]

2.41 The Director or the person to whom any of his or her functions are delegated[90] must comply with any directions of a general nature given by the Treasury;[91] any concession published by the Commissioners and available generally to any person falling within its terms;[92] any interpretation of the law issued by the Commissioners (whether or not published);[93] and any guidance issued by the Commissioners (whether or not published)[94] and must take account of any other material published by the Commissioners.[95]

(d) *Identity of the Director of Border Revenue*

2.42 The Government's intention with respect to the post of Director was 'to ensure that there is a clear, single management line by allowing the chief executive of the UK Border Agency and the Director of Border Revenue to be the same individual'.[96] The Government confirmed that 'under current arrangements for the UK Border Agency

---

83 Ibid, s 7(8)(f).
84 Ibid, s 7(8)(g).
85 Ibid, s 7(8)(h).
86 Ibid, s 9(1).
87 Ibid, s 9(2).
88 PBC Deb 9 June 2009 1st sitting c30, per Phil Woolas MP, Minister of State, Home Office.
89 BCIA 2009, s 9(3).
90 Ibid, s 10(1).
91 Ibid, s 10(2).
92 Ibid, s 10(3)(a).
93 Ibid, s 10(3)(b).
94 Ibid, s 10(4)(a).
95 Ibid, s 10(4)(b).
96 HL Deb 11 February 2009, vol 707 c1131, per Lord West of Spithead, Parliamentary Under-Secretary of State, Home Office.

the Director of Border Revenue will always be its chief executive'.[97] It was said for the Government that:

> the chief executive will be accountable to the Home Secretary in relation to all non-revenue matters, but in respect of revenue matters she or he . . . will act independently, subject, like HM Revenue and Customs, to the general oversight of Treasury Ministers. Therefore, to an extent, there will be a certain schizophrenic element to the role.[98]

That the two posts would be occupied by the same individual was not expressed on the face of the legislation because of the fluidity of the organizational structure and thus the possibility that the structure of the UK Border Agency would not be permanent.[99] 2.43

However, the intended practice is that the post of chief executive of the UK Border Agency would be filled on the basis that the post holder would also be the Director of Border Revenue and it would be done 'by open competition under Civil Service open competition rules'.[100] 2.44

5. Customs Revenue Officials

The Director may designate an immigration officer or any other official in the department of the Secretary of State by whom general customs functions are exercisable as a customs revenue official.[101] As with designation of general customs officials by the Secretary of State, the power to designate and to withdraw or vary a designation is exercisable by notice in writing to the official.[102] A designation may be limited, in particular, as to the functions that are to be exercised or the purpose for which they are to be exercised[103] and may be permanent or for a specified period and may be varied or withdrawn.[104] The Director may only designate an official if satisfied that he or she is capable of effectively carrying out the designated functions; has received adequate training; and is otherwise a suitable person to exercise those functions.[105] A customs revenue official must comply with the directions of the Director.[106] 2.45

Subject to the Director's power to impose limitations on a designation, customs revenue officials have the same functions in relation to a customs revenue matter as 2.46

---

97 HL Deb 22 April 2009 vol 709 c1539, per Lord West of Spithead, Parliamentary Under-Secretary of State, Home Office.

98 HL Deb 25 February 2009, vol 708 c243, per Lord West of Spithead, Parliamentary Under-Secretary of State, Home Office.

99 PBC Deb 9 June 2009 1st sitting c25, per Phil Woolas MP, Minister of State, Home Office.

100 HL Deb 25 March 2009 vol 709 c684, per Lord West of Spithead, Parliamentary Under-Secretary of State, Home Office.

101 BCIA 2009 s 11(1).

102 Ibid, s 12(4).

103 Ibid, s 12(1) and (2).

104 Ibid, s 12(3).

105 Ibid, s 12(5).

106 Ibid, s 13.

an officer of Revenue and Customs would have and may exercise the functions of the Director.[107]

(a) *Construction of Legislation Referring to Customs Officers*

2.47 Legislation, instruments and documents passed or made before the BCIA 2009 was passed and, unless expressly provided to the contrary, passed or made after the BCIA 2009 was passed are to be construed as if references to an officer of Revenue and Customs or to Her Majesty's Revenue and Customs includes a reference to a customs revenue official.[108] However, only certain, specified provisions of the Commissioners for Revenue and Customs Act 2005 are to be construed as applying to customs revenue officials:[109] they are the same provisions as apply to general customs officials (as to which, see above) with the addition of s 25(1A)[110] (an officer may conduct county court proceedings for the recovery of a sum of money); and s 26[111] (a reward may be paid in return for a service which relates to a function of an officer).

6. Constitutional Issues Relating to Customs Revenue Functions

2.48 The House of Lords Select Committee on the Constitution[112] concluded that the Borders, Citizenship and Immigration Bill did not sufficiently respect the 'constitutional convention, or principle . . . that the revenue affairs of individuals should be kept at arm's length from ministers'.[113] Whilst the Government accepted the existence and importance of the principle[114] the proposals contained in the Bill (and in all material respects, subsequently enacted) risked undermining the principle. The Committee contrasted the 'simple, easily understood model for preserving the principle' enacted in respect of the Commissioners of Revenue and Customs in the Commissioners of Revenue and Customs Act 2005 with the 'complex and opaque' arrangements in the Bill.[115] It highlighted in particular that the Director of Border Revenue was 'designated' by the Home Secretary; that the UKBA was an executive agency of the Home Office; that the head of the UKBA 'wears two hats' (as chief executive—accountable to the Home Secretary—and Director of Border Revenue—independent from the Home Secretary—and that designated customs revenue officials could simultaneously be immigration officers and general customs officials.

---

[107] Ibid, s 11(2).

[108] Ibid, s 11(4), (5), and (6).

[109] Ibid, s 11(7).

[110] Ibid, s 11(7)(c).

[111] Ibid, s 11(7)(e).

[112] House of Lords Select Committee on the Constitution, 5th Report (2008–09) *Part 1 of the Borders, Citizenship and Immigration Bill* HL Paper 41 (26 February 2009).

[113] Ibid, para 2.

[114] Ibid.

[115] Ibid, para 8.

3
CUSTOMS POWERS

A. INTRODUCTION

3.01 Powers relating to customs matters are conferred on officials of the United Kingdom Border Agency (UKBA) (i) by deeming references in other legislation to powers of the Her Majesty's Revenue and Customs (HMRC) as being applicable to officials of the UKBA; (ii) by specific provisions for the exchange and disclosure of information and (iii) by the specific application to UKBA officials of other legislation conferring police-like powers on HMRC officials.

B. CONSTRUCTION OF OTHER LEGISLATION

3.02 A wide range of powers is conferred on the Secretary of State, the Director of Border Revenue, general customs officials, and customs revenue officials by operation of the deeming provisions in the Borders, Citizenship and Immigration Act 2009 (BCIA 2009). By those provisions, references to the Commissioners or officers of the Revenue and Customs in enactments, instruments and documents concerned with customs matters and functions are to be construed as including a reference to the Secretary of State,[1] the Director of Border Revenue,[2] general customs officials[3] and customs revenue officials[4] as appropriate. (General customs officials and customs revenue officials are both 'designated customs officials'.[5])

---

[1] BCIA 2009, s 1(4).
[2] Ibid, s 7(5).
[3] Ibid, s 3(5).
[4] Ibid, s 11(4).
[5] Ibid, ss 14(6) and 38.

3.03 Thus, for example, the following provisions of the Customs and Excise Management Act 1979 which confer powers on officers of the Revenue and Customs are now to be construed as conferring the same powers on designated customs officials: s 27 which gives a power to board a ship, aircraft or vehicle, to 'remain therein and rummage any part thereof'; s 28 which gives a power of access to ships, aircraft and vehicles in specified places and to break open any locked containers for which the keys are withheld; ss 29 and 34 which give powers to detain ships, aircraft or vehicles; s 33 which gives a power to board and inspect an aircraft and to inspect goods loaded therein; documents relating to the aircraft and documents relating to goods and passengers carried therein; and s 72 which gives powers to board and search coasting ships and require production of documents.

3.04 The same deeming provision also applies to: s 78 of the Customs and Excise Management Act 1979 which requires any person entering or leaving the UK to answer questions with respect to his or her baggage and anything carried by the person and to produce the baggage for examination; ss 118C, 161, and 161A which give powers to enter and search premises; s 138 which confers powers of arrest in respect of any person who has committed or is reasonably suspected of having committed any offence under the Customs and Excise Acts; ss 139 and 141 which confer powers to seize or detain anything liable to forfeiture under the Customs and Excise Acts, including any ship, aircraft, vehicle, animal, or container used 'for the carriage, handling, deposit or concealment' of such a thing; s 159 which gives a power to 'examine and take account of any goods' which are imported or loaded into any ship or aircraft at any place in the UK and for that purpose, to require any container to be opened or unpacked; s 163 which gives a power to stop and search any vehicle or vessel where there are reasonable grounds to suspect that it is or may be carrying goods on which there is unpaid duty or are in the course of being unlawfully removed from or to a place or are otherwise liable to forfeiture under the Customs and Excise Acts; s 164 which gives a power to search a person on board a ship or aircraft or entering or about to leave the UK, including to conduct a strip search and an intimate search where there are reasonable grounds to suspect that he or she is carrying any article in respect of which there is unpaid duty or the import or export of which is subject to prohibition or restriction.

C. USE AND DISCLOSURE OF INFORMATION

3.05 Part 1 of the BCIA 2009 was said by the Government to establish 'a comprehensive framework covering the use and disclosure of customs information,[6] including personal customs information' and to have done so because 'information is obviously an essential tool in support of law enforcement and national security and is

[6] Defined in the BCIA 2009, ss 14(6) and 38 as 'information acquired or capable of being acquired as a result of the exercise of a general customs function or a customs revenue function'.

key to our ability to secure the border effectively'.[7] The legislative proposals (as eventually enacted) attracted concern that they, together with the accumulation of large databases by the e-borders function, were part of 'a dangerous tendency to collect too much information and to give the various organs of the state too much power to share it with one another without the permission of the person about whom the information was collected'.[8]

1. Supply of Information by the HMRC and Revenue and Customs Prosecution Office

Section 20 of the BCIA 2009 inserts new ss 41A and 41B into the UK Borders Act 2007. That Act already provided for HMRC and the Revenue and Customs Prosecution Office (RCPO) to supply information to the Secretary of State in relation to various immigration and nationality functions,[9] subject to specified restrictions on further disclosure of that information.[10] The new provisions allow the HMRC and RCPO or a person authorized to act on their behalf[11] to supply information[12] to a designated customs official, the Secretary of State, the Director of Border Revenue and a person acting on behalf of any of them[13] for the purpose of the exercise of their customs functions.[14] The provision applies equally to documents or articles coming into the possession of the HMRC or RCPO[15] and allows for the retention or disposal of such documents or articles.[16] 3.06

The recipient of the information, document or article may not further disclose the information, document[17] or article unless the disclosure:[18] is for the purpose of a customs function and does not contravene any restriction imposed by the Commissioners for HMRC or is made for the purpose of civil proceedings whether in or outside the UK and relating to a customs function or[19] is made for the purpose of a criminal investigation or criminal proceedings, whether in or outside the UK or is made in pursuance of a court order or is made with the consent, 3.07

[7] HL Deb 25 March 2009, vol 709 c691, per Lord West of Spithead, Parliamentary Under-Secretary of State, Home Office.

[8] PBC Deb 9 June 2009 1st sitting c31, per Damian Green MP (Conservative), Shadow Minister for immigration.

[9] UK Borders Act 2007, s 40.

[10] Ibid, s 41.

[11] Ibid, new s 41A(5).

[12] Ibid, new s 41A(1).

[13] Ibid, new s 41A(2).

[14] Ibid, new s 41A(1).

[15] Ibid, new s 41A(3).

[16] Ibid, new s 41A(4).

[17] Ibid, new s 41B(1) and (4).

[18] Ibid, new s 41B(2).

[19] The Minister gave as an example of the UKBA needing to make such a disclosure, the disclosure of information to the VAT and duties tribunal if UKBA officials are aware of, or believe there to be, a transgression of VAT duty payment; PBC Deb 9 June 2009, 2nd sitting c45, per Phil Woolas MP, Minister of State, Home Office.

general[20] or specific, of the HMRC or the RCPO or is made with the consent of each person to whom the information relates. The prohibition on further disclosure is also subject to any other enactment permitting disclosure.[21] A person who makes a wrongful disclosure of information received from the HMRC or RCPO may be liable to prosecution.[22]

2. Duty to Share Passenger and Freight Information

3.08 Section 21 of the BCIA 2009 amends Immigration, Asylum and Nationality Act 2006, s 36, which imposes a duty on certain persons to share information relating to the passengers, crew and freight of ships and aircraft. It does so by adding to the list of persons[23] required to share such information designated customs officials; immigration officers; the Secretary of State insofar as he or she has general customs functions, immigration, asylum, or nationality functions and the Director of Border Revenue and any person exercising functions of the Director.

3. Power to Share Customs Information

3.09 A designated customs official,[24] an immigration officer, the Director of Border Revenue, the Secretary of State by whom general customs functions are exercisable, any other Minister of the Crown in his or her department, and a person acting on behalf of any of them[25] may use customs information acquired in connection with a function exercisable by him or her in connection with any other function exercisable by the person.[26] He or she may also disclose customs information to any other

[20] Phil Woolas MP, Minister of State, Home Office, stated: 'the ability to share information under the 2007 Act, in accordance with general consents given by HMRC or RCPO will not lead to unrestricted data sharing but, rather, will enable a class of relevant information to be shared where that is appropriate. It would be impractical and hugely resource intensive if . . . HMRC had to provide specific consent each and every time they supplied information to a person under section 41A of the 2007 Act' PBC Deb 9 June 2009, 2nd sitting c45.

[21] UK Borders Act 2007, new s 41B(3). 'Enactment' does not include legislation of the Scottish Parliament or the Northern Ireland Assembly, see UK Borders Act 2007, new s 41B(6).

[22] Under UK Borders Act 2007, s 42(1), as amended by BCIA 2009, s 20(2).

[23] In the Immigration, Asylum and Nationality Act 2006, s 36(1).

[24] BCIA 2009, s 14(2)(a) and (6). A designated customs official means a general customs official or a customs revenue official.

[25] Ibid, s 14(2). Questioned about who was the first person referred to in s 14(2)(f) ('a person acting on behalf of a person mentioned in paragraphs (a) to (e)'), Lord West of Spithead, Parliamentary Under-Secretary of State, Home Office, stated in the House of Lords at the Committee Stage: 'The UK Border Agency or the border force must have flexibility to respond to the ever changing challenge of protecting our borders. From time to time, the agency will need to use contractors to support and supplement its own staff. It is only right and proper that where the agency needs to do that, the contractors concerned should be able to use and disclose any customs information in so far as that is necessary for them to fulfil their contractual obligations. Any such contractor will be subject to the provisions in the [Act] regulating the use and disclosure of customs information, including [section] 18 which establishes a criminal offence of wrongful disclosure.' HL Comm Deb 25 February 2009, vol 708 c258.

[26] BCIA 2009, s 14(1)(a).

of those persons for the purpose of a function exercisable by that person.[27] Note that the purpose for which the disclosure is made need not be a customs function[28] but may be any function exercised by the person to whom disclosure is made.

The Government promoted this provision as equipping the border force 'with the ability to pool its customs information internally so that any such information acquired by a person to whom the clause applies can pass it to another person to be used for that other person's function' and permitting 'any such person to disclose customs information to another person to whom the [provision] applies for any function exercisable by the recipient. This will enable the UK Border Agency to use its resources as effectively as possible by improving targeting and data sharing across the full range of its immigration and customs functions'. It declined to attach a requirement of 'reasonableness' to any disclosure.[29] 3.10

4. Confidentiality of Customs Information

However, the use and disclosure of customs information is subject to any enactment restricting or prohibiting the use or disclosure of information in Part 1 of the BCIA 2009, any other enactment (not including legislation of the Scottish Parliament, the National Assembly for Wales, or the Northern Ireland Assembly)[30] or an international or other agreement to which the UK is party.[31] 3.11

The BCIA 2009 itself prohibits disclosure of 'personal customs information', (ie customs information relating to a person that identifies the person or, whether by itself or in combination with other information, enables the person to be identified)[32] by a relevant official,[33] the Secretary of State or a Minister in his or her department other than to another relevant official or Minister in the same department.[34] Note that the Secretary of State is not one of the persons to whom personal customs information may be disclosed. 3.12

A person who is or was a relevant official may not disclose personal customs revenue information to a Minister of the Crown.[35] Thus, personal customs information may be disclosed to a Minister (but not the Secretary of State); personal customs revenue information may not be disclosed to either the Minister or the 3.13

---

[27] Ibid, s 14(1)(b).

[28] A customs function is a general customs function or a customs revenue function, see BCIA 2009, s 15(6).

[29] HL Deb 25 February 2009, vol 708 c254, per Lord West of Spithead, Parliamentary Under-Secretary of State, Home Office.

[30] BCIA 2009, s 14(4).

[31] Ibid, s 14(3).

[32] Ibid, s 15(4).

[33] ie a designated customs official, an immigration officer, the Director of Border Revenue, or a person acting on behalf of one of them or on behalf of the Secretary of State, BCIA 2009, s 15(3).

[34] BCIA 2009, s 15(1).

[35] Ibid, s 15(2).

Secretary of State. This is clearly intended to give effect to the constitutional principle that individuals' tax affairs are to be kept at arm's length from Ministers.

5. Exceptions to the Statutory Duty of Confidentiality with Respect to Customs Information

3.14 However, the prohibition on disclosure does not apply to information that the person knows was acquired other than as a result of the exercise of a customs function[36] and it does not apply to information supplied by or on behalf of HMRC or the Revenue and Customs Prosecutions Office.[37]

3.15 Moreover, the prohibition on disclosure is subject to exceptions provided in BCIA 2009, s 16, and to any enactment[38] permitting disclosure where the disclosure would not contravene any restriction imposed by the Commissioners on the disclosure of customs revenue information.[39]

3.16 Section 16 of the BCIA 2009 provides that the prohibitions on disclosure of personal customs information other than to a relevant official or a Minister and on disclosure of personal customs revenue information to a Minister do not apply[40] in a number of circumstances that are set out below. In the case of disclosure of customs revenue information, a further condition has to be satisfied before the prohibition on disclosure is disapplied and that is that the disclosure does not contravene any restriction imposed by the Commissioners for HMRC.[41] However, that further condition does not have to be satisfied if the person making the disclosure knows that the customs revenue information was obtained otherwise than as a result of the exercise of a customs revenue function.[42]

3.17 First of all, the prohibitions do not apply to a disclosure that is made for the purposes of a customs function; a function relating to immigration, asylum, or nationality; a function relating to national security or a function relating to the prevention or detection of crime.[43]

3.18 Secondly, the prohibitions do not apply to a disclosure that is made to a person exercising public functions whether or not within the UK and made for the purposes of any of those functions.[44] There is no definition in the BCIA 2009 of 'public functions'. This appears on its face to be an extremely broad exception to the statutory duty of confidentiality.

---

[36] Ibid, s 15(5).

[37] Ibid, s 15(7).

[38] 'Any enactment' does not include any provision contained in Part 1 to the BCIA 2009 and does not include an Act of the Scottish Parliament, a measure or Act of the National Assembly for Wales or Northern Ireland legislation, BCIA 2009, s 15(6)(b) and (8).

[39] BCIA 2009, s 15(6)(b).

[40] Ibid, s 15(1)(a).

[41] Ibid, s 15(1)(b).

[42] Ibid, s 15(2).

[43] Ibid, s 16(1) and (3).

[44] Ibid, s 16(1) and (4).

Thirdly, the prohibitions do not apply to a disclosure made for the purpose of civil proceedings, whether or not within the UK, relating to a customs function or a function relating to immigration, asylum, nationality, national security or the prevention or detection of crime.[45] 3.19

Fourthly, the prohibitions do not apply to a disclosure that is made for the purpose of a criminal investigation or criminal proceedings, whether or not within the UK.[46] 3.20

Fifthly, the prohibitions do not apply to a disclosure that is made in pursuance of a court order.[47] 3.21

Sixthly, the prohibitions do not apply to a disclosure that is made with the consent of each person to whom the information relates.[48] 3.22

Seventhly, the prohibitions do not apply to a disclosure that is made in order to comply with an obligation of the UK under an international or other agreement.[49] 3.23

Eighthly, the prohibitions do not apply to a disclosure to a person specified in regulations made jointly by the Treasury and the Secretary of State or to a disclosure of a kind specified in such regulations.[50] 3.24

6. Prohibition of Further Disclosure of Customs Information

A person to whom information is disclosed in reliance on the exceptions contained in s 16 of the BCIA 2009 (and set out above) to the prohibitions on disclosure of personal customs information may not further disclose that information other than in the following situations. First, that a relevant official consents to the further disclosure. Such consent may be specific or general.[51] Second, that one of the exceptions contained in s 16 applies to the disclosure.[52] In each of these two situations, if the disclosure is of customs revenue information, the further condition must be satisfied that the disclosure does not contravene any restrictions imposed by the Commissioner for HMRC[53] (unless the person making the disclosure knows that the information was disclosed other than as a result of the exercise of a customs revenue function[54]). The third situation in which further disclosure is not prohibited is one where any other enactment permits disclosure.[55] 3.25

[45] Ibid, s 16(1) and (5)(a).
[46] Ibid, s 16(1) and (5)(b).
[47] Ibid, s 16(1) and (5)(c).
[48] Ibid, s 16(1) and (6).
[49] Ibid, s 16(1) and (7).
[50] Ibid, s 16(1) and (8).
[51] Ibid, s 17(1).
[52] Ibid, s 17(2)(b).
[53] Ibid, s 17(2)(b).
[54] Ibid, s 17(3).
[55] Ibid, s 17(4). An enactment does not include legislation of the Scottish Parliament, the National Assembly for Wales, and the Northern Ireland Assembly, BCIA 2009, s 17(5).

3.26 The provisions authorizing disclosure of customs information do not permit a disclosure contravening the Data Protection Act or which is prohibited by Part 1 of the Regulation of Investigatory Powers Act 2000[56] (ie disclosures related to the interception of communications by post or by a public or private telecommunications system). Information whose disclosure is prohibited by ss 15(1), (2) or 17(1) of this Act is 'exempt information' by virtue of s 44(1)(a) of the Freedom of Information Act 2000,[57] (so that the right of access to information held by a public authority, given by the Freedom of Information Act 2000, does not apply[58]) even if the prohibition was disapplied by one of the exceptions contained in s 16 or another enactment permitted its disclosure.[59]

7. Offence of Wrongful Disclosure

3.27 A person commits an offence if he or she breaches the prohibitions on disclosure by a relevant official, the Secretary of State, or a Minister of personal customs information other than to a Minister or relevant official; on disclosure by a relevant official of personal customs information to a Minister; and on further disclosure of information disclosed in reliance on BCIA 2009, s 16.[60]

3.28 It is a defence for the person to prove that he or she reasonably believed that the disclosure was lawful or that the information had already and lawfully been made available to the public.[61]

3.29 A prosecution for such an offence may only be brought in England or Wales with the consent of the Director of Public Prosecutions or the Director of Revenue and Customs Prosecutions or in Northern Ireland, with the consent of the Director of Public Prosecutions for Northern Ireland.[62]

3.30 A person guilty of an offence is liable on conviction on indictment to imprisonment for up to two years or to a fine or both. If summarily convicted in England, Wales or Scotland, the person is liable to imprisonment for up to 12 months or to a fine not exceeding the statutory maximum whilst if summarily convicted in Northern Ireland, the person is liable to imprisonment for up to six months or to a fine not exceeding the statutory maximum.[63]

3.31 The provision for the offence of wrongful disclosure is without prejudice to the pursuit of any remedy or the taking of any action in relation to a breach of the statutory prohibitions on disclosure.[64]

---

56 Ibid, s 19(1).
57 Ibid, s 19(2).
58 Freedom of Information Act 2000, ss 1(1)(a) and 2(3)(h).
59 BCIA 2009, s 19(3).
60 Ibid, s 18(1).
61 Ibid, s 18(2).
62 Ibid, s 18(3).
63 Ibid, s 18(5).
64 Ibid, s 18(4).

D. INVESTIGATIONS AND DETENTION

Sections 22–24 of the BCIA 2009 give to UKBA officials similar powers, subject to similar safeguards, to those exercised by HMRC in relation to the investigation of offences and detention of persons. They do so by applying various provisions of the Police and Criminal Evidence Act 1984 (PACE) to UKBA officials, including provisions relating to the searching of premises, seizure of property, powers of arrest, searching of persons, places of detention, designation of custody officers and imposition of custody time limits. 3.32

1. The Secretary of State's Order Making Power

Section 23 of the BCIA 2009 gives the Secretary of State power to provide, by order (ie a statutory instrument subject to the affirmative resolution procedure[65]), for the Police and Criminal Evidence Act 1984 (PACE) and the Police and Criminal Evidence (Northern Ireland) Order 1989 (SI 1989/1341 (NI 12) to apply (subject to modifications) to investigations of offences conducted by designated customs officials and immigration officers and to persons detained by designated customs officials and immigration officers.[66] Phil Woolas MP, Minister of State, Home Office, referred to it as allowing 'the creation in future of a comprehensive framework for UKBA, including immigration'.[67] 3.33

The Government indicated that it intends to use this order making power to make provision in respect of immigration (as opposed to customs) powers of detention, replacing the Immigration (PACE Codes of Practice) Direction 2000[68] so as 'to bring together in one place the PACE powers and safeguards to be applied in relation to the border force customs and immigration functions'.[69] However, in the same debate, the same Minister said that PACE provisions would not be extended to the exercise of administrative powers, including powers of detention, by immigration officers.[70] In his letter of 23 February to the Joint Committee on Human Rights he said: 3.34

Most people detained by immigration officers are held in connection with administrative immigration processes, rather than as part of any criminal investigation. It would not be appropriate to apply the provisions of PACE and the Codes to those administrative processes,

[65] Ibid, ss 23(1) and 37(1), (3), and (4)(d)

[66] Ibid, s 23(1).

[67] PBC Deb 9 June 2009 2nd sitting c52.

[68] And the Immigration (PACE Codes of Practice No 2 and Amendment) Direction 2000, both made under Immigration and Asylum Act 1999, s 145.

[69] HL Comm Deb 25 February 2009 cc262–3, per Lord West of Spithead, Parliamentary Under-Secretary of State, Home Office. See also cc266–7 where Lord West of Spithead said 'we will make an order under Clause 22 [now section 23] to replace the Immigration (PACE Codes of Practice) Direction 2000 and the Immigration (PACE Codes of Practice No 2 and Amendment) Direction 2000.

[70] Ibid.

or to any persons detained in connection with them: nor is it intended that any order made in due course under Clause 22 of the Bill [now section 23] should alter that position.[71]

Nor would PACE and the relevant provisions of the codes be applied to immigration officers' powers to detain and search individuals under s 2 of the UK Borders Act 2007 because 'such officers do not carry out any of the substantive functions of a police constable. They act in support, not in place of the police.'[72] It seems that the intention is to use the order making power to extend PACE to any criminal investigation conducted by immigration officers, and to persons detained by those officers in connection with any such investigation.[73]

2. Application of the PACE Orders

3.35 In the absence of a bespoke order for immigration officers and designated customs officials made under s 23, the BCIA 2009 provides for the orders which applied the Police and Criminal Evidence Act 1984 and the Police and Criminal Evidence (Northern Ireland) Order to customs officers to be modified and applied in relation to immigration officers and designated customs officials.[74] It thereby seeks to ensure a 'seamless application of PACE to those officers transferring from HMRC to the UK Border Agency, until a further bespoke PACE application order is made in relation to the border force customs and immigration functions'.[75] The provision applying the existing PACE orders may be amended or repealed 'by order'[76]—presumably once bespoke orders have been made.

3.36 The Government declined to apply the provisions of PACE to cover private contractors providing services relating to investigations and detention of persons because they did not have the statutory powers and responsibility possessed by UKBA officials. Responsibility for services provided by contractors would rest with the UKBA officials.[77]

3.37 Various provisions of PACE or, for Northern Ireland, the Police and Criminal Evidence (Northern Ireland) Order 1989 were applied to the investigation of offences and to detention by officers of Revenue and Customs by 'the PACE orders', ie the PACE (Application to Revenue and Customs) Order 2007[78] and the Police and Criminal Evidence (Application to Revenue and Customs) Order

[71] Letter from Lord West of Spithead, Parliamentary Under-Secretary of State, Home Office, 23 February 2009, appended to the JCHR Legislative Scrutiny: Borders, Citizenship and Immigration Bill 9th Report (2008–09) HL Paper 62, HC 375 (24 March 2009).

[72] Ibid.

[73] PBC Deb 9 June 2009, 2nd sitting c57, per Phil Woolas MP, Minister of State, Home Office.

[74] BCIA 2009, s 22.

[75] HL Comm Deb 25 February 2009 vol 708 c262, per Lord West of Spithead, Parliamentary Under-Secretary of State, Home Office.

[76] BCIA 2009, s 23(5).

[77] HL Comm Deb 25 February 2009 vol 708 c267, per Lord West of Spithead, Parliamentary Under-Secretary of State, Home Office.

[78] SI 2007/3175, by article 3(1) applying the provisions of PACE in Schedule 1 to the Order.

(Northern Ireland) 2007.[79] Schedule 1 to the PACE orders listed the provisions of PACE or the 1989 Order that were to apply, by article 3(1) of the PACE orders, to investigations conducted by officers of the Revenue and Customs and to persons detained by such officers.

Section 22 of the BCIA 2009 applies the PACE orders (subject to modifications) to criminal investigations conducted by designated customs officials relating to a general customs matter or a customs revenue matter[80] and to persons detained by designated customs officials.[81] It does not apply the entirety of the PACE orders because some of the powers conferred by them relate to inland customs matters, such as the powers relating to production orders in tax investigations that would not be required by UKBA.[82] 3.38

To that end, the BCIA 2009 requires certain terms in the PACE orders to be read according to the different context to which they are being applied. Thus, references to an officer of Revenue and Customs are to be read as references to a designated customs official;[83] references to the Commissioners are to be read as references to the Secretary of State in relation to general customs matters or the Director of Border Revenue in relation to customs revenue matters;[84] references to HMRC or to Revenue and Customs are to be read as references to the Secretary of State, the Director of Border Revenue, and designated customs officials;[85] references to an office or a designated office of Revenue and Customs are to be read as references to an office or a designated office of the UK Border Agency;[86] references to a relevant indictable offence are to be read as references to an indictable offence that relates to a general customs matter or a customs revenue matter;[87] references to a relevant investigation are to be read as references to a criminal investigation conducted by a designated customs official that relates to a general customs matter;[88] references to a person being in Revenue and Customs detention are to be read as references to a person being in UK Border Agency detention;[89] references to an officer of Revenue and Customs of at least the grade[90] of officer are to be read as 3.39

[79] SR 2007/464.

[80] BCIA 2009, s 22(1)(a).

[81] Ibid, s 22(1)(b).

[82] PBC Deb 9 June 2009 2nd sitting c53, per Phil Woolas MP, Minister of State, Home Office.

[83] BCIA 2009, s 22(3)(a).

[84] Ibid, s 22(3)(b).

[85] Ibid, s 22(3)(c).

[86] Ibid, s 22(3)(d) and (e).

[87] Ibid, s 22(f).

[88] Ibid, s 22(g).

[89] Ibid, s 22(h).

[90] Part 2 of Schedule 2 to the PACE order includes a table setting out 'where in the Act an act or thing is to be done by a constable of a rank specified in column 1, that same act or thing shall, in the application of the Act to Revenue and Customs, be done by an officer of Revenue and Customs of at least an equivalent grade specified in column 2'. The BCIA 2009, s 22(3) then provides how those ranks and grades are to be read for designated customs officials. In certain circumstances, a person may be authorized to exercise a power which PACE requires to be exercised by a person of higher rank, PACE 1984, s 107.

references to a designated customs official of at least the grade of immigration officer or executive officer;[91] references to an officer of Revenue and Customs of at least the grade of higher officer are to be read as references to a designated customs official of at least the grade of immigration officer or executive officer;[92] references to an officer of Revenue and Customs of at least the grade of senior officer are to be read as references to a designated customs official of at least the grade of immigration inspector or senior executive officer[93] and any other references to an officer of Revenue and Customs occupying a specified post or grade are to be read as references to the Secretary of State.[94]

3.40 As far as the investigation of offences and detention of persons are concerned, the effects of the PACE orders as modified by the BCIA 2009 include the following.

(a) *Powers to Search Premises and Seize Articles*

3.41 A designated customs official can apply to a justice of the peace for a search warrant[95] and to a circuit judge for an order giving him or her access to 'excluded material or special procedure material'[96] (ie certain types of confidential material). He or she may enter and search any premises for the purpose of executing an arrest warrant or arresting a person for an indictable offence;[97] may enter and search any premises occupied or controlled by a person arrested for an indictable offence;[98] if lawfully on any premises, may seize anything which is on the premises if (inter alia) he or she has reasonable grounds to believe that it is evidence relating to an offence that he or she is investigating,[99] including information stored in electronic form.[100] When searching premises in reliance on a warrant, a designated customs official may search any person found on the premises where he or she has reasonable cause to believe that the person is in possession of material which is likely to be of substantial value to the investigation.[101] Designated customs officials' powers to seize items are not limited to items that are evidence of offences in relation to which they have functions.[102] The designated official is obliged, if requested to do so, to provide a record of what is seized and a photograph or photocopy of

[91] BCIA 2009, s 22(3)(i).

[92] Ibid, s 22(3)(j).

[93] Ibid, s 22(3)(k).

[94] Ibid, s 22(3)(l).

[95] PACE 1984, s 8, subject to the safeguards in s 15 and if issued, to be executed in accordance with s 16.

[96] Ibid, s 9. The definition of excluded material and special procedure material is modified by article 6 of the PACE orders.

[97] Ibid, s 17.

[98] Ibid, s 18, modified by article 8 of the PACE orders.

[99] Ibid, s 19.

[100] Ibid, s 20.

[101] PACE (Application to Revenue and Customs) Order 2007, SI 2007/3175, art 18.

[102] PACE orders, art 5.

seized material.[103] He or she may retain seized material for as long as necessary in all the circumstances.[104]

(b) *Powers of Arrest*

3.42 A designated customs official may arrest without warrant anyone who is about to commit or is in the act of committing an offence or whom he or she has reasonable grounds to suspect is or is about to commit an offence or whom the designated customs official reasonably suspects to be guilty of an offence.[105]

(c) *Use of Reasonable Force*

3.43 Where any provision of PACE, as applied to designated customs officials, confers a power on a designated customs official and does not provide that the power may only be exercised with the consent of some other person, the official may use reasonable force, if necessary, in the exercise of the power.[106]

(d) *Detention of Suspects*

3.44 A person arrested by a designated customs official must be taken to an office of the UKBA and, if detained for more than six hours, must be taken to a designated office of the UKBA.[107] A person is in UK Border Agency detention if taken to a UKBA office after being arrested or, having attended a UKBA office voluntarily, is arrested there.[108] A person may be transferred between UKBA detention and Revenue and Customs detention and between UKBA detention and police detention.[109] The Government confirmed that a person transferred between non-designated UKBA and HMRC offices could not be detained for six hours in each but only for a total of six hours.[110]

3.45 A person arrested for an offence may not be kept in detention except in accordance with the provisions of Part IV of PACE including: that he or she is to be released if the grounds for detention cease to apply;[111] the Secretary of State is required to designate UKBA offices for the purpose of detaining arrested persons and to designate offices that appear to him or her to provide enough accommodation

---

103 PACE 1984, s 21.

104 Ibid, s 22.

105 Ibid, s 24. This power does not limit any other power of arrest conferred on designated customs officials by any other enactment, eg Customs and Excise Management Act 1979, s 138(1), PACE (Application to Revenue and Customs) Order 2007, SI 2007/3175, art 17.

106 PACE (Application to Revenue and Customs) Order 2007, SI 2007/3175, art 16.

107 PACE 1984, s 30. An office of the UKBA is 'premises wholly or partly occupied by designated customs officials', BCIA 2009, s 22(4)(b).

108 BCIA 2009, s 22(4)(a).

109 Ibid, s 22(6).

110 HL Deb 25 March 2009 vol 709 c698, per Lord West of Spithead, Parliamentary Under-Secretary of State, Home Office.

111 PACE 1984, s 34.

for that purpose;[112] a designated customs official must be appointed by the Secretary of State as custody officer at each designated office[113] and he or she is responsible for determining whether to charge, release, or authorize detention of the arrested person.[114] The custody officer is responsible for ensuring that the detained person is treated in accordance with PACE and any relevant code of practice and that a custody record is kept.[115] Periodic reviews of the person's detention are to be carried out by the custody officer in respect of a person charged and by a designated customs official of at least immigration officer or executive officer grade in respect of a person who has not been charged.[116]

(e) *Custody Time Limits*

3.46 A person may not be kept in UK Border Agency detention for more than 24 hours without being charged[117] unless a designated customs official of at least the rank of inspector or senior executive officer has reasonable grounds for believing that further detention is necessary to preserve evidence or obtain evidence by questioning in relation to the offence for which the person was arrested; that the offence is indictable and that it is being investigated diligently and expeditiously.[118] In that case, detention for up to 36 hours may be authorized. Thereafter, a designated customs official may apply to a magistrates' court for a warrant of further detention which may authorize up to 36 hours' further detention;[119] application may be made to extend the warrant up to a maximum of 96 hours' detention from the earlier of the time of the person's arrival at the UKBA office and the time of the person's arrest.[120] Each UKBA office is required to keep written records showing on an annual basis the numbers of people detained for more than 24 hours and subsequently released without charge and of warrants for further detention.[121]

3.47 Nothing in Part IV of PACE affects the right of any detained person to apply for habeus corpus.

(f) *Questioning and Treatment of Persons by Designated Customs Officials*

3.48 The custody officer is to ascertain and make a record of everything that a person has with him when brought under arrest to, or arrested at, a UKBA office and the

[112] Ibid, s 35, modified by the PACE (Application to Revenue and Customs) Order 2007, SI 2007/3175, art 9, but not by the Northern Ireland order.

[113] Ibid, s 36, modified by the PACE (Application to Revenue and Customs) Order 2007, SI 2007/3175, art 10, but not by the Northern Ireland order.

[114] Ibid, s 37.

[115] Ibid, s 39.

[116] Ibid, s 40.

[117] Ibid, s 41, modified by the PACE (Application to Revenue and Customs) Order 2007, SI 2007/3175, art 11, but not by the Northern Ireland order.

[118] Ibid, s 42.

[119] Ibid, s 43.

[120] Ibid, s 44.

[121] Ibid, s 50, the PACE (Application to Revenue and Customs) Order 2007, SI 2007/3175, art 12, and the Northern Ireland order, art 9.

person may be searched by a designated customs official.[122] A designated customs official of immigration officer or executive officer grade may authorize the carrying out of an intimate search if there are reasonable grounds for believing that the detained person has concealed on him anything which could cause injury to him or herself or to others.[123] Intimate samples may be taken from a person if a designated customs official of at least the grade of immigration officer or executive officer authorizes the taking of samples and the person consents.[124] A non-intimate sample may be taken with the authority of a designated customs official of at least immigration officer or executive officer grade, and without the person's consent in various circumstances including if the person is in detention in consequence of arrest for a recordable offence or the person is held on the authority of a court.[125] Fingerprints, impressions of footwear or samples taken from a person need not be destroyed after they have fulfilled the purpose for which they were taken unless the person from whom they were taken is not suspected of having committed the offence investigated.[126]

A person detained is entitled to have one friend or relative or other person known to him or her and likely to take an interest in the person's welfare informed of his or her arrest and detention.[127] 3.49

A person arrested and held in custody at a UK Border Agency Office is entitled to consult a solicitor privately at any time.[128] 3.50

The PACE codes of practice are applicable to investigations by designated customs officers because a person other than a police officer charged with the duty of investigating an offence is obliged to have regard to any relevant provision of a code.[129] They are admissible in evidence in criminal and civil proceedings and if any question of a code appears to the court to be relevant to any question arising, it shall be taken into account in determining that question.[130] 3.51

A court is required to give a warning to the jury of a special need for caution if the case against the accused depends wholly or substantially on a confession by him or 3.52

[122] Ibid, s 54.

[123] Ibid, s 55, the PACE (Application to Revenue and Customs) Order 2007, SI 2007/3175, art 13 and the Northern Ireland order, art 10.

[124] Ibid, s 62.

[125] Ibid, s 63.

[126] Ibid, s 64, modified by the PACE (Application to Revenue and Customs) Order 2007, SI 2007/3175, art 14.

[127] Ibid, s 56.

[128] Ibid, s 58.

[129] Ibid, s 67(9). Lord West of Spithead, Parliamentary Under-Secretary of State, Home Office, specifically referred to this provision in relation to investigation of offences by immigration officers in his letter of 23 February 2009 to the JCHR, JCHR Legislative Scrutiny: Borders, Citizenship and Immigration Bill 9th (2008–09) HL Paper 62 HC 375 (24 March 2009).

[130] PACE 1984, s 67.

her and the court is satisfied that the person is mentally handicapped and the confession was not made in the presence of an independent person.[131]

(g) *Exceptions*

3.53 Designated customs officials do not have power to charge a person with any offence, to release a person on bail or to detain a person after he or she has been charged with an offence.[132]

3. Scotland

3.54 The provisions of PACE do not apply in Scotland. The powers of the HMRC to investigate offences and detain suspects are contained in the Criminal Law (Consolidation)(Scotland) Act 1995. BCIA 2009, s 24, adds a new s 26C to that Act so as to make it applicable to criminal investigations conducted by designated customs officials.

4. Short Term Holding Facilities

3.55 The Immigration and Asylum Act 1999 (IAA 1999) defined a 'short term holding facility' as 'a place used solely for the detention of detained persons for a period of not more than seven days or for such other period as may be prescribed'.[133] 'Detained persons' means persons detained or required to be detained under powers in the Immigration Acts.[134] The BCIA 2009 amends the definition of 'short term holding facilities' so that in addition, a short term holding facility means a place for the detention of persons other than detained persons (ie persons detained other than under the Immigration Acts) who may be detained 'for any period'.[135] In fact, the Government gave an assurance that these facilities would not in fact be used to hold people for more than seven days.[136]

3.56 In the House of Commons, Phil Woolas MP, Minister of State, Home Office, stated:

> Short-term holding facilities fall into two categories—the residential facilities at Dover, Manchester, Harwich and Colnbrook near Heathrow, and the holding rooms at most ports and certain UK Border Agency offices. All are subject to a statutory maximum stay of seven days. At present, short-term holding facilities may be used to hold only individuals who have been detained for immigration purposes under UKBA's administrative powers of detention,

---

[131] Ibid, s 77, modified by the PACE (Application to Revenue and Customs) Order 2007, SI 2007/3175, art 15.

[132] Article 4 of the PACE orders, read in the light of BCIA 2009, s 22.

[133] IAA 1999, s 147.

[134] Ibid; for the 'Immigration Act' see UKBA 2007, s 61(2).

[135] BCIA 2009, s 25.

[136] PBC Deb 9 June 2009 c58, per Phil Woolas MP, Minister of State, Home Office.

and those who have been detained under section 2 of the UK Borders Act 2007, pending the arrival of a police officer.

By modifying the definition of short-term holding facilities, we are removing that constraint so as to allow other categories of persons to be held in those facilities. As a consequence, short-term holding facilities will be able to hold a range of individuals, subject to the prescribed periods of detention and protections relevant in each case. That could include individuals arrested in connection with immigration or customs offences, individuals detained under section 2 of the UK Borders Act as liable to arrest and pending the arrival of a police officer or, as now, individuals detained in detention under the Immigration and Asylum Act 1999.[137]

The Government emphasized that this provision would not affect the treatment of persons detained under powers in the Immigration Acts but would 'simply allow the UK Border Agency and HMRC to use short term holding facilities to detain persons following arrest where this is in accordance with the provisions that we are making in relation to the application of PACE and the associated codes of practice'.[138] It was also said that 'the short term holding facilities are UKBA accommodation that we currently use for the short term detention of a person detained under the Immigration Acts so we are saying that those can now be utilised by all people in the border agency'.[139] 3.57

137 HC Deb 14 July 2009 vol 496 c179, per Phil Woolas MP, Minister of State, Home Office.

138 HL Comm Deb 25 February 2009 vol 708 c287, per Lord West of Spithead, Parliamentary Under-Secretary of State, Home Office.

139 Ibid, c289, per Lord West of Spithead, Parliamentary Under-Secretary of State, Home Office.

4

INSPECTION AND OVERSIGHT AND MISCELLANEOUS MATTERS

A. INTRODUCTION

4.01 There are provisions in the Borders, Citizenship and Immigration Act 2009 (BCIA 2009), concerned with inspection, that adapt existing oversight arrangements to the changes in the operation of border functions instituted by Part 1 of the Act.

B. INSPECTIONS BY THE CHIEF INSPECTOR OF THE UK BORDER AGENCY

4.02 Section 48 of the UK Borders Act 2007 required the Secretary of State to appoint a person as Chief Inspector of the Border and Immigration Agency to monitor and report on the efficiency and effectiveness of the Agency. BCIA 2009, s 28, makes various amendments to that provision to further the Government's intention 'that the chief inspector should have oversight of the full range of functions to be exercised by the [UK Border] agency, including customs functions for which the agency will have prime responsibility at the border'.[1]

4.03 First of all, it changes the Chief Inspector's title to 'Chief Inspector of the UK Border Agency'[2] and provides that the person holding the office of Chief Inspector

[1] HL Comm Deb 25 February 2009, vol 708 c292, per Lord West of Spithead, Parliamentary Under-Secretary of State, Home Office.

[2] BCIA 2009, s 28(1), amending UKBA 2007, s 48(1).

of the Border and Immigration Agency when the BCIA 2009 is passed is to be treated as if appointed Chief Inspector of the UK Border Agency.[3]

Secondly, in place of the original compendious term for the object of inspection ie 'the Border and Immigration Agency'[4] the BCIA 2009 requires the Chief Inspector to 'monitor and report on the efficiency and effectiveness of the performance of functions by' designated customs officials and officials of the Secretary of State exercising customs functions; immigration officers and officials of the Secretary of State exercising functions relating to immigration, asylum, or nationality; the Secretary of State in so far as the Secretary of State has general customs functions; the Secretary of State in so far as the Secretary of State has functions relating to immigration, asylum, or nationality; the Director of Border Revenue; and any person exercising functions of the Director.[5] 4.04

Thirdly, the Chief Inspector is required to monitor and report on the efficiency and effectiveness of services provided by contractors engaged in relation to those functions.[6] 4.05

Fourthly, the list of matters that the Chief Inspector is required to consider and make recommendations about is extended to include: practice and procedure in relation to the prevention, detection, and investigation of offences; practice and procedure in relation to the conduct of criminal proceedings and whether customs functions have been appropriately exercised by the Secretary of State and the Director of Border Revenue.[7] 4.06

Fifthly, the Chief Inspector is not required to report on the functions of those he is otherwise required to monitor at removal centres, short term holding centres and under escort arrangements and detention facilities in so far as they are monitored by HM Chief Inspector of Prisons, HM Inspectors of Constabulary, the Scottish inspectors, or the Northern Ireland inspectors.[8] The intention, thereby, is to avoid duplication of inspection regimes leaving primary oversight of detention facilities to the expertise of the prisons inspectorates.[9] 4.07

C. INSPECTIONS BY HER MAJESTY'S INSPECTORS OF CONSTABULARY

The Secretary of State may make regulations conferring functions on HM Inspectors of Constabulary, the Scottish inspectors or the Northern Ireland inspectors in relation to designated customs officials and officials of the Secretary of State exercising 4.08

[3] BCIA 2009, s 28(10).
[4] UKBA 2007, s 48(2) (as originally enacted).
[5] BCIA 2009, s 28(2), inserting a new subsection (1A) into s 48 of the UKBA 2007.
[6] Ibid, s 28(2), inserting a new subsection (1B) into s 48 of the UKBA 2007.
[7] Ibid, s 28(3)(d), inserting new subsections (2)(ga), (gb), and (gc) into s 48 of the UKBA 2007.
[8] Ibid, s 28(4), inserting a new subsection (2A) into s 48 of the UKBA 2007.
[9] PBC Deb 9 June 2009 c63, per Phil Woolas MP, Minister of State, Home Office.

customs functions; immigration officers and officials of the Secretary of State exercising functions in relation to immigration, asylum or nationality; the Secretary of State in so far as he or she has general customs functions and functions relating to immigration, asylum or nationality; the Director of Border Revenue and any person exercising functions of the Director; and contractors providing services for any of them relating to the discharge of those functions.[10]

4.09 The regulations may make similar provision to those relating to the inspectors of constabulary in the Police Act 1996,[11] the Police (Scotland) Act 1967[12] and the Police (Northern Ireland) Act 1998,[13] ie for the conduct of inspections and reporting to the Secretary of State on the efficiency and effectiveness of those inspected; the carrying out of any other duties as directed by the Secretary of State for the purpose of furthering their efficiency and effectiveness.[14] The regulations may enable a Minister to require an inspection to be carried out and must make provision for the inspectors' reports to be published and for an annual report by the inspectors.[15]

4.10 However, inspections are not to address a matter of a kind which the comptroller and auditor general may examine under section 6 of the National Audit Act 1983,[16] ie 'the economy, efficiency and effectiveness with which [the person inspected] has used its resources in discharging its functions'.[17]

4.11 An inspection in Scotland must be carried out jointly by HM Inspectors of Constabulary and the Scottish inspectors.[18]

D. COMPLAINTS AND MISCONDUCT

4.12 By Police and Justice Act 2006, s 41, as originally enacted, the Secretary of State may[19] by regulations confer powers on the Independent Police Complaints Commission (IPCC) relating to the exercise by immigration officers of specified enforcement functions and the exercise by officials of the Secretary of State of specified enforcement functions relating to immigration and asylum.

4.13 Enforcement functions include in particular: powers of entry; powers to search persons or property; powers to seize or detain property; powers to arrest or detain

10 BCIA 2009, s 29(1).
11 ss 54–56.
12 ss 33–34.
13 ss 41–42.
14 BCIA 2009, s 29(2).
15 Ibid, s 29(3).
16 Ibid, s 29(4).
17 National Audit Act 1983, s 6(1).
18 BCIA 2009, s 29(5).
19 And indeed, has, by the Independent Police Complaints Commission (Immigration and Asylum Enforcement Functions) Regulations 2008, SI 2008/212.

persons; powers to examine persons or otherwise obtain information and powers in connection with removal from the UK.[20]

However, these regulations may not confer functions on the Independent Police Complaints Commission in relation to the exercise by any person of a function conferred on him by or under Part 8 of the IAA 1999.[21] Part 8 of the IAA 1999 is concerned with the organization, management, running of and detention in removal centres and the escorting of detainees to and from places of detention, including for their removal from the UK. 4.14

The BCIA 2009 amends Police and Justice Act 2006, s 41. First of all, it enables the Secretary of State to make regulations conferring functions on the IPCC relating to 'the provision of services pursuant to arrangements relating to the discharge of a' specified enforcement function of immigration officers, the Secretary of State or officials of the Secretary of State.[22] In other words, the Secretary of State will be able to extend the functions of the IPCC to inspect any contractual services provided in relation to the discharge of those functions.[23] 4.15

Secondly, it enables the Secretary of State to make regulations conferring powers on the IPCC in relation to the exercise of customs functions by designated officials and officials of the Secretary of State; the exercise of customs revenue functions by the Director of Border Revenue and any person exercising functions of the Director and 'the provision of services pursuant to arrangements relating to the discharge' of those functions.[24] 4.16

The IPCC's jurisdiction is limited to England and Wales. The Government declined to accept proposed amendments that would give extra-territorial jurisdiction so as to apply to officials working overseas, in particular, operating juxtaposed controls and to contractors engaged in enforcing removals from the UK. Promoting the amendment, Lord Avebury (Liberal Democrat) had highlighted the existence of documented cases of assaults upon people being removed from the UK by private contractor escorts taking place outside the UK, particularly on aircraft after taking off[25] and the need for extra-territorial jurisdiction to deal with such matters.[26] The Government's position was that: 4.17

> the Prisons and Probation Ombudsman is the correct body to oversee complaints, incidents and conduct matters relating to detention and escorting functions undertaken by UKBA's officers, officials and contractors . . . This oversight is not restricted by geographical

[20] Police and Justice Act 2006, s 41(2).

[21] Ibid, s 41(3).

[22] BCIA 2009, s 30(1)(a), inserting a new s 41(1)(c) into the Police and Justice Act 2006.

[23] HL Comm Deb 25 February 2009 vol 708 c295, per Lord West of Spithead, Parliamentary Under-Secretary of State, Home Office; PBC Deb 9 June 2009 2nd sitting c66, per Phil Woolas MP, Minister of State, Home Office.

[24] BCIA 2009, s 30(1)(b), inserting a new s 41(2A) into the Police and Justice Act 2006.

[25] *Outsourcing Abuse: The use and misuse of state sanctioned force during the detention and removal of asylum seekers* (2008) Birnberg Peirce and Partners, Medical Justice and National Coalition of Anti-Deportation Campaigns.

[26] HL Comm Deb 25 February 2009 vol 708 cc293–6.

boundaries and . . . ensures that there is suitable scrutiny of matters arising while immigration subjects are detained, escorted and removed from the UK.[27]

4.18 With regard to alleged misconduct by officials in the juxtaposed controls, complaints are investigated by the authorities in the host state and all evidence gathered is handed to the UK Border Agency professional standards unit to investigate but without independent oversight.[28] As far as private contractors working in the juxtaposed controls were concerned, it was said by the Government that their exercise of powers to search freight was subject to oversight by a Crown servant (currently, a senior customs official) appointed as monitor. However,

> consideration is being given on whether an independent system of oversight can be put in place in respect of matters arising at the juxtaposed controls that involve border force officers, officials and/or contracted staff and which, though they do not warrant criminal investigation, represent allegations of serious misconduct.[29]

E. MISCELLANEOUS PROVISIONS

1. Prosecution of Offences

4.19 The BCIA 2009 gives to the Attorney General power, by order, to assign to the Director of Revenue and Customs Prosecutions a function of instituting or assuming the conduct of criminal proceedings in England and Wales or providing legal advice relating to a criminal investigation by various persons, of a kind specified in the order.[30] The various persons are: designated customs officials; immigration officers; officials of the Secretary of State; the Secretary of State; the Director of Border Revenue; a person acting on behalf of any of them; a constable.[31]

4.20 The functions assigned to the Director of Revenue and Customs Prosecutions by virtue of this Act are to be treated as functions of the Director under the Commissioners for Revenue and Customs Act 2005[32] and proceedings conducted by the Director in consequence of this Act are to be treated as proceedings conducted under the Commissioners for Revenue and Customs Act 2005.[33] Consequently, the provisions made in that Act for the discharge of the Director's

---

27 HL Deb 25 March 2009 vol 709 c703, per Lord West of Spithead, Parliamentary Under-Secretary of State, Home Office.

28 HL Comm Deb 25 February 2009 vol 708 c295, per Lord West of Spithead, Parliamentary Under-Secretary of State, Home Office.

29 HL Deb 25 March 2009 vol 709 cc703–4, per Lord West of Spithead, Parliamentary Under-Secretary of State, Home Office.

30 BCIA 2009, s. 31(1).

31 Ibid, s. 31(2).

32 Ibid, s 31(3)(a). Commissioners for Revenue and Customs Act 2005, s 35, defines the functions of the Director.

33 BCIA 2009, s 31(3)(b).

functions will apply, eg as to the obligation to have regard to the Code for Crown Prosecutors[34] and the appointment of a 'Revenue and Customs Prosecutor' to exercise functions of the Director.[35]

2. Property, Rights, Liabilities, Facilities, and Services

The Commissioners may make one or more schemes for the transfer of property, rights and liabilities of a specified description from HMRC to the Secretary of State, the Director of Border Revenue or designated customs officials.[36] Such schemes may include providing for anything done or being done (including legal proceedings) by or in relation to a transferor to be treated as done or being done by the transferee. They may also provide for references to a transferor in an agreement or instrument or other document to be treated as references to the transferee. 4.21

HMRC may make facilities and services available to any person by whom functions relating to immigration, asylum or nationality or customs functions are exercisable for the purposes of the exercise of any of those functions.[37] A person by whom functions relating to immigration, asylum or nationality or customs functions are exercisable may make facilities and services available to HMRC for the purpose of the exercise of a function by HMRC.[38] 4.22

3. Payment of Customs Revenues

The BCIA 2009 requires the Director of Border Revenue and the Secretary of State to pay money received by way of revenue or security for revenue (ie money paid as security for a tax or duty) in the exercise of their customs revenue and general customs functions to the Commissioners for HMRC.[39] The Treasury may, by order, require such payments to be made into the Consolidated Fund and may also, by order, amend or repeal the provision for payment of revenue to the Commissioners for HMRC.[40] 4.23

4. Children

UKBA 2007, s 21, as originally enacted requires the Secretary of State to issue a code of practice designed to ensure that in exercising functions in the UK the Border and 4.24

[34] Commissioners for Revenue and Customs Act 2005, s 36(2).
[35] Ibid, s 37.
[36] BCIA 2009, s 26(1).
[37] Ibid, s 27(1).
[38] Ibid, s 27(1).
[39] Ibid, s 32(1) and (2).
[40] Ibid, s 33.

Immigration Agency takes appropriate steps to ensure that while children are in the UK they are safe from harm.

4.25 BCIA 2009, s 34, amends s 21 of the UKBA 2007 so as to substitute a list of persons for 'the Border and Immigration Agency'. The persons listed are: designated customs officials and officials of the Secretary of State exercising customs functions; immigration officers and officials of the Secretary of State exercising functions relating to immigration, asylum, or nationality; the Secretary of State in so far as the Secretary of State has general customs functions and functions relating to immigration, nationality, or asylum and the Director of Border Revenue and any person exercising functions of the Director.[41]

4.26 Once BCIA 2009, s 55, comes into force, this section ceases to have effect. It is intended as a temporary measure whilst the coming into force of s 55 (duty regarding the welfare of children) is delayed pending consultation on the guidance to be issued under that section.[42]

5. Power to Modify Enactments

4.27 The Secretary of State may, by order (ie statutory instrument subject to the affirmative resolution procedure[43]) modify an enactment in so far as it applies in relation to relevant persons or the exercise of functions by relevant persons.[44]

4.28 Relevant persons are the Secretary of State by whom general customs functions are exercisable, officials in his or her department, the Director of Border Revenue, and designated customs officials and immigration officers.[45]

4.29 Such an order may, in particular, extend an exemption or protection afforded by an enactment to a relevant person and provide for the disclosure of information to or the doing of other things in relation to relevant persons.[46]

4.30 Before making such an order that relates to a general customs matter or a customs revenue matter or the exercise of a customs function, the Secretary of State must consult the Commissioners for HMRC.[47]

6. Power to Make Supplementary Provision

4.31 BCIA 2009, s 36, gives the Secretary of State a further order (ie statutory instrument subject to the affirmative resolution procedure[48]) making power to make such incidental, supplementary, consequential, transitional or transitory provision as he or

---

41 Ibid, s 34.
42 PBC Deb 11 June 2009 c75, per Phil Woolas MP, Minister of State, Home Office.
43 BCIA 2009, s 37(1), (3), and (4)(e).
44 Ibid, s 35(1).
45 Ibid, s 35(2).
46 Ibid, s 35(3).
47 Ibid, s 35(4).
48 BCIA 2009, s 37(1), (3) and (4)(f).

she considers appropriate for the general or particular purposes of Part 1 of the BCIA 2009 or in consequence of or for giving full effect to Part 1.[49] Such an order may amend, repeal, revoke or otherwise modify any enactment, including the BCIA 2009.[50] 4.32

[49] BCIA 2009, s 36(1).
[50] BCIA 2009, s 36(2).

5
ACQUISITION OF BRITISH CITIZENSHIP BY NATURALISATION

A. THE PATH TO CITIZENSHIP

1. Introduction

5.01 In the Green Paper *The Path to Citizenship: Next Steps in Reforming the Immigration System*[1] (the Green Paper) the Home Office outlined its proposals in respect of the path to British citizenship,[2] as part of its wider programme of alteration to the

[1] February 2008.

[2] It is not always clear whether the 'citizenship' referred to in the title of the Green Paper is British citizenship (the statutorily defined primary status in British nationality law) or citizenship in the broader and vaguer sense of membership of the community.

immigration system, which included changes to ensure that those who come to the United Kingdom do so in its interests, and changes in respect of the policing of the immigration system and the protection of borders. The purpose of the alterations was said to be:

> 1. . . . to strengthen our shared values and citizenship . . .
>
> 5. . . . we think the current system does not provide enough of an incentive for a migrant to progress to British citizenship. We want to encourage people with the right qualifications and commitment to take up citizenship so that they can become fully integrated into our society.[3]

The Borders, Citizenship and Immigration Act 2009 (BCIA 2009) contains the modifications to the British Nationality Act 1981 (BNA 1981), introduced as part of the alterations to the path to citizenship. However, some of the changes to this path will need to be implemented by changes to the rules for the grant of leave to enter or remain under the Immigration Rules[4] (or their successor) and the policies for the grant of leave to enter or remain outside of the Rules. 5.02

In addition, the path to citizenship contemplates two alternative end points: British citizenship or permanent residence. Only the requirements for the former are found in the BCIA 2009 and its modifications to the BNA 1981. In respect of the latter, while permanent residence leave[5] has been defined as indefinite leave to enter or remain *for the purposes of nationality law* by the BCIA 2009 (see para 5.72 below), further reform of the Immigration Rules and policies may lead to permanent residence being recast as a substantive category under immigration law. 5.03

The Green Paper proposals contain (a) matters now reflected in the BCIA 2009 in respect of nationality law, (b) matters now abandoned, and (c) matters that await further Immigration Rules or the making of policy. So, for example, probationary citizenship leave[6] (see para 5.71 below) awaits definition under future immigration rules. The intention of the Government is to make the modified BNA 1981 and the Immigration Rules work together but the necessary amendment is yet to occur in respect of the latter. In the discussion of the Green Paper below, it is indicated where the proposals fall within (a), (b), or (c) as set out above. 5.04

The concern of the Government has not simply been with modifying the rules for the acquisition of British citizenship as a form of British nationality. Its concern in respect of citizenship emerged in an earlier Green Paper, *The Governance of Britain*[7] (July 2007), as part of a discussion about citizenship, national identity, common British values, a possible British Bill of rights and duties, and the constitution. In the 5.05

[3] At p 6.
[4] HC 395 of 1993–94 as amended.
[5] BNA 1981, Sch 1, para 11(4), as inserted by BCIA 2009, s 49(3).
[6] Ibid, para 11(3), as inserted by BCIA 2009, s 49(3).
[7] Cm 7170, paras 180–93.

context of a brief consideration of the social, cultural, and functional aspects of being a British citizen that Green Paper stated:

> 187 . . . more could be done to create a simpler, fairer and more meaningful system, ensuring that the benefits and rights of citizenship are valued and offered to those prepared to make a contribution to the UK's future.[8]

5.06 In his citizenship review for the Government, *Citizenship: Our Common Bond* (11 March 2008), Lord Goldsmith QC (Labour) proposed a reform drawing a sharp distinction between temporary residents and British citizens, with the latter enjoying rights not accorded to the former. In essence he proposed a moment of decision for the temporary resident, who would be compelled to acquire citizenship in order to settle permanently. In such a system, the status of permanent resident was to be effectively abolished:

> 26 . . . I propose that government should give consideration to moving towards a system of rules whereby people who have come to the UK either have limited leave to be here or they have to apply to become citizens . . .[9]

5.07 At the Second Reading of the Bill in the House of Lords, Lord Goldsmith QC (Labour) articulated a general proposition that:

> [c]itizenship is a highly important topic in an era when shared cultural and historical links often no longer seem enough to bind us together; the nature of our society has changed. Citizenship is more than rules on nationality. It is not about Britishness . . . It is about how one creates a society in which its members feel that they belong and, therefore, share the same concerns, hopes and aspirations as their fellow citizens.[10]

5.08 During the Second Reading of the Bill in the House of Commons, Jacqui Smith MP, Secretary of State for the Home Department, spelt out the Government's aspirations by more direct reference to narrow, material benefits accruing to the state:

> Our earned citizenship proposals . . . deliver simple steps and set the right balance between demonstrating commitment to the UK and gaining access to privileges—privileges like our benefits system, where we estimate that our proposals could result in savings of at least £350 million in the first five years.[11]

5.09 It is not possible to understand the significance of the changes wrought by the BCIA 2009 to the BNA 1981 without an understanding of the proposed changes to the Immigration Rules and policies that confer leave to enter or remain, which will underpin whether a migrant is eligible to apply for naturalisation as a British citizen. Accordingly, the Government proposals in respect of the path to British citizenship are considered below as part of the necessary context.

---

[8] Ibid.

[9] *Citizenship: Our Common Bond* (11 March 2008) Lord Goldsmith QC.

[10] HL Deb 11 February 2009 vol 707 c1146.

[11] HC Deb 2 June 2009 vol 493 c175.

The proposals in the Green Paper in respect of British citizenship were to be furthered together with simplification of immigration laws, with the plan being to publish a draft partial Bill on both for pre-legislative scrutiny by the end of the summer 2008 and to introduce a full Bill to Parliament by the end of November 2008.[12] This did not occur as planned and the BCIA 2009 contains a smaller portfolio of matters than the draft partial Bill as originally contemplated (see para **5.41** below). 5.10

The Green Paper proposed three key routes to naturalisation as a British citizen:[13] 5.11

1. highly skilled and skilled workers (Tier 1 and Tier 2) under the Points-Based System (PBS), and their dependants (the work route);
2. family members of British citizens and permanent residents (the family route); and
3. persons in need of protection: refugees and those granted humanitarian protection (the protection route).

These routes are based on the categories of leave to enter or remain that already exist under the Immigration Rules[14] in respect of such persons. In order to provide for these categories alone (subject to limited exceptions) to lead to probationary citizenship and naturalisation as a British citizen under the BNA 1981 as modified by the BCIA 2009, amendments to the Immigration Rules will need to be made, to specify or identify the categories of leave that are to count for the purposes of qualifying temporary residence leave[15] (see para **5.70** below) and probationary citizenship leave[16] (see para **5.71** below). The necessary amendments to the Immigration Rules have not yet been made. 5.12

Within each route to naturalisation as a British citizen, the Green Paper stated that there should be three stages in the journey:[17] 5.13

1. Temporary residence;
2. Probationary citizenship; and
3. British citizenship/permanent residence.

The Green Paper contemplated that: 5.14

> 10 . . . the journey to citizenship will enable migrants to demonstrate a more visible and a more substantial contribution to Britain as they pass through successive stages. At each stage,

[12] Green Paper *The Path to Citizenship: Next Steps in Reforming the Immigration System* (February 2008), p 6, para 3.

[13] Ibid, para 7.

[14] HC 395 of 1993–94 as amended.

[15] BNA 1981, Sch 1, para 11(2), as inserted by BCIA 2009, s 49(3).

[16] Ibid, para 11(3), as inserted by BCIA 2009, s 49(3).

[17] Green Paper *The Path to Citizenship: Next Steps in Reforming the Immigration System* (February 2008), p 6, para 7.

the journey will incorporate appropriate requirements that determine whether a migrant can progress.[18]

5.15 In accordance with the proposals in the Green Paper, the BNA 1981 as modified by the BCIA 2009, defines temporary residence leave, probationary citizenship leave, and permanent residence leave for the purposes of nationality law.[19] However, as noted at para **5.04** above, modifications to the Immigration Rules will need to be made, to specify the categories of leave that count for these purposes. The necessary amendments to the Immigration Rules have not yet been made.

2. Probationary Citizenship

(a) *Introduction*

5.16 Probationary citizenship as proposed in the Green Paper is a new, additional, time-limited period interpolated between temporary residence and British citizenship or permanent residence. This proposal is now reflected in the BNA 1981, Sch 1, para 11(3), as inserted by the BCIA 2009, s 49, where probationary citizenship leave is not a form of probationary nationality but is defined as a form of limited leave to enter or remain (see para **5.71** below). The Green Paper proposed that migrants who are ineligible or who fail to qualify for probationary citizenship would be expected to leave the UK.[20] The necessary amendments to the Immigration Rules, to specify the categories of leave to enter or remain that count as probationary citizenship leave and to govern the periods of time in respect of which such leave may be granted, have not yet been made.

5.17 In evidence to the Home Affairs Committee, the Immigration Law Practitioners' Association (ILPA) stated:

> a. The proposed new 'probationary citizenship' stage is unnecessary and adds complication since it is nothing more than a new name for 'temporary leave' which is also a stage on the route to citizenship.[21]

(b) *The Work Route*

5.18 The Green Paper proposed that persons entering the United Kingdom under the work route (Tier 1 or Tier 2 of the PBS) would be eligible for probationary citizenship after five years, *provided* they can demonstrate a contribution to the economy including by payment of tax.[22] Once probationary citizenship is granted under the work route, migrants would be required to be self-sufficient but would not be

---

[18] Ibid, para 10.

[19] BNA 1981, Sch 1, para 11(2)–(4), as inserted by BCIA 2009, s 49(3).

[20] Green Paper *The Path to Citizenship: Next Steps in Reforming the Immigration System* (February 2008), p 19, para 103.

[21] HC Home Affairs Committee 5th Report (2008–09) HC 425 Ev 169.

[22] Green Paper *The Path to Citizenship: Next Steps in Reforming the Immigration System* (February 2008), p 26, para 146.

restricted to the employment for which they entered the UK.[23] As noted above (para **5.04**), the necessary modifications to the Immigration Rules have not yet been made, to give effect to this proposal.

There is to be no route to probationary citizenship, nor therefore to British citizenship, for those in Tier 4 (Students) or Tier 5 (Youth Mobility and Temporary Workers) of the PBS, their dependents, or visitors.[24] However, at present students are able to switch into Tier 1 and Tier 2, providing an indirect route to citizenship for them. A student who switches into Tier 2 would be expected to complete a further five years in that category before being eligible to apply for probationary citizenship.[25] 5.19

Tier 3 (Low Skilled Workers filling specific temporary labour shortages) of the PBS has never been implemented as a route to work in the UK. It will not be implemented while restrictions remain in place on access to the labour market for nationals of Bulgaria and Romania,[26] following the accession of those states to the European Union on 1 January 2007. It will only be introduced in the future if needed.[27] The Green Paper states that migrants in Tier 3 would not have a route to British citizenship or permanent residence under the proposals.[28] 5.20

(c) *The Protection Route*

The Green Paper proposed that persons entering under the protection route (refugees and those granted humanitarian protection) would be eligible to apply for probationary citizenship after five years, *provided* they can show they are still in need of protection. Otherwise they would be be required to leave the UK.[29] This last proposed requirement to leave the UK takes no account of the need to protect any rights deserving protection under Article 8 (right to respect for private and family life) of the Convention for the Protection of Human Rights and Fundamental Freedoms (the Human Rights Convention)[30] arising out of the life lived by the migrant in the UK, through the provision of further leave to remain. As noted above (para **5.04**), the necessary amendments to the Immigration Rules have not yet been made, to give effect to the proposal for the protection route. 5.21

(d) *The Family Route*

The Green Paper proposed that persons entering under the family route (family members of British citizens and permanent residents) would be eligible to become probationary citizens after two years, *provided* they can demonstrate that they can 5.22

23 Ibid, p 27, para 152.

24 Ibid, p 20, fig 1.

25 Ibid, p 26, para 146.

26 Accession (Immigration and Worker Authorisation) Regulations 2006, SI 2006/3317.

27 Green Paper *The Path to Citizenship: Next Steps in Reforming the Immigration System* (February 2008), p 21.

28 Ibid, para 107.

29 Ibid, p 26, para 147.

30 Rome, 4 November 1950; TS 71 (1953); Cmd 8969.

support themselves or be supported by the sponsor and that their relationship with the sponsor is still subsisting.[31] Once probationary citizenship was granted under the family route, migrants would be required to continue to satisfy those requirements.[32] As noted above (para **5.04**), the necessary amendments to the Immigration Rules have not yet been made, to give effect to the proposal for the family route.

3. Three Immigration Categories that Avoid Probationary Citizenship

5.23 The Green Paper proposed that there would be three categories of persons who would be able to progress directly to permanent residence without passing through a stage of probationary citizenship:[33]

1. Those discharged from HM Forces who have completed four years service;
2. Victims of domestic violence who were admitted as a partner of a British citizen or permanent resident; and
3. Bereaved partners who were admitted as a partner of a British citizen or permanent resident where the sponsor has died during the two-year probationary period.

5.24 The necessary amendments to the Immigration Rules have not yet been made, to give effect to the proposal.

4. Earned Citizenship Requirements

(a) *Introduction*

5.25 The four areas where changes in the requirements for progression to citizenship, that is progression to probationary citizenship and thereafter progression through probationary citizenship to British citizenship, proposed in the Green Paper were:[34]

1. The English language requirement: the current test for settlement to apply to those seeking probationary citizenship;
2. Paying tax and becoming self-sufficient: with minimum time periods at each stage to demonstrate the strength of the migrant's contribution to the British economy or relationship to a British citizen or permanent resident, together with a record of self-sufficiency;
3. Obeying the law: denying access to probationary citizenship to a person who has served a custodial sentence and requiring them to leave the United Kingdom and slowing down progress to naturalisation for minor offences; and

[31] Green Paper *The Path to Citizenship: Next Steps in Reforming the Immigration System* (February 2008), p 26, para 148.

[32] Ibid, p 27, para 153.

[33] Ibid, p 23, para 126.

[34] Ibid, pp 6–7, para 10.

4. Joining in with the British way of life: speeding up the journey through probationary citizenship where the migrant has demonstrated commitment to the UK by playing an active part in the community.

(b) *The English Language Requirement*

Persons who are currently exempt from the requirement to demonstrate English language ability and knowledge of life in the UK before being granted settlement, such as bereaved spouses/civil partners, would be exempt from such requirements in respect of probationary citizenship but would have to fulfil the requirements to qualify for British citizenship or permanent residence, unless exempt by virtue of age or disability.[35] Thus in the proposed system, a bereaved spouse/civil partner would have to pass the language and life in the UK test in order to be in the UK without restriction on time (as a permanent resident), whereas prior to such an alteration, a bereaved spouse/civil partner may be in the UK without a restriction on time (as a settled person with indefinite leave to remain[36]) without having to pass such a test. The necessary amendments to the Immigration Rules have not yet been made, to give effect to the proposal. 5.26

(c) *Paying Tax and Becoming Self-sufficient*

The Green Paper acknowledged that migrants are on average net fiscal contributors but stated that there was a need to take into account transitional pressures placed by migrants on public services and the need to ensure that individuals do not place undue demands on benefits and services. With that in mind the Green Paper set out the Government's proposal to restrict access to certain benefits until migrants reach the British citizenship/permanent residence stage and to create a fund, to which migrants would have to contribute, to manage the transitional impact of migration.[37] 5.27

The Green Paper noted that citizenship reform was linked to the Government agenda to increase the cohesiveness of communities and to the work of the Department for Communities and Local Government in this regard.[38] 5.28

The Green Paper also contemplated prohibiting probationary citizens on the work route and the family route from access to benefits and housing and restricting at access to further and higher education their 'home rate', see paras **5.204–5.206** below. In essence, migrants would have to wait longer before becoming entitled to benefits and housing as British citizens or permanent residents. The statutory machinery for the regulation of access to benefits and housing is separate from the BNA 1981, although it interacts with requirements of the Immigration Rules 5.29

[35] Ibid, p 26, para 142.

[36] Immigration Rules, paras 287–9, HC 395 of 1993–94 as amended.

[37] Green Paper *The Path to Citizenship: Next Steps in Reforming the Immigration System* (February 2008), p 7, para 11.

[38] Ibid, p 12, paras 44–45; see also the report of the Commission on Integration and Cohesion *Our Shared Future* (14 June 2007).

(see para 5.207 below). The necessary amendments to the Immigration Rules have not yet been made, to give effect to the proposal.

(d) *Obeying the Law*

5.30 The Green Paper proposed that temporary residents would be prohibited from progressing to probationary citizenship if they have criminal convictions falling within deportation criteria (and that such persons would be deported from the UK). Where such persons cannot be removed for legal reasons, those with such convictions or those who are excluded from asylum or international protection would nonetheless be prohibited from progressing to probationary citizenship. For others with lesser offences who have served a custodial sentence (subject to the provisions of the Rehabilitation of Offenders Act 1974) probationary citizenship would be refused and they would be subject to removal at the end of their residence, save where removal would breach obligations arising under the Refugee Convention[39] or the Human Rights Convention, in which case individuals would be required to complete five years as probationary citizens before being eligible to apply for permanent residence.[40]

5.31 A similar approach was to be taken for those who were probationary citizens so that those falling within deportation criteria would be deported and those imprisoned for a lesser offence would be refused British citizenship or permanent residence and removed.[41]

5.32 The Green Paper also contemplated various approaches to non-custodial offences and considered whether to stop or delay the path to citizenship for those whose children commit criminal offences.[42]

5.33 The BCIA 2009 does not make any changes to the BNA 1981 in respect of criminal activity, with regard to the period of time that must be spent in the United Kingdom in order to be eligible to apply for naturalisation as a British citizen. Criminal activity continues to be considered as part of the requirement to be of good character.[43] Further, the amendments to the Immigration Rules to regulate, by reference to the requirement to obey the law, access to and progression through probationary citizenship leave, on the route to British citizenship, have not yet been made. In addition, it is not yet clear whether all, or if not which, proposals made in the Green Paper on this issue, will be adopted.

[39] Geneva, 28 July 1951; UNTS 2545 (1954) and Protocol Relating to the Status of Refugees of 31 January 1967 (UNTS 8791 (1967).

[40] Green Paper *The Path to Citizenship: Next Steps in Reforming the Immigration System* (February 2008), p 28, paras 161–2.

[41] Ibid, para 163.

[42] Ibid, pp 28–9, paras 164–6.

[43] See BNA 1981, Sch 1, paras 1(1)(b) and 3(3); see also the Nationality Instructions, Chapter 18, Annex D.

(e) *Joining in with the British Way of Life*

5.34 The Green Paper canvassed the idea that those probationary citizens who had demonstrated some form of active citizenship or community involvement would be able to apply for British citizenship after a minimum of one year as a probationary citizen; for those who had not, a minimum period of three years would apply. The equivalent periods for those wishing to be permanent residents would be three years where active citizenship was demonstrated and five years in its absence.[44] The position set out in the Green Paper is considered further in the discussion of the activity condition as provided for as part of the provisions for applying for naturalisation as a British citizen as a result of amendments made to the BNA 1981 by the BCIA 2009 (see para **5.192** below). Amendments to the Immigration Rules, to regulate access to permanent residence by reference to an activity condition, have not yet been made.

5. British Citizenship or Permanent Residence

5.35 The Green Paper proposed that persons with permanent residence might remain in the United Kingdom indefinitely or progress to British citizenship upon satisfaction of the relevant criteria. Migrants who obtain permanent residence would be able to apply for British citizenship at a later date.[45] However, the Government wanted to encourage persons who wished to settle in the United Kingdom to progress to British citizenship rather than choosing permanent residency, on the basis that the former aided successful integration. The Green Paper stated:

> 123. We recognise though that some people will feel unable to apply for British citizenship—because of restrictions on holding more than one nationality in the law of their country of origin—and we have taken this into account in the proposed architecture. We intend to provide a clear route for migrants to become permanent residents, as an alternative route to British citizenship, but all migrants will need to spend longer as probationary citizens if they choose this route. A shorter progression time to British citizenship from probationary citizenship is intended to encourage migrants to choose British citizenship above permanent residence.[46]

5.36 The Green Paper proposed that probationary citizens would be able to apply for British citizenship after a minimum of one year but those who wished to become permanent residents (whether by choice or because they were unable to become British citizens) would have to spend a minimum of three years as probationary citizens. The ability to take advantage of the minimum time period would be dependent on satisfaction of the activity condition (see paras **5.192–5.203** below).[47]

[44] Green Paper *The Path to Citizenship: Next Steps in Reforming the Immigration System* (February 2008), p 29, paras 169–170.

[45] Ibid, p 20, fig 1.

[46] Ibid, p 23.

[47] Ibid, pp 26–7, paras 149–50.

Amendments to the Immigration Rules, to regulate access to permanent residence by reference to the time spent as a probationary citizen, have not yet been made.

5.37 The critical disadvantage in the proposals for those persons on the work route or the family route, who spend longer as probationary citizens on account of seeking to be permanent residents rather than British citizens, is that they would be denied access to benefits and housing for so long as they are probationary citizens. Thus they would spend longer without access to benefits or housing than those able to naturalise as British citizens.

6. Dependants

5.38 Under the proposals in the Green Paper, migrants entering under the work route would be restricted to bringing only partners and children. Dependants of migrants entering under the work route or the protection route, who arrived and remained with the principal migrant, would need to spend the same amount of time in each category and stage as the principal migrant applying for probationary citizenship. Thus under the work route, in order to progress to probationary citizenship, they would need to spend five years on temporary residence leave in their own right, supported by the principal applicant; to have demonstrated the requisite English language ability; to have the required knowledge of life in the UK; and to have obeyed the law. Thereafter, as probationary citizens they would be able to apply for British citizenship after a minimum of one year but those who wish to become permanent residents would have to spend a minimum of three years as probationary citizens; both options being further subject to having been supported by the principal applicant and to having obeyed the law.[48] Amendments to the Immigration Rules, to regulate the position of dependants, have not yet been made.

7. The First Consultation Exercise

5.39 The Green Paper set out some questions as part of a limited consultation exercise. The Analysis of Consultation Responses and the Government Response to the Consultation were both published on 14 July 2008. From the Analysis of Consultation Responses, it is clear that the respondents did not particularly welcome the Government's proposals. On many key questions, the percentage of respondents who took an adverse view was higher than those in favour among both British citizens and non-British citizens, with the latter recording higher percentages for an adverse view than their British citizen counterparts. For example, 50 per cent of British citizens did *not* think probationary citizenship was a good idea and only 38 per cent were in favour, while 74 per cent of non-British citizens thought it not a good idea with only 15 per cent in favour.[49]

---

[48] Ibid, p 27, paras 154–6.

[49] *The Path to Citizenship: Next Steps in Reforming the Immigration System: Analysis of Consultation Responses* (14 July 2008) pp 10–11.

Notwithstanding the decidedly mixed responses from the consultation, the Government's Response to the Consultation pressed on, setting out the path to British citizenship that it intended to implement, the latter being largely as discussed in the Green Paper.[50] A particular feature of the proposals, mentioned in the Response, which did not eventually appear in the BCIA 2009, was the proposal to provide for a means to slow down progression to British citizenship by one year for persons convicted of a crime resulting in a non-custodial sentence.[51] In addition, the prohibition on probationary citizens having access to state support was defined as a prohibition on access to non-contributory benefits, social assistance, local authority housing, or homelessness assistance. It is not clear what is meant by social assistance as a separate item in this context. 5.40

8. The Draft (Partial) Immigration and Citizenship Bill

In May 2008 the Government's Draft Legislative Programme for 2008–09[52] made reference to a Citizenship, Immigration and Borders Bill, ambitiously setting out its main aims as being to:[53] 5.41

- support the concept of earned citizenship—setting out the eligibility requirements for UK citizenship;
- support the establishment of the UK Border Agency;
- replace ten separate pieces of immigration law—of which some of the earlier provisions have already been partially superseded by subsequent Acts—with a single Act of Parliament; and
- provide for sharper and more consistent immigration rules, which can continue to be quickly adjusted in response to changing circumstances.

In July 2008, at the time it responded to the consultation responses to the Green Paper *The Path to Citizenship: Next Steps in Reforming the Immigration System: Analysis of Consultation Responses*, the Government also published a slightly less ambitious draft (Partial) Immigration and Citizenship Bill,[54] covering much but not all of the proposed territory referred to in the Draft Legislative Programme for 2008–09. Part 3 of the draft Bill set out proposals for the alteration of the requirements for naturalisation as a British citizen, in line with the path to citizenship proposals for earned citizenship.[55] The draft Bill was for the most part concerned with immigration as opposed to British nationality or British citizenship. The focus of the draft Bill was the proposed replacement of almost all existing immigration statutes with a single statute that, in addition, would simplify immigration law. 5.42

[50] *The Path to Citizenship: Next Steps in Reforming the Immigration System: Government Response to Consultation* (14 July 2008) pp 4–5.
[51] Ibid, p 16.
[52] Cm 7372.
[53] Ibid, p 57.
[54] Cm 7373.
[55] See *Making Change Stick: An Introduction to the Immigration and Citizenship Bill* (14 July 2008).

In respect of immigration law, the draft Bill had been foreshadowed by the Home Office paper *Simplifying Immigration Law: An Initial Consultation*,[56] the paper *Simplifying Immigration Law: The Responses to the Initial Consultation*,[57] and by additional material in the Green Paper *The Path to Citizenship: Next Steps in Reforming the Immigration System*.[58]

5.43 However, the draft (Partial) Immigration and Citizenship Bill, with its proposals for simplification of immigration law, did not form the basis of the actual Bill brought forward. Instead the *Borders, Citizenship and Immigration Bill*,[59] with its far narrower focus, was introduced in the House of Lords on 14 January 2009. Part 2 of the BCIA 2009 has the title 'Citizenship' and it is evident from the headings within that Part that this is a reference to British citizenship.

9. A Points-Based System for Naturalisation as a British Citizen

5.44 During the Second Reading of the Bill in the House of Commons, Jacqui Smith MP, Secretary of State for the Home Department, intimated that the Government was to advance proposals for a Points-Based System for the path to settlement and British citizenship.[60] After the BCIA 2009 received Royal Assent on 21 July 2009, the Home Office published a further consultation document *Earning the Right to Stay: A New Points Test for Citizenship* (the Points Test Paper) (3 August 2009). The paper sought views (from 3 August to 26 October 2009) on:

- introducing a new, points based test for earned citizenship to better manage the numbers allowed to settle permanently in the UK (as British citizens or permanent residents);
- delivering the earned citizenship system in partnership with local authorities;
- supporting those who are on the path to citizenship to integrate into their new communities; and
- managing the impacts (*sic*) of migration on the developing world.[61]

5.45 One Government concern as set out in the Points Test Paper is to manage population growth by strengthening mechanisms to control who is allowed to stay in the UK on a permanent basis and to break the (so-called) automatic link between temporary residence and permanent settlement (as a British citizen or permanent resident).[62] The main proposal is to introduce a points test at the point of entry to the probationary citizenship stage. The Points Test Paper states that the threshold for satisfaction of the test could be altered from time to time in the current interests of the country and economy.[63] Presently, there is no 'automatic link', as opposed to a

[56] June 2007.
[57] December 2007.
[58] February 2008.
[59] HL Bill 15.
[60] HC Deb 2 June 2009 vol 493 c169 and c175.
[61] *Earning the Right to Stay: A New Points Test for Citizenship* (3 August 2009), p 6, para 3.
[62] Ibid, paras 4–5.
[63] Ibid, p 7, paras 6–7.

further test, between temporary residence and permanent settlement, so the basis for the proposal is not understood.

For those on the family route or the protection route to citizenship, a sufficient number of points would be awarded on the basis of continuing family relationship or protection needs as the case may be. However for those on the work route a more complex points system is contemplated whereby points might be awarded for attributes including: 5.46

- Earning potential;
- Special artistic, scientific or literary merit;
- Qualifications;
- Shortage occupation;
- English (above existing requirements); and
- Having lived and worked in a part of the UK in need of further immigration, eg Scotland.[64]

The Points Test Paper also contemplates deducting points for 5.47

> 10 . . . failure to integrate into British life; for criminal or anti-social behaviour, or in circumstances where an active disregard for UK values is demonstrated.

The highly subjective value judgments that would be involved in awarding and, particularly, in deducting points are a cause of deep concern. Further, the proposals for deducting points have the potential to inhibit acts of protest, free association, free speech, and dissent that might be thought to provide the foundation of a free and democratic society (see para **1.37**). 5.48

The Points Test Paper also considers migration and international development issues and identifies a need to manage the negative impacts of migration on developing countries (such as 'brain-drain' from the Third World).[65] It is possible that points may be awarded to those in their country of origin undertaking work with developmental benefit.[66] How such a scheme would fit in with the requirement to be present in the qualifying period remains unclear. 5.49

In addition to the introduction of a points test, there is also a proposal to split the requirement for a sufficient knowledge of English and life in the United Kingdom into two stages, with tests higher than those currently imposed being applied as a requirement for naturalisation as a British citizen. In respect of the life in the United Kingdom test the focus would be on practical information at the probationary citizenship stage with more difficult historical and political topics being included at the British citizenship stage.[67] The Points Test Paper also proposed that the introduction of the pre-application English language requirement for spouses, civil partners, unmarried and same sex partners, fiancé(e)s, and proposed civil partners be 5.50

[64] Ibid, para 9.
[65] Ibid, p 29, para 4.2.
[66] Ibid, p 30, para 4.10.
[67] Ibid, p 9, paras 22–4.

brought forward to summer 2011;[68] that it will apply to those seeking leave to enter *and* to those seeking leave to remain; and that it should require applicants to demonstrate that they can speak English to the required level, without the additional requirement for competency in listening, writing, and reading required by those entering under the Points-Based System.[69]

5.51 The Points Test Paper proposes an enhanced role for local authorities that builds on the Nationality Checking Service (NCS), which currently checks applications for citizenship before they are sent. It is stated that local authorities could play a role in verifying whether the activity condition has been met, providing further advice to migrants and coordinating opportunities for integration to migrants.[70]

5.52 The Points Test Paper proposals build on the Green Paper and the modifications to the BNA 1981 made by the BCIA 2009. It is to the latter that consideration must now be given.

B. COMMON PROVISIONS IN PART 2 OF THE BORDERS, CITIZENSHIP AND IMMIGRATION ACT 2009

1. The Territorial Extent of Part 2 (Citizenship) of the BCIA 2009

5.53 BCIA 2009, s 57(1), provides that, subject to further provisions, the Act extends to England and Wales, Scotland, and Northern Ireland. An amendment, modification, or repeal by the Act has the same effect as the enactment or relevant part of the enactment to which it relates (ignoring the extent by virtue of an Order in Council made under any of the Immigration Acts).[71]

5.54 By Order in Council, Her Majesty may provide for the provisions of Part 2 of the BCIA 2009 to extend, with or without modifications, to any of the Channel Islands or the Isle of Man.[72] However this does not apply where a provision is extended to a place by virtue of the provisions for an amendment, modification, or repeal, referred to in para **5.53** above.[73]

2. Commencement of Part 2 (Citizenship) of the BCIA 2009

5.55 The BCIA 2009 received Royal Assent on 21 July 2009. The provisions in Part 2 (Citizenship) come into force on such day as the Secretary of State appoints by order.[74] Any repeal provided for by BCIA 2009, s 56 and the Schedule, comes into

[68] Ibid, p 9, para 25.

[69] Ibid, p 23, paras 3.16–3.18.

[70] Ibid, p 8, paras 14–17.

[71] BCIA 2009, s 57(3): see also UK Borders Act, s 61(2), for the definition of 'the Immigration Acts'.

[72] Ibid, s 57(5).

[73] Ibid, s 57(6).

[74] Ibid, s 58(2).

force in the same way as the provision of the Act to which it relates.[75] Orders for the purposes of commencement must be made by statutory instrument,[76] may appoint different days for different purposes, and may include transitional or incidental provision or savings.[77]

As of August 2009, the Government intends to commence the provisions of Part 2 that relate to naturalisation no earlier than July 2011[78] and the remaining provisions in January 2010. 5.56

3. Transitional Provisions on Commencement of Part 2 (Citizenship) of the BCIA 2009

As originally introduced in the House of Lords[79] and as brought later to the House of Commons,[80] the Bill contained very little by way of transitional provision in respect of the modifications to the provisions for the acquisition of citizenship by naturalisation. Transitional provision was limited to provision in respect of the qualifying period and for periods of leave to enter or remain so that periods before commencement could be taken into account. 5.57

In that context, the Joint Committee on Human Rights noted that it was not clear what the effect would be on those whose applications for citizenship were pending on the date at which the Act comes into force and on those with limited leave to remain who have not yet qualified for indefinite leave to remain. The Committee recalled its earlier concern[81] about the injustice done by retrospective changes to the Immigration Rules[82] in respect of the Highly Skilled Migrant Programme and the subsequent proceedings in the High Court. The Government was urged not to ride roughshod over migrants' legitimate expectations of settlement and to introduce clear transitional provisions that met the legitimate expectations of those already in the system.[83] 5.58

Subsequently and after much pressure,[84] the Government introduced some transitional provisions into the Bill during its passage in the House of Commons.[85] 5.59

Provision is made for those already in the immigration system at a particular stage and who are applying for British citizenship by naturalisation. An order 5.60

---

[75] Ibid, s 58(5).

[76] Ibid, s 58(7).

[77] Ibid, s 58(8).

[78] HC Deb 14 July 2009 vol 496 c244.

[79] Borders, Citizenship and Immigration Bill [HL] HL Bill 15.

[80] Borders, Citizenship and Immigration [HL] Bill 86.

[81] JCHR 20th Report Highly Skilled Migrants: Changes to the Immigration Rules (2006–07) HL Paper 173 HC 993; see also *R (on the application of HSMP Forum Limited) v Secretary of State for the Home Department* [2008] EWHC 664 (Admin) (High Court) and *R (on the application of HSMP Forum (UK) Limited) v Secretary of State for the Home Department* [2009] EWHC 711 (Admin) (High Court) (Judgment in the latter case post-dates the 20th Report of the JCHR).

[82] HC 395 of 1993–94 as amended.

[83] JCHR Legislative Scrutiny: Borders, Citizenship and Immigration Bill, 9th Report (2008–09) HL Paper 62 HC 375, p 15, para 1.52.

[84] eg PBC 3rd Sitting 11 June 2009 cc76–92; PBC 4th Sitting 11 June 2009 cc95–103.

[85] HC Deb 14 July vol 496 cc232–3.

commencing BCIA 2009, ss 39–41, must include provisions that the amendments made thereby do not have effect in relation to an application for naturalisation as a British citizen if:[86]

(a) The date of the application is before the date on which those sections come into force, that is the date of commencement, in accordance with the order; or
(b) The date of the application is before the end of the twenty-four month period beginning with the date of commencement and the application is made by a person who:
    (i) on the date of commencement has indefinite leave to remain in the United Kingdom; or
    (ii) is given indefinite leave to remain in the United Kingdom on an application, the date of which is before the date of commencement and which is decided after the date of commencement (under pre-commencement rules).

5.61 In an order commencing BCIA 2009, ss 39–41, the transitional provisions may in particular provide:

(a) that the qualifying period for the purposes of the BNA 1981, Sch 1, paras 1 and 3 includes time before that commencement (see paras **5.55–5.56** above); and
(b) for leave to enter or remain in the United Kingdom granted before that commencement to be treated as qualifying temporary residence leave or probationary citizenship leave for the purposes of BNA 1981, Sch 1.

5.62 However, those who merely have limited leave to enter or remain, on commencement, will need to satisfy the modified requirements for probationary citizenship leave and thereafter British citizenship or permanent residence leave. An example of how this is intended to work in practice was given in written evidence to the Joint Committee on Human Rights by Phil Woolas MP, Minister of State, Home Office:

> Migrants who are currently in the UK and have existing limited leave to enter or remain which is regarded, under the new earned citizenship system, as a qualifying immigration status, will be able to count that time towards the qualifying period for naturalisation as a British citizen. For example a person here under Tier 2 of the Points-Based System before the earned citizenship clauses in the Bill are commenced will be able to count that time as a type of qualifying temporary residence leave, and therefore count this towards the revised qualifying periods for naturalisation.[87]

5.63 The provisions for making transitional provision for commencing BCIA 2009, ss 39–41 do not apply to an order commencing those sections for the purpose only of enabling regulations to be made under the BNA 1981.[88]

---

[86] BCIA 2009, s 58(9)–(11). See also UKBA news update 23 September 2009.

[87] JCHR Government replies to the Second, Fourth, Eighth, Ninth and Twelfth Reports of Session 2008–09 17th Report, (2008–09) HL Paper 104 HC 592, Written Evidence p 8.

[88] BCIA 2009, s 58(12).

In respect of the acquisition of British citizenship through the female line, in an order commencing BCIA 2009, s 45, transitional provisions may in particular provide that BCIA 2009, s 45, is to apply to an application made, but not determined, under the BNA 1981, s 4C, before that commencement (see para **6.50**).[89] 5.64

C. HUMAN RIGHTS CONCERNS RELATING TO THE NATURALISATION PROVISIONS

Pursuant to obligations under Human Rights Act 1998, s 19, statements have been made prior to the Second Reading in each House of Parliament by the Minister in charge of the Bill,[90] that in the view of the Minister concerned the Bill is compatible with Convention rights.[91] 5.65

In the Explanatory Notes accompanying the Bill as introduced in the House of Lords[92] and the Explanatory Notes to the Bill as brought from the House of Lords to the House of Commons,[93] the Government stated its belief that the proposals in respect of what is now Part 2 (Citizenship) did not raise any Human Rights Convention issues. The Joint Committee on Human Rights noted that in consequence, there was no human rights analysis by the Government about the impact of its proposals. Whilst the Committee recognized that human rights law does not confer any free-standing right to be a citizen of any county, it considered that the provisions in respect of earned citizenship nonetheless raised numerous, significant human rights issues.[94] The concerns of the Committee in respect of the provisions for 'Earned Citizenship' as set out in the Bill related to:[95] 5.66

(a) access to benefits (see **para 5.204** below);
(b) the Activity Condition/Community Activity requirement (see **para 5.192** below);
(c) retrospectivity (see **para 5.58** above); and
(d) compatibility with the Refugee Convention (see **para 5.215** below).

The Government addressed the issues raised by the Committee in an undated letter from Phil Woolas MP, Minister of State, Home Office.[96] These human rights 5.67

---

[89] Ibid, s 58(14).

[90] Lord West of Spithead, Parliamentary Under-Secretary of State, Home Office, in the House of Lords and Jacqui Smith MP, Secretary of State for the Home Department, in the House of Commons.

[91] For the definition of 'Convention Rights' see Human Rights Act 1998, s 1.

[92] Explanatory Notes to the Borders, Citizenship and Immigration Bill [HL] as introduced in the House of Lords on 14 January 2009 [HL Bill 15], para 222.

[93] Explanatory Notes to the Borders, Citizenship and Immigration Bill [HL] as brought from the House of Lords on 23 April 2009 [Bill 86], para 268.

[94] JCHR Legislative Scrutiny: Borders, Citizenship and Immigration Bill, 9th Report (2008–09) HL Paper 62 HC 375, p 12, para 1.36.

[95] Ibid, pp 12–16, paras 1.37–1.57.

[96] JCHR Government replies to the Second, Fourth, Eighth, Ninth and Twelfth Reports of Session 2008–09, 17th Report (2008–09) HL Paper 104 HC 592, Written Evidence pp 5–10.

matters are considered below in the context of our consideration of the substantive provisions of the Act.

D. THE NEW VOCABULARY OF IMMIGRATION TERMS FOR THE PURPOSES OF NATURALISATION AS A BRITISH CITIZEN

1. Introduction

5.68 The definitions of the forms of status relating to the requirements for naturalisation as a British citizen are to be found in BNA 1981, Sch 1, para 11, as inserted by BCIA 2009, s 49(3). The immigration terms applied for the purposes of naturalisation as a British citizen are:

(a) Qualifying temporary residence leave
(b) Probationary citizenship leave
(c) Permanent residence leave
(d) Qualifying CTA entitlement
(e) Commonwealth right of abode
(f) Permanent EEA entitlement and
(g) Temporary EEA entitlement.

5.69 A reference to having leave to enter or remain in the United Kingdom is to be construed in accordance with the Immigration Act 1971.[97] In the 1971 Act, those not having the right of abode (whereby they are free to live in, and come and go into and from, the UK) may only live, work, and settle in the UK by permission (ie 'leave'), and subject to such regulation and control of their entry into, stay in, and departure from the UK as is imposed by the Immigration Act 1971.[98] (A separate body of law governs EU free movement rights—those with such rights neither require 'leave' nor possess 'the right of abode' under the 1971 Act.)

2. Qualifying Temporary Residence Leave

5.70 A person has qualifying temporary residence leave if he has *limited* leave to enter or remain in the United Kingdom *and* the leave is granted for a purpose by reference to which a grant of probationary citizenship leave may be made (ie the temporary residence leave is for a purpose which may qualify the holder for a grant of probationary citizenship leave, as not all leave to enter or remain may lead to probationary

[97] BNA 1981, Sch 1, para 11(9), as inserted by BCIA 2009, s 49(3).

[98] Immigration Act 1971, s 1; see also the Immigration Act 1971, s 3, for the general provisions for regulation and control, the Immigration Rules HC 395 of 1993–94 as amended, and the Immigration Directorate Instructions found on the UK Border Agency website at <http://www.bia.homeoffice.gov.uk/>.

citizenship leave).[99] Until necessary amendments are made to the Immigration Rules,[100] accommodating 'the path to citizenship' provided for by the BCIA 2009, is not possible to specify the purposes which will suffice for limited leave to be 'qualifying temporary residence leave' (by reference to which probationary citizenship leave may be granted). It seems clear that limited leave granted for the purposes of the work route, the family route, and the protection route will be included. In addition, some forms of limited leave, for purposes such as UK ancestry leave[101] (see para **5.132**) will fall outside these three routes of the 'path to citizenship' but will nonetheless be included as qualifying temporary residence leave. However, there will be limited leave granted for other purposes that will be excluded from forming a path to probationary citizenship and thus to naturalisation.

3. Probationary Citizenship Leave

A person has probationary citizenship leave if he has limited leave to enter or remain in the United Kingdom *and* the leave is of a description identified in the Immigration Rules[102] as probationary citizenship leave.[103] This period of leave is time-limited. A person who remains in the UK beyond its expiry without securing an alternative basis to remain will be required to leave the United Kingdom. Prior to amendments being made to the Immigration Rules, it is not possible to state the types of leave that will be identified as probationary citizenship leave. It seems clear that further grants of leave after qualifying temporary residence leave under the work route, the family route, and the protection route will be included. 5.71

4. Permanent Residence Leave

A person has permanent residence leave if he has indefinite leave to enter or remain in the United Kingdom.[104] Indefinite leave is leave to enter or remain in the UK, being leave granted under the Immigration Act 1971 that is not limited as to duration.[105] Permanent residence is to be the alternative to British citizenship under the path to citizenship reforms of which the BCIA 2009 forms a part. It is contemplated that a person with probationary citizenship leave will spend a longer period of time on the path to permanent residence than he would on the path to British citizenship (see para **5.35** above). Whether this policy aspiration is implemented remains to be seen. For present purposes, indefinite leave to enter or remain, as defined for 5.72

[99] BNA 1981, Sch 1, para 11(2), as inserted by BCIA 2009, s 49(3).

[100] Presently, HC 395 of 1993–94 as amended.

[101] Presently, HC 395 of 1993–94 as amended, paras 186–93; see *The Path to Citizenship: Next Steps in Reforming the Immigration System Government Response to Consultation* (14 July 2008), pp 10–11.

[102] Made under the Immigration Act 1971, s 3.

[103] BNA 1981, Sch 1, para 11(3), as inserted by BCIA 2009, s 49(3).

[104] Ibid, para 11(4), as inserted by BCIA 2009, s 49(3).

[105] Immigration Act 1971, s 33(1).

immigration purposes in the Immigration Act 1971, is described as permanent residence leave for the purposes of naturalisation as a British citizen.

5. Qualifying CTA Entitlement

5.73 A person has a qualifying CTA (Common Travel Area) entitlement if he:[106]

(a) is a citizen of the Republic of Ireland;
(b) last arrived in the United Kingdom on a 'local journey' from the Republic of Ireland;[107]
(c) and on that arrival was a citizen of the Republic of Ireland and was entitled to enter by virtue of the Immigration Act 1971, s 1(3).

5.74 Irish citizens who posses a qualifying CTA entitlement do not require leave to enter or remain in the UK (whether as qualifying temporary residence leave or probationary citizenship leave) for the purposes of making an application for naturalisation as a British citizen under the modified provisions under the BNA 1981, ss 6(1) or 6(2), nor do they require a temporary or permanent EEA entitlement (to which they may be entitled as Irish citizens) for the purposes of making an application for naturalisation as a British citizen under the modified provisions under BNA 1981, s 6(1).

5.75 The Common Travel Area (CTA) comprises the United Kingdom, the Channel Islands, the Isle of Man, and the Republic of Ireland. Arrival in and departure from the UK on a local journey from or to another part of the CTA is not subject to immigration control under the Immigration Act 1971. In addition, a person does not require leave to enter the UK on so arriving, unless another part of the CTA has been excluded for any purpose through the exercise of powers under the Immigration Act 1971.[108]

5.76 In relation to the CTA, a journey is a 'local journey' if, but only if, it begins and ends in the CTA and *is not* made by a ship or aircraft which:[109]

(a) in the case of a journey to a place in the UK, began its voyage from, or has during its voyage called at, a place not in the CTA; or
(b) in the case of a journey from a place in the UK, is due to end its voyage in, or call in the course of its voyage at, a place not in the CTA.

106 BNA 1981, Sch 1, para 11(5), as inserted by BCIA 2009, s 49(3).

107 'Local journey' is defined by reference to the meaning given in the Immigration Act 1971, s 11(4).

108 Immigration Act 1971, ss 1(3), 9, and 11(4); see also the Immigration (Control of Entry through Republic of Ireland) Order 1972, SI 1972/1610 and the Immigration Rules HC 395 of 1993–94 as amended, para 15.

109 Immigration Act 1971, s 11(4).

6. Commonwealth Right of Abode

A person has a Commonwealth right of abode if he has the right of abode in the United Kingdom by virtue of Immigration Act 1971, s 2(1)(b).[110] By the latter a person has the right of abode in the UK if he is a Commonwealth citizen who immediately before the commencement of the BNA 1981 (on 1 January 1983) was a Commonwealth citizen having the right of abode in the United Kingdom by virtue of Immigration Act 1971, ss 2(1)(d) or 2(2) as then in force, and has not ceased to be a Commonwealth citizen in the interim. The full text of Immigration Act 1971, s 2, as in force immediately before the commencement of the BNA 1981 is set out in Appendix 2. 5.77

Commonwealth citizenship is a status that includes persons who are British citizens, British overseas territories citizens, British Nationals (Overseas), British Overseas citizens, British subjects, or citizens of Commonwealth countries (under any enactments in force in any country in question) listed in the BNA 1981, Sch 3.[111] All British citizens have the right of abode in the UK. Otherwise it is only British subjects and citizens of Commonwealth countries who may have that right (because citizens of the UK and Colonies with the right of abode became British citizens on 1 January 1983, and since that date the right of abode is only obtainable by obtaining British citizenship itself). 5.78

Citizens of Commonwealth countries who posses the right of abode do not require leave to enter or remain in the UK (whether as qualifying temporary residence leave or probationary citizenship leave) for the purposes of making an application for naturalisation as a British citizen under the modified provisions under the BNA 1981 s 6(1) or (2). The same is true in respect of British subjects with the right of abode registering as British citizens under BNA 1981, s 4. 5.79

7. Permanent EEA Entitlement

A person has a permanent EEA entitlement if the person is entitled to reside in the United Kingdom permanently by virtue of any provision made under European Communities Act 1972, s 2(2).[112] Presently, the right of permanent residence is contained in Directive 2004/38/EC of the European Parliament and of the Council of 30 April 2004 (the Directive), Articles 16 and 17[113] and its domestic analogue, the Immigration (European Economic Area) Regulations 2006, SI 2006/1003, reg 15, the latter being made under European Communities Act 1972, s 2(2). 5.80

The free movement provisions of which the permanent right of residence forms a part, apply not only to European Union citizens and their family members but also 5.81

[110] BNA 1981, Sch 1, para 11(6), as inserted by BCIA 2009, s 49(3).
[111] Ibid, 1981, s 37.
[112] Ibid, Sch 1, para 11(7), as inserted by BCIA 2009, s 49(3).
[113] [2004] OJ L158/77.

nationals of Iceland, Liechtenstein, Norway, and Switzerland and their family members.

5.82 By Immigration Act 1988, s 7(1), a person shall not require leave to enter or remain in the United Kingdom under the Immigration Act 1971 in any case in which he is entitled to do so by virtue of any provision made under European Communities Act 1972, s 2(2), *or* an enforceable Community right.[114] Insofar as an enforceable Community right arises *otherwise* than by virtue of any provision made under European Communities Act 1972, s 2(2), it would not fall within the definition of either a permanent EEA entitlement (or a temporary EEA entitlement, see para **5.83** below) for the purposes of an application for naturalisation as a British citizen. Whether such an outcome is compatible with Community law remains to be seen.

8. Temporary EEA Entitlement

5.83 A person has a temporary EEA entitlement if the person does not have a permanent EEA entitlement but is entitled to reside in the United Kingdom by virtue of any provision made under European Communities Act 1972, s 2(2).[115] Presently, the rights of residence are mostly, although not exclusively, contained in Directive 2004/38/EC of the European Parliament and of the Council of 30 April 2004 (the Directive),[116] and its domestic analogue the Immigration (European Economic Area) Regulations 2006, SI 2006/1003, the latter being made under European Communities Act 1972, s 2(2). However, there are rights of residence that do not fall within these provisions—see for example Case 200/02 *Kunqian Catherine Zhu and Man Lavette Chen v Secretary of State for the Home Department* [2004] ECR I-09925 and rights arising by reference to Article 49 of the EC Treaty as in Case 60/00 *Mary Carpenter v Secretary of State for the Home Department* [2002] ECR I-06279. Whether the apparent exclusion of these and other such rights for the purposes of an application for naturalisation as a British citizen is compatible with Community law remains to be seen (see para **5.82** above).

E. THE REQUIREMENTS FOR NATURALISATION UNDER S 6(1) OF THE BRITISH NATIONALITY ACT 1981

1. Introduction

5.84 The lead provisions of the BCIA 2009 on nationality law (ss 39–49, comprising Part 2 (Citizenship)) amend the law on naturalisation as a British citizen. Sections 39 and 41 amend the BNA 1981 Sch 1 requirements for naturalisation under BNA 1981

[114] See European Communities Act 1972, s 2(1).

[115] BNA 1981, Sch 1, para 11(8), as inserted by BCIA 2009, s 49(3).

[116] [2004] OJ L158/77.

s 6(1), while ss 40 and 41 amend BNA 1981 s 6(2), and the corresponding Schedule 1 requirements for naturalisation based on marriage, etc. Certain existing requirements are retained. Others are substituted through new provisions. In certain respects the amendments are liberal (eg s 6(2) naturalisation will be open to a wider variety of people), while in other respects the amendments tighten the law (eg in some cases limited leave will not count towards residence for naturalisation purposes) and reduce flexibility (eg generally requiring absences not to exceed 90 days a year, whereas previously the allowance was not on a per annum basis).

Section 6(1) of the BNA 1981 provides the primary route to naturalisation as a British citizen. The provision itself is unaltered by the BCIA 2009 and provides that if on an application for naturalisation as a British citizen made by a person who is of full age (aged 18 or over) and capacity,[117] the Secretary of State is satisfied that the applicant fulfils the requirements of Schedule 1 of the BNA 1981 for naturalisation as a citizen, he *may*, if he thinks fit, grant him a certificate of naturalisation as such a citizen. 5.85

2. Section 6(1): Certain Requirements Remaining the Same

The BCIA 2009 amends the relevant provisions of Schedule 1 of the BNA 1981 to substitute new requirements for old whilst retaining others. The requirements that are retained unaltered, in addition to being of full age and capacity, are found in the BNA 1981, Sch 1, para 1(b), (c), (ca), and (d). They are that the applicant: 5.86

1. is of good character;[118]
2. has sufficient knowledge of the English, Welsh, or Scottish Gaelic language;[119]
3. has sufficient knowledge of life in the United Kingdom;[120] and
4. meets future intentions requirement.[121]

The future intentions requirement is that either: 5.87

1. his intentions are that, in the event of a certificate of naturalisation being granted his home or (if he has more than one) his principal home will be in the United Kingdom; or
2. he intends, in the event of such a certificate being granted, to enter into, or continue in, Crown service under the government of the United Kingdom, or service under an international organisation of which the United Kingdom or its government is a member, or service in the employment of a company or association established in the United Kingdom.

---

[117] See Nationality Instructions, Chapter 18, Annex A.
[118] See Nationality Instructions, Chapter 18, Annex D.
[119] See ibid, Annex E.
[120] Ibid.
[121] See ibid, Annex F, Annex F(i), and Annex F(ii).

5.88 Although the requirement to have a sufficient knowledge of the English, Welsh, or Scottish Gaelic language as a requirement for naturalisation under the BNA 1981, s 6, remains unaltered by the BCIA 2009, JUSTICE noted in a memorandum to the Home Affairs Committee that:

> . . . there are approximately 58,652 Scots Gaelic speakers in the UK, as compared to approximately one million people in the UK who speak Urdu. If the purpose of a language requirement is to ensure that new citizens are able to communicate with at least some of their fellow citizens, then it is unclear why preference should be given to a language spoken by 0.01% of its population over one spoken by 0.5%. . .[122]

3. Section 6(1): New Requirements as to Presence and Status

5.89 The new requirements being substituted are introduced into the BNA 1981 by s 39 of the BCIA 2009. Schedule 1 of the BNA 1981 is modified so that a new paragraph 1(2) is substituted specifying requirements to be met and paragraph 1(3) is omitted. Thereafter paragraph 2 is the subject of renovation so that in some respects provision is made for the exercise of discretion where the new requirements are not met. In addition a new paragraph 2A is inserted to define *qualifying immigration status* (see para **5.91** below).

5.90 The substituted presence and status requirements that must be met as a result of the amendments are found in the substituted paragraph 1(2)(a)–(f) of Schedule 1 of the BNA 1981. These are that:

1. the applicant was in the United Kingdom at the beginning of the *qualifying period* (see para **5.177** below);
2. the applicant was not absent from the United Kingdom for more than 90 days *in each year* of the qualifying period (see para **5.123** below);
3. the applicant had *qualifying immigration status* for the whole of the qualifying period (see para **5.91** below);
4. on the date of application, the applicant has a specified status or entitlement (see para **5.93** below);
5. where on the date of application the applicant has probationary citizenship leave granted for the purpose of taking employment in the United Kingdom, he has been in continuous employment (see para **5.128** below) since the date on which that leave was granted;[123] and
6. the applicant was not in the United Kingdom at any time in the qualifying period in breach of immigration laws (see para **5.110** below).

Regarding the qualifying periods for naturalisation under s 6(1), see Section G, below.

---

[122] HC Home Affairs Committee 5th Report HC 425, Ev 145.

[123] 'Employment' includes 'self-employment', see BNA 1981, Sch 1, para 2(5), as inserted by BCIA 2009, s 39(10).

4. Qualifying Immigration Status: for the Purpose of the s 6(1) Presence and Status Requirements

Qualifying immigration status is defined for the purposes of the presence and status requirements of the BNA 1981, Sch 1, para 1(2) by paragraph 2A, inserted into the BNA 1981, Sch 1 by the BCIA 2009, s 39(11). Paragraph 2A(1) provides that a person has a qualifying immigration status if the person has (see paras **5.68–5.83** above for the definition of each term below): 5.91

1. Qualifying temporary residence leave;
2. Probationary citizenship leave;
3. Permanent residence leave;
4. A qualifying CTA entitlement;
5. A Commonwealth right of abode; or
6. A temporary or permanent EEA entitlement.

By the BNA 1981, Sch 1, para 2A(2), a person required to have a qualifying immigration status for the whole of the qualifying period need not have the same qualifying immigration status for the whole of that period. 5.92

5. The Status or Entitlement Required on the Date of the s 6(1) Application

The specified status or entitlement that an applicant must possess on the date of application may be (see para **5.90** above):[124] 5.93

1. probationary citizenship leave;
2. permanent residence leave;
3. a qualifying CTA entitlement;
4. a Commonwealth right of abode; or
5. a permanent EEA entitlement.

6. The Requirements as to Presence and Status Prior to Modification by the BCIA 2009

Prior to the amendments made by the BCIA 2009, the requirements as to presence and status were that:[125] 5.94

1. the applicant was in the United Kingdom at the beginning of the period of five years ending with the date of the application;
2. the number of days on which he was absent from the UK in that period does not exceed 450;
3. the number of days on which he was absent from the United Kingdom in the period of 12 months so ending does not exceed 90;

[124] BNA 1981, Sch 1, para 1(2)(d), as inserted by BCIA 2009, s 39(2).

[125] Ibid, para 1(1)(a) and para 1(2), prior to amendment by the BCIA 2009; see also Nationality Instructions, Chapter 18, Annex B, Annex B(i), and Annex B(ii).

4. he was not at any time in the period of 12 months so ending subject under the immigration laws to any restriction on the period for which he might remain in the United Kingdom; and
5. he was not at any time in the period of five years so ending in the United Kingdom in breach of the immigration laws.

7. Technical or Deemed Absences

5.95 Although an applicant for naturalisation may be in the United Kingdom, rather than absent, for a material time, BNA 1981, Sch 1, para 9(1), which remains unaltered by the BCIA 2009, makes provision in particular circumstances for a person to be treated as absent from the UK so that time spent in the UK does not count for the purposes of fulfilling the requirement to be present in the UK for a given period. However, in respect of a technical or deemed absence, a person may be treated as being in the UK for the whole or any part of any period during which he would fall to be treated as absent in the exercise of discretion under BNA 1981, Sch 1, para 2(b).[126]

5.96 Subject to the exercise of this discretion, a person shall be treated as having been absent from the UK during any period when:[127]

(a) he was in the UK and either was entitled to an exemption under the Immigration Act 1971, s 8(3) or s 8(4) (exemptions for diplomatic agents, etc and members of armed forces), or was a member of the family and formed part of the household of a person so entitled;

(b) he was detained in any place of detention in the UK in pursuance of a sentence passed on him by a court in the UK or elsewhere for any offence, or when liable to be so detained he was unlawfully at large or absent without leave and for that reason liable to be arrested or taken into custody;

(c) he was detained in any hospital in the UK under a hospital order made under Part III of the Mental Health Act 1983 or section 175 or 376 of the Criminal Procedure (Scotland) Act 1975 or Part III of the Mental Health (Northern Ireland) Order 1986 being an order made in connection with his conviction of an offence, or when liable to be so detained he was unlawfully at large or absent without leave and for that reason liable to be arrested or taken into custody; or

(d) he was detained under any detention power conferred by UK immigration laws, or any period when his actual detention under any such power being required or specifically authorized, he was unlawfully at large and for that reason liable to be arrested.

---

126 See also Nationality Instructions, Chapter 18, Annex B.

127 BNA 1981, Sch 1, para 9(1); See also Nationality Instructions, Chapter 18, Annex B.

8. Armed Forces Cases and Exceptional Crown Service: the Alternative to the Presence and Status Requirements for s 6(1) Naturalisation

Prior to the amendments made by the BCIA 2009, the BNA 1981, Sch 1, para 1(3) provided for an alternative to the residence requirements where the applicant for naturalisation was serving outside the United Kingdom in Crown Service under the government of the United Kingdom.[128] This provision is omitted by the BCIA 2009. However, in its place provision is made for an alternative (to the presence and status requirements) in respect of those in the armed forces or Crown service. The statutory power exists 'in the special circumstances of a particular case that is an armed forces case or an exceptional Crown Service case'. 5.97

This wording comes from the BCIA 2009, s 39(9), which makes new provision for the alternative requirement to the presence and status requirements found in the BNA 1981, Sch 1, para 1(2). Paragraph 1(3) of Schedule 1 of the BNA 1981 is omitted by the BCIA 2009, s 39(3). In its place the new alternative requirement is introduced as paragraph 2(2) of Schedule 1 of the BNA 1981, inserted by the BCIA 2009, s 39(9). 5.98

The substituted provision provides that if in the special circumstances of a particular case that is (a) an armed forces case or (b) an exceptional Crown Service case the Secretary of State thinks fit, he may waive the need to fulfil *any or all* of the residence and status requirements.[129] 5.99

An armed forces case is a case where the applicant is or has been a member of the armed forces on the date of application.[130] 5.100

A member of the armed forces means:[131] 5.101

1. a member of the regular forces within the meaning of the Armed Forces Act 2006 (Royal Navy, the Royal Marines, the regular army, or the Royal Air Force),[132] or
2. a member of the reserve forces within the meaning of the Armed Forces Act 2006 (the Royal Fleet Reserve, the Royal Naval Reserve, the Royal Marines Reserve, the Army Reserve, the Territorial Army, the Royal Air Force Reserve, or the Royal Auxiliary Air Force)[133] who is subject to service law by virtue of the Armed Forces Act 2006, s 367(2) (a), (b), or (c); that is in permanent service on call-out under any provision of the Reserve Forces Act 1980 or the Reserved Forces Act 1996 or under any other call-out obligation of an officer; in home defence service on call-out under the Reserve Forces Act 1980, s 22; or in full-time service under a commitment entered into under the Reserve Forces Act 1996, s 24.

---

[128] See also the Nationality Instructions, Chapter 18, Annex C.
[129] BNA 1981, Sch 1, para 2(2), as inserted by BCIA 2009, s 39(9).
[130] Ibid, para 2(3), as inserted by BCIA 2009, s 39(9).
[131] Ibid s 50(1A), as inserted by BCIA 2009, s 49(1).
[132] Armed Forces Act 2006, s 374.
[133] Ibid.

5.102 However, a person is not to be regarded as a member of the armed forces if the person is treated as a member of a regular or reserve force by virtue of:[134]

1. the Armed Forces Act, s 369 (members of British overseas territories' forces serving with UK forces); or
2. the Visiting Forces (British Commonwealth) Act 1933, s 4(3).

5.103 'Crown service under the government of the United Kingdom' is defined by BNA 1981, s 50(1), as Crown service under Her Majesty's government in the United Kingdom, under Her Majesty's government in Northern Ireland, or under the Scottish Administration.

5.104 An exceptional Crown service case is a case where on the date of application, the applicant is serving outside the United Kingdom in Crown service under the Government of the United Kingdom and the Secretary of State considers the applicant's performance in service to be exceptional.[135]

5.105 In a letter of 19 March 2009 to Lord Avebury (Liberal Democrat), Lord Brett, Government Whip, Government Spokesman for the Home Office, set out the criteria that an exceptional Crown service applicant will be expected to meet. The criteria specified there are those already found in guidance made in respect of the Crown service alternative requirement contained in BNA 1981, Sch 1, para 1(3) (prior to its omission by amendment by the BCIA 2009), such guidance being found in the Nationality Instructions, Chapter 18, Annex C, para 2; save that the letter of Lord Brett omits the criterion of loyalty contained in those instructions.[136]

9. The Exercise of Discretion where the Requirements for s 6(1) Naturalisation are not Satisfied

5.106 Prior to amendment by BCIA 2009, s 39, the power of the Secretary of State to exercise discretion where a requirement for naturalisation was not met was found in BNA 1981, Sch 1, para 2. This paragraph is modified by BCIA 2009, s 39, by way of substitution, addition, and omission; although some parts are also retained.

5.107 As was the case prior to modification, there is no power to dispense with the requirement to be in the United Kingdom at the beginning of the qualifying period (unless the absence is deemed absence: see para **5.108**(b) below). Thereafter there is power to exercise discretion in respect of individual requirements. In the application of the powers to exercise discretion prior to modification, the policies to be followed are found in the Nationality Instructions, Chapter 18, and its various annexes. It is expected that substituted guidance will be made available on commencement of the new provisions as to how discretion may be exercised in respect of each requirement.

[134] BNA 1981, s 50(1B), as inserted by BCIA 2009, s 49(1).
[135] Ibid, Sch 1, para 2(4), as inserted by BCIA 2009, s 39(9).
[136] Nationality Instructions, Chapter 18, Annex C, para 2.5.

The modified paragraph 2(1) provides that if in the special circumstances of any particular case the Secretary of State thinks fit he may do any or all of the following things: 5.108

(a) Treat the applicant as fulfilling the requirement not to be absent from the United Kingdom for more than 90 days *in each year* of the qualifying period although the number of days on which he was absent in a year of the qualifying period exceeds 90;

(b) Treat the applicant as having been in the United Kingdom for the whole or any part of any period during which he would otherwise fall to be treated as having been absent under paragraph 9(1) of Schedule 1 of the BNA 1981 (that is where he is treated as technically absent, albeit actually present) (see para **5.95** above);[137]

(c) Treat the applicant as fulfilling the requirement to have had qualifying immigration status for the whole of the qualifying period where such status has only been held for part of that period;

(d) Treat the applicant as fulfilling the requirement for having a specified status or entitlement on the date of application, where he had probationary citizenship leave but it expired in the qualifying period;

(e) Treat the applicant as fulfilling the requirement to have been in continuous employment since the date on which leave was granted, where probationary citizenship leave was granted for the purpose of taking employment in the United Kingdom, although he has not been in continuous employment since the date of the grant of leave;[138]

(f) Treat the applicant as fulfilling the requirement not to be in the United Kingdom at any time in the qualifying period in breach of immigration laws, although he was in breach of the immigration laws in that period; and

(g) Waive the need to fulfil either or both of the requirements to have sufficient knowledge of the English, Welsh, or Scottish Gaelic language and sufficient knowledge of life in the United Kingdom, if he considers that because of the applicant's age or physical or mental condition it would be unreasonable to expect him to meet one or more of those requirements.[139]

The existence of a power to exercise discretion, where probationary citizenship leave has expired prior to an application for naturalisation, is a reminder that probationary citizenship leave is a time-limited period and that applications for naturalisation after its expiry may be entertained less favourably, the longer the period of time between its expiry and an application for naturalisation. In a letter of 19 March 2009 5.109

[137] This provision is wholly unaltered by the BCIA 2009.

[138] 'Employment' includes 'self-employment', see BNA 1981, Sch 1, para 2(5), as inserted by BCIA 2009, s 39(10).

[139] This provision is wholly unaltered by the BCIA 2009.

to Baroness Hanham (Conservative), Lord West of Spithead, Parliamentary Under-Secretary of State, Home Office, stated that:

> . . . we think it reasonable to allow a discretion for us to waive this requirement where a person would qualify for naturalisation but for having applied for naturalisation a few days after their probationary citizenship has expired . . .
>
> We plan to allow a similar discretion in relation to qualifying for probationary citizenship—so if a migrant applies for this status and would have qualified but for the fact that they applied a small number of days after their temporary residence expired, we will allow that person to progress.

10. The Requirement not to be in the United Kingdom in Breach of Immigration Laws

5.110 It is a requirement for naturalisation under both BNA 1981 s 6(1) and s 6(2) not to be in the United Kingdom in breach of the immigration laws during any time in the qualifying period (see paras **5.90** and **5.161**). In respect of both routes discretion may be exercised to treat the applicant as fulfilling the requirement although he was in the UK in breach of immigration laws in the qualifying period (see paras **5.108** and **5.170**).

5.111 BCIA 2009, s 48(1), inserts section 50A into the BNA 1981 to define 'breach of immigration laws' in this context. Prior to this innovation the meaning of unlawful presence in the United Kingdom for nationality purposes was found in Nationality, Immigration and Asylum Act 2002, s 11. The latter ceases to have effect (BCIA 2009, s 48(2)) and is repealed (BCIA 2009, Sch, Part 2), save that it continues to have effect for certain purposes. Many but not all of the provisions found in BNA 1981, s 50A, are the same as those found in Nationality, Immigration and Asylum Act 2002, s 11.

5.112 Section 50A of the BNA 1981 applies for the construction of a reference to being in the United Kingdom 'in breach of the immigration laws' in:[140]

(a) BNA 1981, s 4(2) or (4) (acquisition of British citizenship by registration by a British overseas territories citizen, a British National (Overseas), a British Overseas citizen, a British subject, or a British protected person);

(b) BNA 1981, s 50(5) (a person is not to be treated for the purpose of any provision of the BNA 1981 as ordinarily resident in the United Kingdom or in a British overseas territory at a time when he is in the United Kingdom or, as the case may be, in that territory in breach of the immigration laws); or

(c) Schedule 1 (requirements for naturalisation).

[140] BNA 1981, s 50A(1), as inserted by BCIA 2009, s 48(1).

Subject to saving provisions in respect of Nationality, Immigration and Asylum Act 2002, s 11 (see para **5.120** below), BNA, s 50A, applies only for the purpose of determining on or after the relevant day whether:[141] 5.113

(a) a person born on or after the relevant day is a British citizen under BNA 1981, s 1(1):
(b) on an application under BNA 1981, ss 1(3) or 4(2), made on or after the relevant day, a person is entitled to be registered as a British citizen; or
(c) on an application for naturalisation under BNA 1981, s 6(1) or (2), made on or after the relevant day, the applicant fulfils the requirements of BNA 1981, Sch 1 for naturalisation as a British citizen.

The relevant day for the purposes of determining the matters set out in para **5.113** above, is the day appointed for commencement of BCIA 2009, s 48.[142] 5.114

BNA 1981, s 50A, applies without prejudice to the generality of:[143] 5.115

(a) a reference to being in a place outside the United Kingdom in breach of immigration laws; and
(b) a reference in a provision other than those specified in para **5.112** above to being in the United Kingdom in breach of immigration laws.

By BNA 1981, s 50A(4),[144] a person is in the United Kingdom in breach of the immigration laws if, and only if, the person: 5.116

(a) is in the United Kingdom;
(b) does not have the right of abode in the UK (within the meaning of the Immigration Act 1971, s 2);
(c) does not have leave to enter or remain in the UK (whether or not the person previously had leave);
(d) does not have a qualifying CTA entitlement (see para **5.73** above);[145]
(e) is not entitled to reside in the UK by virtue of any provision made under the European Communities Act 1972, s 2(2) (whether or not the person was previously entitled);
(f) is not entitled to enter and remain in the UK by virtue of the Immigration Act 1971, s 8(1) (crew) (whether or not the person was previously entitled); and
(g) does not have the benefit of an exemption under the Immigration Act 1971 s 8(2) to (4) of that Act (diplomats, soldiers and other special cases) (whether or not the person previously had the benefit of an exemption).

---

[141] Ibid, s 50A (2) and (3), as inserted by BCIA 2009, s 48(1).
[142] Ibid, s 50A(8), as inserted by the BCIA 2009, s 48(1).
[143] Ibid, s 50A(7), as inserted by the BCIA 2009, s 48(1).
[144] As inserted by BCIA 2009, s 48(1).
[145] 'Qualifying CTA entitlement' defined in BNA 1981, s 50A(5), as inserted by BCIA 2009, s 48(1), in the same terms as also defined in BNA 1981, Sch 1, para 11(5), as inserted by BCIA 2009, s 49(3).

5.117 The inclusion of the reference to a qualifying CTA entitlement is an addition to the provisions previously found in the Nationality, Immigration and Asylum Act 2002, s 11, and reflects innovations made elsewhere in the BNA 1981 in the requirements for naturalisation.

5.118 The reference to residence in the UK by virtue of any provision made under the European Communities Act 1972, s 2(2), replaces the references to the Immigration (European Economic Area) Regulations 2000, SI 2000/2326, found in Nationality, Immigration and Asylum Act 2002, s 11. While the innovation of defining rights arising under Community law by reference to European Communities Act 1972, s 2(2), as opposed to subordinate legislation, relieves Parliament of the need to make future amendments to the provision when new subordinate legislation is substituted to give effect to Community obligations, the provision still does not cater for those who have a right to reside by virtue of an enforceable Community right arising otherwise than by provisions made under European Communities Act 1972, s 2(2) (see para **5. 82** above).

5.119 The provisions deeming a person not to be in the United Kingdom before disembarkation, while in a controlled area, or while under immigration control, found in Immigration Act 1971, s 11(1), apply for the purposes of BNA 1981, s 50A, as they apply for the purposes of the Immigration Act 1971.[146] Thus a person to whom Immigration Act 1971, s 11, applies, is not unlawfully present, as he is deemed not to have entered at all, unlawfully or otherwise. For example, a person who presents himself at port, is refused leave to enter, but who is granted temporary admission to the UK under Immigration Act 1971, Sch 2, para 21(1), while he makes further representations for leave, is not unlawfully present in the United Kingdom.

5.120 Notwithstanding its repeal, Nationality, Immigration and Asylum Act 2002, s 11, continues to have effect for the purpose of determining on or after the relevant day whether:[147]

(a) a person *born before* the relevant day is a British citizen under BNA 1981, s 1(1);

(b) on an application for registration as a British citizen under BNA 1981, ss 1(3) or 4(2) *made but not determined before* the relevant day, a person is entitled to be so registered;

(c) on an application for naturalisation as a British citizen under BNA 1981 s 6(1) or (2) *made but not determined before* the relevant day, the applicant fulfils the requirements of the BNA 1981, Sch 1; or

(d) in relation to an application for registration as a British citizen under BNA 1981, s 1(3), or naturalisation as a British citizen under BNA 1981 s 6(1) or (2) *made on or after* the relevant day, a person was in the United Kingdom 'in breach of the immigration laws' at a time before 7 November 2002, being the date of

[146] BNA 1981, s 50A(6), as inserted by BCIA 2009, s 48(1).
[147] BCIA 2009, s 48(3).

commencement of Nationality, Immigration and Asylum Act 2002, s 11.[148] Where the latter continues to have effect for the purpose of determining this matter on or after the relevant day, BNA 1981, s 50A, does not apply for the purposes of determining the matter.

The relevant day for the purposes of the continuing effect of the subsection (3) is the date for commencement of BCIA 2009, s 48.[149] 5.121

In respect of the withholding and withdrawal of support under community care, health, housing, children, local government, and asylum support legislation, Nationality, Immigration and Asylum Act 2002, Sch 3, specifies categories of persons ineligible for specified forms of assistance and support. Among them are persons unlawfully in the UK. As section 11 of the Nationality, Immigration and Asylum Act 2002 is repealed by BCIA 2009, Sch, Part 2, the reference to it in Nationality, Immigration and Asylum Act 2002, Sch 3, para 7(a), is substituted so that BNA 1981, s 50A, is specified in its place as supplying the definition of persons in the UK in breach of immigration laws for the purposes of determining persons unlawfully in the UK who are ineligible for support.[150] 5.122

11. Commentary on the New Requirements (s 6(1) and (2))

(a) *The Requirements as to Presence in the United Kingdom*

The requirement not to be absent from the United Kingdom for more than 90 days *in each year* of the qualifying period replaces the pre-existing requirement in thc BNA 1981 not to be absent for more than 450 days in the five years ending with the date of an application under BNA 1981, s 6(1), or not to be absent for more than 270 days in the three-year period ending with the date of application under BNA 1981, s 6(2); and the requirement under both routes not to be absent in the 12 months so ending for more than 90 days.[151] 5.123

Prior to amendment there was discretion in the special circumstances of any particular case to treat the applicant as fulfilling these requirements,[152] the guidance as to the exercise of that discretion being given in the Nationality Instructions.[153] Following the amendments made by the BCIA 2009, there is also a discretion to 5.124

[148] See Nationality, Immigration and Asylum Act 2002, s 11(4), which has the effect that a person who on commencement of s 11 on 7 November 20002, *is or has been any time* since he last entered the United Kingdom (ie he need no longer be) an EEA national who is a qualified person within the meaning of the Immigration (European Economic Area) Regulations 2000, SI 2000/2326, or the family member of such a person, is not subject to the effect of s 11 for the purposes of considering whether he is unlawfully present. Thus such a person is not unlawfully present simply on the basis that he is no longer exercising a right of residence under the Immigration (European Economic Area) Regulations 2000.

[149] BCIA 2009, s 48(5).

[150] BCIA 2009, 48(6).

[151] BNA 1981, Sch 1, paras 1(2) and 3, prior to amendment by the BCIA 2009.

[152] Ibid, paras 2(a) and 4, prior to amendment by the BCIA 2009.

[153] Chapter 18, Annex B.

treat the applicant as satisfying the requirement not to be absent from the United Kingdom although the number of days on which he was absent in a year of the qualifying period exceeds 90.

5.125 In respect of the exercise of that discretion, in a letter of 19 March 2009 to Lord Avebury (Liberal Democrat), Lord Brett, Government Whip, Government Spokesman for the Home Office, stated that the guidance to the existing exercise of discretion had worked well and that the Government considered it sensible to continue with something similar:

In particular we propose that discretion may be exercised in the following broad circumstances:

- If the applicant has exceeded the 90 day limit by only a few days we would look to ignore this, particularly if there was evidence or an explanation as to why, and especially where there is also evidence which demonstrates that a person has a close link with the United Kingdom by establishing their home, family and a large part of their estate here.
- If a person was unable to travel back to the UK due to poor weather conditions or ill-health whilst abroad, and this took them over the limits, we would waive the excess absences where there was evidence to support this.

As with all discretion it is not possible to cover every scenario and, as such, providing a definitive list of circumstances in which discretion will be exercised is not possible . . . Where absences are considered excessive we will require—as now—that migrants provide evidence which they consider justifies this, and we will take this into consideration when assessing the application as a whole.

5.126 At the Committee Stage of the Bill, Lord Brett stated:

. . . we will not examine the requirement too closely where the absences take place in the early part of the qualifying period—that is, in the entry into the probationary citizenship stage, which has already been examined. We are not concerned about absences from the UK before the start of the qualifying period.[154]

(b) *A Qualifying CTA (Common Travel Area) Entitlement*

5.127 A qualifying CTA (Common Travel Area) entitlement permits Irish citizens who enter the United Kingdom under the Common Travel Area (CTA) arrangements without needing to obtain leave to enter, to be able to apply for naturalisation as a British citizen without needing to obtain leave to remain. Where an Irish citizen who has previously entered the UK under the CTA arrangements, leaves, then returns and does not re-enter the UK on a 'local journey' (from the Channel Islands, the Isle of Man, or the Republic of Ireland)[155] but from an EU Member State, Lord Brett, Government Whip, Government Spokesman for the Home Office, in a letter of 19 March 2009 to Lord Avebury (Liberal Democrat) stated:

[154] HL Comm Deb 2 March 2009 vol 708 c513.
[155] Immigration Act 1971, s 1(3).

. . . that as the definition of qualifying immigration status includes both a CTA entitlement and an EEA entitlement, then, such person would be able to aggregate both forms of status towards the overall qualifying period . . .

(c) *'Continuous Employment'*

For naturalisation under BNA 1981, s 6(1), it is a requirement that where on the date of application the applicant has probationary citizenship leave granted *for the purpose of taking employment* in the United Kingdom, he must have been in *continuous employment* since the date on which that leave was granted.[156] This was of concern when the Bill was in passage and requires consideration. Although, there is a discretion to treat the applicant as fulfilling the requirement where he has not been in continuous employment since the date for the grant of that leave, it is not precisely clear (a) what will count as 'continuous employment' and (b) how discretion will be exercised where the requirement is not met. 5.128

In evidence noted by the Home Affairs Committee,[157] the Immigration Law Practitioners' Association (ILPA) observed[158] that there are already different requirements for migrants with regard to periods of employment insofar as Tier 2 PBS applicants have 60 days to find another job (where not actively involved or complicit in dishonesty by the former sponsor) where their employer loses their sponsor licence, before their leave is curtailed,[159] whereas EEA nationals from states that acceded to the European Union on 1 May 2004 and 1 January 2007 are treated as legally working for certain purposes where intervening periods during which they were not legally working do not exceed 30 days.[160] ILPA argued that a requirement that a person continues to be lawfully present (with leave to enter or remain and abiding by the conditions of such leave) should be sufficient. 5.129

In a letter of 19 March 2009 to Lord Avebury (Liberal Democrat), Lord Brett, Government Whip, Government Spokesman for the Home Office, stated: 5.130

You asked if a worker who loses his employment and then finds a new sponsor to employ him within the 60 days is to be treated as having been in continuous employment under the Bill . . . in such a case the individual will be regarded as having "continuous employment".

In respect of those with leave under Tier 1 of the PBS, Lord Brett stated: 5.131

. . . Although those in Tier 1 are not restricted to having a sponsor, they must meet the points test for Tier 1 again when they apply for further leave to remain. I do not think that these factors make the continuous employment in the Bill unnecessary; rather they are wholly

---

156 BNA 1981, Sch 1, para 1(2)(e) as inserted by BCIA 2009, s 39(2).

157 HC Home Affairs Committee 5th Report (2008–09) HC 425 p 11.

158 ILPA Briefing on the Borders, Citizenship and Immigration Bill, Clause 37 (Continuous Employment), February 2009, pp 1–2.

159 UK Border Agency Guidance for Sponsor applications—Tier 2, Tier 4, and Tier 5 of the Points Based System, paras 544–5.

160 Accession (Immigration and Worker Registration) Regulations 2004, SI 2004/1219, reg 2(8) and Accession (Immigration and Worker Authorisation) Regulations 2006, SI 2006/3317, reg 2(12).

consistent with it and underline the Government's clear policy that migrants who are here to work must be economically active. As such we are clear that a person can meet the continuous employment condition where they change jobs/types or self-employment during the qualifying period.

5.132 In respect of certain other specific groups, Lord Brett, stated:

We will ensure that any definition of continuous employment takes into account the position of certain groups such as Entrepreneurs who may be a company director and therefore not 'employed', or Investors who may not have been employed in any capacity. In addition, routes outside the Points-Based System, such the ancestry route which does not require that any employment undertaken must have been continuous, will be factored into the definition.

. . . All overseas domestic workers currently have an avenue to settlement in the UK after 5 years' continuous employment.

Overseas domestic workers in private households will, under requirements for obtaining probationary citizenship in this category, be able to leave their employer and seek domestic work with another employer. This continues to enable overseas domestic workers to remove themselves from abusive situations.

5.133 In respect of the exercise of discretion to treat the applicant as fulfilling the requirement although he has not been in continuous employment since the date for the grant of that leave Lord Brett stated:

. . . any discretion will be used sparingly and only in truly deserving cases . . . The guidance we publish will include examples . . . but each case will ultimately be considered on its individual merits.

5.134 As noted by the Home Affairs Committee, the Joint Council for the Welfare of Immigrants (JCWI) raised a further concern about the potential for discrimination, which was that the requirement:

. . . may lead to indirect discrimination on grounds of race or gender . . . given its propensity for disproportionate impacts on women who most obviously may need to take time out of the labour market due to pregnancy and child-care responsibilities, or certain ethnic groups (and women), given their greater tendency to be located in insecure employment as a result of labour market discrimination.[161]

5.135 At the Second Reading of the Bill in the House of Commons, Neil Gerrard MP (Labour) voiced concern about the potential for exploitation by employers:

Concerns have been expressed—certainly by a number of trade unions—about what that might mean: the potential for exploitation, and the potential for people to be locked into working conditions that are even unlawful. Indeed, we know that that happens now. Someone who has a dubious immigration status or is scared about what might happen to them if they lose their job can end up working in unlawful conditions, not being paid the minimum wage

[161] HC Home Affairs Committee 5th Report (2008–09) HC 425 Ev 193.

and so on. They are scared to complain, however, because they are scared of the consequences. They are scared that they will lose their job, apart from anything else. If another consequence is going to be that they lose their qualifying period for citizenship and have to go back to the beginning of the process, that will act as a further incentive not to complain.[162]

At the Committee stage in the House of Lords, Lord Brett, addressing some of the concerns raised, stated: 5.136

. . . we recognise that there may be circumstances, especially in the current economic climate, where economically productive migrants cease to be in employment for short periods and through no fault of their own. That is why Clause 37(7) gives us the discretion to waive this requirement in compelling circumstances . . .[163]

At the Report stage in the House of Lords, Lord Brett added: 5.137

This requirement is wholly consistent and underlines the Government's clear policy that migrants who enter via the work route—for example, tiers 1 or 2 of the points-based system—are here to work or to be economically active. This is what the points-based system makes clear.

. . . I was asked for further detail on how we exercise discretion to waive the requirements for individuals to have been in continuous employment. I reiterate that we expect that any discretion will be exercised sparingly and in deserving cases . . . In assessing whether to apply discretion, we would take into account a number of factors, including the person's overall employment record while in the UK; the length of time for which they have been out of work; and the explanation or evidence offered by the individual. I think that that deals with several points raised by the noble Lord, Lord Avebury, about redundancy and bankruptcy, which is not necessarily anything that the individual migrant worker has any control over.[164]

The Home Affairs Committee concluded: 5.138

4 . . . for those migrants who abide by the conditions of their leave, short periods of joblessness, particularly in the current economic climate, should not automatically restart the clock on their qualifying period to citizenship. Whilst we welcome the discretionary power in the Bill to, in 'compelling circumstances', waive the requirement for an individual to have been in continuous employment, the conditions in which the exercise of that discretion is envisaged remain ill-defined. The Government must be more transparent by setting out a specific time period within which individuals can be between jobs without breaking the continuous employment requirement for citizenship. We suggest that this period should be in line with existing conditions, such as the 60 days granted to migrants under tier 2 of the points-based system.[165]

---

162 HC Deb 2 June 2009 vol 493 c189.

163 HL Comm Deb 2 March 2009 vol 708 c526.

164 HL Deb 25 March 2009 vol 709 c734.

165 HC Home Affairs Committee 5th Report (2008–09) HC 425, p 25.

F. THE REQUIREMENTS FOR NATURALISATION UNDER S 6(2) OF THE BRITISH NATIONALITY ACT 1981

1. Introduction

5.139 As noted above in introducing the previous section (see para **5.84**), BCIA 2009, ss 40 and 41, amend BNA 1981, s 6(2), and the corresponding Schedule 1 requirements for naturalisation based on marriage, etc. Certain existing requirements are retained. Others are substituted by new requirements.

5.140 Prior to amendment by the BCIA 2009, BNA 1981, s 6(2), provided a route to naturalisation for a person married to a British citizen and for a civil partner of a British citizen. As a result of the amendments introduced by the BCIA 2009, this is broadened out to embrace other family members with whom the applicant has a family association and, further, the applicant's associate need not be a British citizen.

5.141 Prior to amendment, the route to naturalisation under BNA 1981, s 6(2), was quicker than that under BNA 1981, s 6(1), as presence in the United Kingdom was only required for three years ending on the date of application as opposed to five years in respect of s 6(1).[166] Under the amendments made by the BCIA 2009, the route under BNA 1981, s 6(2), remains the quicker route but the periods of time when a person is required to be present have altered for both routes (see Section G below).

2. Alterations to the BNA 1981, s 6(2)

5.142 Following amendment by BCIA 2009, s 40(1), s 6(2) of the BNA 1981 provides a route for naturalisation so that the Secretary of State may, if he thinks fit, grant an application for naturalisation as a British citizen, made by a person:

(a) Who is of full age (aged 18 or over) and capacity[167] (as was the case prior to amendment);
(b) Who on the date of application has a *relevant family association*; and
(c) Where the Secretary of State is satisfied that the applicant fulfils the requirements of BNA 1981, Sch 1, for naturalisation as a citizen (as was the case prior to amendment, although the content of the Schedule referred to has changed, see below para **5.154**).

5.143 Thereafter, BNA 1981, s 6(3) and (4), are inserted by BCIA 2009, s 40(2), to make further provision for the definition of a *relevant family association* and to make provision to treat a person as having a relevant family association where one no longer exists.

---

166 BNA 1981, Sch 1, paras 1(2)(a) and 3(a).
167 Nationality Instructions, Chapter 18, Annex A.

3. A Relevant Family Association

Section 6(3) of the BNA 1981 provides that for the purposes of BNA 1981, s 6 and Sch 1, a person has a relevant family association if he has: 5.144

1. a connection of a prescribed description
2. to a person of a prescribed description.

The powers to prescribe a description of a connection and to prescribe a description of a person are conferred upon the Secretary of State. The powers are exercisable by regulations made by statutory instrument under the negative resolution procedure.[168] By BNA 1981, s 50(1), 'prescribed' means prescribed by regulations made under BNA 1981, s 41. 5.145

In an important innovation, the person with whom the applicant for naturalisation must have a relevant family association need not be a British citizen. In a memorandum submitted to the Delegated Powers and Regulatory Reform Committee, the Home Office stated: 5.146

> 41 . . . There is a power to prescribe a description of person B, which could be used, for example, to prescribe that person B was a British citizen or a person with permanent residence in the UK.[169]

The Home Office memorandum justified the use of regulations to set out relevant family associations as they were likely to be detailed and subject to amendment and as there was a need to maintain flexibility: 5.147

> 43 . . . For example, if the regulations prescribe the connection by reference to a category of the immigration rules under which a person has leave to enter or remain, any changes to the name of that category in the immigration rules would necessitate a change to the description of the relevant family association. This will also give the flexibility to add new relevant family associations as considered appropriate.[170]

In its 4th Report the Delegated Powers and Regulatory Reform Committee set out the Government's response to the 3rd Report, as set out in a letter to the Chairman from Lord West of Spithead, Parliamentary Under-Secretary of State, Home Office: 5.148

> 8 . . . We think it is relevant that we intend to use the regulations to widen the scope of section 6(2), and therefore the groups of applicant who will benefit from the shorter qualifying period. It is our current intention to include, not only spouses and civil partners of British citizens, but also other groups such as unmarried and same-sex partners of British citizens or person with permanent residence leave.[171]

---

[168] BNA 1981, s 41(1)(a).

[169] HL Delegated Powers and Regulatory Reform Committee 3rd Report (2008–09) HL Paper 29, Appendix 1, p 18.

[170] Ibid.

[171] HL Delegated Powers and Regulatory Reform Committee 4th Report (2008–09) HL Paper 48, Appendix 2, p 8.

5.149 In a letter of 19 March 2009 to Lord Avebury (Liberal Democrat) Lord Brett, Government Whip, Government Spokesman for the Home Office, stated that relevant family association is likely to include the following groups:

> a. spouses of British citizens and permanent residents;
> b. unmarried and same-sex partners of British citizens and permanent residents;
> c. bereaved spouses and civil partners, unmarried and same-sex partners of British citizens and permanent residents;
> d. victims of domestic violence or British citizens and permanent residents; and
> e. persons exercising access rights to a child resident in the UK.
>
> We are also considering whether to include further groups such as elderly dependent relatives.

5.150 At the Committee Stage of the Bill, Lord Brett stated:

> . . . the regulations are likely to include other conditions recognising unmarried partners if they have been in a relationship for two years, which is the normal term—we do not intend to change it.[172]

5.151 In its 3rd Report the Delegated Powers and Regulatory Reform Committee drew the attention of the House of Lords to the clause to consider whether it was satisfied that the negative resolution procedure afforded an adequate level of parliamentary control.[173] The Home Office memorandum submitted to the Committee had considered that the negative resolution procedure was the appropriate level of scrutiny, comparable to the regime for outlining which dependents of asylum seekers or supported persons are entitled to support under the Immigration and Asylum Act 1999, s 94.[174]

4. The Discretion to Treat a Person as Having a Relevant Family Association

5.152 Section s 6(4) of the BNA 1981[175] provides that in the special circumstances of any particular case, the Secretary of State may treat a person as having a relevant family association on the date of the application although the relevant family association ceased to exist before that date.

5.153 In respect of the exercise of discretion to treat the applicant as fulfilling the requirement to have had a relevant family association (including the specific provisions that apply in respect of a partner of a British citizen or a person with permanent residence leave, see para **5.162** below) where the relevant family association has ceased to exist, in a letter of 19 March 2009 to Lord Avebury (Liberal Democrat)

[172] HL Comm Deb 2 March 2009 vol 708 c547.

[173] HL Delegated Powers and Regulatory Reform Committee 3rd Report (2008–09) HL Paper 29 p 5, para 12.

[174] Ibid, Appendix 1, p 18, para 44.

[175] Inserted by BCIA 2009, s 40(2).

Lord Brett, Government Whip, Government Spokesman for the Home Office, stated:

> . . . it is not the purpose of guidance to set out all of the possible scenarios where discretion may be exercised . . . one example where we may use discretion is in the case of a partner who separated from their British citizen partner a (sic) shortly before they were due to complete their qualifying time period under the family route . . .

5. Alterations to the Requirements in BNA 1981, Schedule 1, for Naturalisation under s 6(2) (ie on the Basis of a Relevant Family Association)

(a) *Introduction*

BCIA 2009, s 40(3)–(5), amends the relevant provisions of Schedule 1 of the BNA 1981 in respect of s 6(2) naturalisation. Schedule 1 of the BNA 1981 is modified so that paragraphs 3 and 4 are substituted and a new paragraph 4A is inserted. 5.154

(b) *Requirements that are Unaltered in Substance*

Three requirements, which are unaltered in substance from those obtaining prior to the BCIA 2009, but which are now found in BNA 1981, Sch 1, para 3(1)(c)–(e) are that: 5.155

1. a person is of good character;[176]
2. he has sufficient knowledge of the English, Welsh, or Scottish Gaelic language;[177] and
3. he has sufficient knowledge of life in the United Kingdom.[178]

(c) *New Requirements as to Presence and Status*

Thereafter, the substituted presence and status requirements that must be met are found in modified BNA 1981, Sch 1, para 3(1)(a) and 3(2). These are that: 5.156

1. the applicant was in the United Kingdom at the beginning of the *qualifying period*;
2. the applicant was not absent from the United Kingdom for more than 90 days *in each year* of the qualifying period;
3. Subject to a proviso (see para **5.162** below), the applicant had a *relevant family association* (see para **5.144** above) for the whole of the qualifying period *and* had a *qualifying immigration status* (see para **5.171** below) for the whole of the qualifying period;
4. on the date of application, the applicant has a specified status or entitlement, namely:

[176] See Nationality Instructions, Chapter 18, Annex D.
[177] See Nationality Instructions, Chapter 18, Annex E.
[178] Ibid.

(a) probationary citizenship leave based on the applicant having the relevant family association (see para **5.71** above and paras **5.157–5.158** below);
(b) permanent residence leave based on the applicant having the relevant family association (see para **5.72** above and paras **5.157–5.158** below);
(c) a qualifying CTA entitlement (see para **5.73** above); or
(d) a Commonwealth right of abode (see para **5.77** above); and

5. the applicant was not in the United Kingdom at any time in the qualifying period in breach of immigration laws (see para **5.110** above).

5.157 In respect of probationary citizenship leave based on the applicant having a relevant family association and permanent residence leave based on the applicant having a relevant family association, there is an interplay between the particular type of leave to be granted (as an immigration matter), which must be based on a relevant family association and the requirements for naturalisation under this route (a nationality matter).

5.158 Where (a) probationary citizenship leave based on a relevant family association or (b) permanent residence leave based on a relevant family association is relied upon, such leave is based on a relevant family association if it was *granted* on the basis of the person having a relevant family association.[179]

5.159 There is no provision equivalent to that for those applying to naturalise under BNA 1981, s 6(1), that enables an applicant to rely on possession of a permanent EEA entitlement on the date of application in order to satisfy the requirement for a specified status or entitlement on the date of application.

5.160 Although an applicant for naturalisation may be in the United Kingdom, rather than absent, for a material time, BNA 1981, Sch 1, para 9(1), which remains unaltered by the BCIA 2009, makes provision in particular circumstances for a person to be treated as absent from the UK so that time spent in the UK does not count for the purposes of fulfilling the requirement to be present in the UK for a given period (see para **5.95** above).

(d) *The Requirements as to Presence and Status Prior to Modification by the BCIA 2009*

5.161 Prior to the amendments made by the BCIA 2009, the requirements as to presence and status were that:[180]

(a) the applicant was in the United Kingdom at the beginning of the period of three years ending with the date of the application;
(b) the number of days on which he was absent from the UK in that period does not exceed 270;
(c) the number of days on which he was absent from the United Kingdom in the period of 12 months so ending does not exceed 90;

[179] BNA 1981, Sch 1, para 4A(2), as inserted by BCIA 2009, s 40(5).

[180] Ibid, para 3(1)(a), prior to amendment by the BCIA 2009; see also Nationality Instructions, Chapter 18, Annex B, Annex B(i), and Annex B(ii).

(d) that on the date of application he was not subject under the immigration laws to any restriction on the period for which he might remain in the United Kingdom; and
(e) he was not at any time in the period of three years so ending in the United Kingdom in breach of the immigration laws.

(e) *The Interplay for Partners between the Requirement for a Relevant Family Association and the Requirements as to Presence and Status*

In respect of the requirement for a *relevant family association* for the purposes of the presence and status requirements (see para **5.144** above), specific provision is made where the applicant relies on a relationship with *a partner* by BNA 1981, Sch 1, para 3(5).[181] Where the relevant family association specified in the regulations is that the applicant is the partner of a British citizen or a person with permanent residence leave: 5.162

(a) the requirement to have a relevant family status for the whole of the qualifying period is only met if the applicant was that person's partner for the whole of the qualifying period; and
(b) in respect of the requirement to have *qualifying immigration status* for the whole of the *qualifying period*, the applicant can rely on (i) qualifying temporary residence leave based on a relevant family association, (ii) probationary citizenship leave based on a relevant family association, or (iii) permanent citizenship leave based on a relevant family association; *only* if that partnership is the relevant family association upon which the leave to which the status related to it is based (NB a qualifying CTA entitlement and a Commonwealth right of abode are not subject to this requirement).

The applicant is a person's partner where:[182] 5.163

(a) The person is the applicant's spouse or civil partner or is in a relationship of a description specified in regulations for these purposes; and
(b) The marriage, civil partnership or other relationship satisfies any conditions specified in those regulations.

However, the relationship by reference to which the applicant and the other person are partners need not be of the same description for the whole of the qualifying period.[183] Unmarried partners who marry each other during the qualifying period may satisfy the requirements in respect of the qualifying period. 5.164

[181] Inserted by BCIA 2009, s 40(3).
[182] BNA 1981, Sch 1, para 3(6), as inserted by BCIA 2009, s 40(3).
[183] Ibid, para 3(7); as inserted by BCIA 2009, s 40(3).

6. A New Future Intentions Requirement

5.165 Prior to the BCIA 2009, there was no future intentions requirement to be met for those seeking to naturalise under BNA 1981, s 6(2). Such a requirement only existed for those seeking to naturalise under s 6(1). Following amendments made by the BCIA 2009, there is now such a requirement for those persons seeking to naturalise under s 6(2).

5.166 The requirements that must be met in respect of future intentions as a result of the amendments are found in BNA 1981, Sch 1, para 3(1)(b) and 3(3). They are that in the event of a certificate of naturalisation as a British citizen being granted:

(a) the applicant intends that his home (or where he has more than one) his principal home, will be in the United Kingdom;
(b) the applicant intends to enter into or continue in service of a specified description (see para **5.167** below); or
(c) the person with whom the applicant has a *relevant family association* intends to enter into or continue in service of a specified description (see para **5.167** below), and the applicant intends to reside with him during the period that person is in the service in question.

5.167 The 'service' referred to in respect of the future intentions requirement is specified in BNA 1981, Sch 1, para 3(4) as:

(a) Crown Service under the Government of the United Kingdom;
(b) Service under an international organisation of which the United Kingdom or Her Majesty's government in the United Kingdom is a member, or
(c) Service in the employment of a company or association established in the UK.

5.168 As may be seen, an applicant may intend to reside with a person in service outside the UK, rather than be in such service himself.

5.169 The description of service provided for the purposes of naturalisation under BNA 1981, s 6(2), follows that provided for naturalisation under s 6(1).[184] The Nationality Instructions, Chapter 18, Annex F, Annex F(i) and Annex F(ii) provide further guidance as to how such service is presently understood for the purposes of BNA 1981, s 6(1).

7. The Exercise of Discretion where the Requirements for s 6(2) Naturalisation are not Satisfied

5.170 In respect of the discretion that may be exercised by the Secretary of State where the requirements for naturalisation under s 6(2) are not met, BNA

[184] Ibid, para 1(1)(d).

1981, Sch 1, para 4[185] provides that if in the special circumstances of any particular case the Secretary of State thinks fit he may do any or all of the following things:

(a) Treat the applicant as fulfilling the requirement not to be absent from the United Kingdom for more than ninety days in each year of the qualifying period although the number of days on which he was absent in a year of the qualifying period exceeds ninety (see para **5.156** above);

(b) Treat the applicant as having been in the United Kingdom for the whole or any part of any period during which he would otherwise fall to be treated as having been absent under paragraph 9(1) of Schedule 1 of the BNA 1981 (that is where he is treated as technically absent, albeit actually present) (see para **5.160** above);

(c) Treat the applicant as fulfilling the requirement to have had a relevant family association (including the specific provisions that apply in respect of a partner of a British citizen or a person with permanent residence leave) for the whole of the qualifying period, where the relevant family association of an applicant has ceased to exist (for example on relationship breakdown) (see para **5.156** above);

(d) Treat the applicant as fulfilling the requirement to have had a qualifying immigration status for the whole of the qualifying period (including the specific provisions that apply in respect of a partner of a British citizen or a person with permanent residence leave), where the applicant has had a qualifying immigration status for only part of the qualifying period (see para **5.156** above);

(e) Treat the applicant as fulfilling the requirement to have a specified status or entitlement on the date of application, where he has had probationary citizenship leave but it expired in the qualifying period (see para **5.156** above);

(f) Treat the applicant as fulfilling the requirement not to be in the United Kingdom at any time in the qualifying period in breach of immigration laws, although he was in breach of the immigration laws in that period (see para **5.156** above);

(g) Waive the need to fulfil either or both of the requirements to have sufficient knowledge of the English, Welsh or Scottish Gaelic language and sufficient knowledge of life in the United Kingdom, if he considers that because of the applicant's age or physical or mental condition it would be unreasonable to expect him to meet one or more of those requirements[186] (see para **5.155** above); and

(h) Waive the need to fulfil *any or all* of the presence and status requirements (other than the requirement not to be in the UK in breach of immigration law at any time during the qualifying period), including the specific provisions that apply in respect of a partner of a British citizen or a person with permanent residence

[185] Substituted by BCIA 2009, s 40(4).
[186] This provision is wholly unaltered by the BCIA 2009.

leave, if on the date of application the person with whom the applicant has a relevant family association is serving in specified service outside the United Kingdom and the qualifying territories, and that person's recruitment for that service took place in the United Kingdom. The service in question is that under BNA 1981, s 2(1)(b): that is Crown service under the Government of the United Kingdom or a qualifying territory and other designated service (see para **5.156** above).[187]

8. Qualifying Immigration Status: for the Purpose of the s 6(2) Presence and Status Requirements

5.171 Qualifying immigration status is defined for the purposes of the presence and status requirements of BNA 1981, Sch 1, para 3, by Sch 1, para 4A[188] of that Act. Paragraph 4A(1) provides that a person has a qualifying immigration status if the person has:

(a) Qualifying temporary residence leave based on a relevant family association (see paras **5.70** above and **5.174** below);
(b) Probationary citizenship leave based on a relevant family association (see paras **5.71** above and **5.173–5.174** below);
(c) Permanent residence leave based on a relevant family association (see paras **5.72** above and **5.173–5.174** below);
(d) A qualifying CTA entitlement (see para **5.73** above); or
(e) A Commonwealth right of abode (see para **5.77** above).

5.172 Unlike the provisions applying to applicants for naturalisation under BNA 1981, s 6(1), for applicants seeking to naturalise under BNA 1981, s 6(2), a temporary or permanent EEA entitlement does not satisfy the requirement for a qualifying immigration status.

5.173 In respect of qualifying temporary residence leave based on a relevant family association, probationary citizenship leave based on a relevant family association, and permanent residence leave based on a relevant family association, there is an interplay between the particular type of leave to be granted (as an immigration matter), which must be based on a relevant family association and the requirements for naturalisation under this route (a nationality matter).

5.174 Where (a) qualifying temporary residence leave, (b) probationary citizenship leave, or (c) permanent residence leave, in each case based on a relevant family association is relied upon, such leave is based on a relevant family association if it was *granted* on the basis of the person having a relevant family association.[189]

[187] See the British Citizenship (Designated Service) Order 2006, SI 2006/1390; see also the Nationality Instructions, Chapter 18, Annex B, para 6.

[188] Inserted by BCIA 2009, s 40(5).

[189] BNA 1981, Sch 1, para 4A(2), as inserted by BCIA 2009, s 40(5).

A person who is required to have a qualifying immigration status and a relevant family association for the whole of the qualifying period, need not have the same qualifying immigration status or the same relevant family association (subject to the specific provisions that apply in respect of a partner of a British citizen or a person with permanent residence leave, see paras **5.162–5.164** above) for the whole of that period.[190] 5.175

Where a person relies on having more than one qualifying immigration status for the whole of the qualifying period and relies upon more than one of:[191] 5.176

(a) qualifying temporary residence leave based on a relevant family association;
(b) probationary citizenship leave based on a relevant family association;
(c) permanent residence leave based on a relevant family association;

subject to the specific provisions that apply in respect of a partner of a British citizen or a person with permanent residence leave (see paras **5.162–5.164** above), it is not necessary for the leave to which each status relates to be based on the same relevant family association. Further, where specific provisions apply in respect of a partner of a British citizen or a person with permanent residence leave, the relationship by reference to which the persons referred to are partners need not be of the same description in respect of each grant of leave. Thus a partner who had temporary citizenship leave as an unmarried partner and who is thereafter granted probationary citizenship leave as a spouse of the same person would satisfy the requirement to have held a qualifying immigration status throughout the whole of the qualifying period.

G. THE QUALIFYING PERIODS FOR NATURALISATION UNDER S 6(1), (2)

1. The Basic Provisions

The qualifying periods for naturalisation as a British citizen under both routes provided for in BNA 1981, s 6(1) and 6(2), are set out in BNA 1981, Sch 1, para 4B.[192] 5.177

The qualifying period is a period of years ending with the date of application for naturalisation.[193] 5.178

In respect of each routes—s 6(1) and s 6(2) (where there is a relevant family association)—there are two periods of different length specified as the qualifying periods, dependent on whether the applicant has met the *activity condition*. 5.179

[190] Ibid, para 4A(3), as inserted by BCIA 2009, s 40(5).
[191] Ibid, para 4A(4), as inserted by BCIA 2009, s 40(5).
[192] Inserted by BCIA 2009, s 41(1).
[193] BNA 1981, Sch 1, para 4B(1), as inserted by BCIA 2009, s 41(1).

5.180 For applicants seeking to naturalise under s 6(1), the qualifying periods are:[194]

(a) eight years, where a person does not meet the activity condition; and
(b) six years, where a person meets the activity condition.

5.181 For applicants seeking to naturalise under s 6(2), the qualifying periods are:[195]

(a) five years, where a person does not meet the activity condition; and
(b) three years, where a person meets the activity condition.

5.182 An applicant meets the activity condition if the Secretary of State is satisfied that the applicant:[196]

(a) has participated, otherwise than for payment, in prescribed activities; or
(b) is to be treated as having so participated.

5.183 At the Committee Stage in the House of Commons, Phil Woolas MP, Minister of State, Home Office, confirmed that qualifying periods may be aggregated:

> Somebody who spends two periods in the UK with a qualifying immigration status, and who in between is lawfully in the UK with an immigration status that is not a qualifying one, can have the two qualifying periods aggregated . . . For example, an applicant who entered under the work route, stopped working after three years to commence a two-year period of study and then resumed work, could count both periods spent as a worker towards the qualifying period.[197]

2. Subordinate Regulations

5.184 In order to further regulate and amend the provisions introduced in respect of the requirement to participate in prescribed activities or be treated as having so participated, provisions are inserted into the BNA 1981, s 41(1), to confer power upon the Secretary of State to make provision by regulations for:[198]

(a) Substituting a different number of years for any of the qualifying periods specified for the purposes for naturalisation under BNA 1981 s 6(1) and s 6(2), both where the activity condition is met and where it is not met;
(b) Determining whether a person has participated, for the purposes of an application for naturalisation, in prescribed activities; and
(c) Determining whether a person is to be treated, for the purposes of an application for naturalisation, as having participated in prescribed activities.

5.185 Further provision is also made for the Secretary of State to make regulations for substituting a different number of years for any of the qualifying periods specified

---

194 Ibid, para 4B(2) and (3), as inserted by BCIA 2009, s 41(1).
195 Ibid.
196 Ibid, para 4B(5), as inserted by BCIA 2009, s 41(1).
197 PBC Deb 4th Sitting 11 June 2009 c108.
198 BNA 1981, s 41(1)(bc), (bd), and (be), as inserted by BCIA 2009, s 41(2).

for the purpose of naturalisation under s 6(1) and s 6(2), both where the activity condition is met and where it is not met.[199] It is expressly provided that in respect of both s 6(1) and s 6(2) regulations may provide for the period of years to be *the same* where the activity condition is met and where it is not met.

Further, regulations made for (a) determining whether a person has participated in prescribed activities, and (b) determining whether a person is to be treated as having participated in prescribed activities:[200] 5.186

(a) may make provision applying in relation to the time before commencement of BCIA 2009, s 41; the latter being the statutory provision governing the qualifying period; and
(b) may enable the Secretary of State to make arrangements for such persons as he thinks appropriate to determine whether in accordance with those regulations a person has, or is to be treated as having, participated in an activity.

Regulations, whether alone or with any other provision, made for:[201] 5.187

(a) prescribing activities for the purposes of the activity condition;
(b) substituting a different number of years for any of the qualifying periods specified for the purposes for naturalisation under s 6(1) and s 6(2) of the BNA, both where the activity condition is met and where not met);
(c) determining whether a person has participated, for the purposes of an application for naturalisation, in prescribed activities; and
(d) determining whether a person is to be treated, for the purposes of an application for naturalisation, as having participated in prescribed activities;

must be made under the affirmative resolution procedure. The power to make regulations for the above purposes is conferred upon the Secretary of State and the regulations are to be made by statutory instrument.

In a memorandum supplied to the Delegated Powers and Regulatory Reform Committee, the Home Office justified the use of regulations for these matters, rather than setting them out in the primary legislation, on account of the provision necessarily being detailed and there being a need to have flexibility: 5.188

49 . . . The department may for example want to adjust the list of activities an applicant can complete to reduce their qualifying period for naturalisation, or adjust the groups of people who will automatically be treated as having carried out those activities. The department has established a design group with the voluntary sector and local government to advise on what the prescribed activities should be, the level of commitment needed, and how completion of the activities should be verified. The department will be monitoring the practical application of these matters with the third sector and other interested parties, and therefore believe a

[199] Ibid, s 41(1B), as inserted by BCIA 2009, s 41(3).
[200] Ibid, s 41(1C), as inserted by BCIA 2009, s 41(3).
[201] Ibid, s 41(7) as amended, and s 41(8) as modified by BCIA 2009, s 41(4) and (5) respectively.

regulation-making power is the appropriate way to ensure that requirements can be updated in line with the operational realities.[202]

5.189 In its 3rd Report, at paragraph 14, the Delegated Powers and Regulatory Reform Committee drew attention to the provisions to make regulations to substitute different qualifying periods and the separate provision to substitute the same qualifying periods *regardless* of whether the activity condition was satisfied. On account of shorter qualifying periods being contemplated where the activity condition was satisfied, the Committee sought to draw the latter provisions to the attention of the House of Lords, so that more details could be obtained from the Minister.[203]

5.190 In its 4th Report the Delegated Powers and Regulatory Reform Committee presented the Government's response as set out in a letter to the Chairman from Lord West of Spithead, Parliamentary Under-Secretary of State, Home Office:

> 10. The Government is fully committed to introducing Active Citizenship and it is a key part of the new Path to Citizenship. Nevertheless, we are conscious that this is a novel area of policy and as such recognise the need to put in place appropriate safeguards should any operational difficulties emerge.
>
> 11. To mitigate this risk we have already put in place a design group including representatives from local authorities and the third sector to advise us on the practicalities including the range of activities, the level of commitment and the most appropriate way we can verify that activities have taken place.
>
> 12. However, we believe it is sensible to have the power to take account of the possibility that significant operational difficulties could necessitate the cessation of the condition. We believe that this power is extremely unlikely to be used, but that it represents a sensible safeguard.[204]

5.191 On account of its concern as to the nature of the proposed prescribed activities, the Home Affairs Committee was not satisfied with the proposal to prescribe activities in regulations made under the affirmative resolution procedure. The Committee recommended that the Bill be amended so that the detailed nature of the prescribed activities could be laid under the super-affirmative resolution procedure, whereby a proposed instrument is laid before Parliament for a prescribed period to allow for scrutiny and amendments before a draft instrument is laid for approval, to allow greater scrutiny.[205] This suggestion was not taken up.

---

[202] HL Delegated Powers and Regulatory Reform Committee 3rd Report (2008–09) HL Paper 29, Appendix 1, pp 19–20.

[203] Ibid, p 5.

[204] HL Delegated Powers and Regulatory Reform Committee 4th Report (2008–09) HL Paper 48, Appendix 2, p 8.

[205] HC Home Affairs Committee 5th Report (2008–09) HC 425, pp 14–15.

H. THE ACTIVITY CONDITION

1. Introduction

The introduction of an activity condition by BCIA 2009, s 41, as an optional requirement for naturalisation allows for the qualifying period to be reduced by two years for both the routes (BNA 1981, s 6(1) and s 6(2)) where the applicant has satisfied it. The activity condition is met if the Secretary of State is satisfied that the applicant has participated otherwise than for payment in prescribed activities or is to be treated as having so participated. 5.192

An applicant who does not satisfy the activity condition will need to spend a longer period of time with probationary citizenship leave before progressing to British citizenship (or permanent residence). During this time the applicant will not have access to benefits or housing. Therefore although voluntary, in many cases there will be circumstantial pressure to satisfy the activity condition. There will be pressure on migrants denied benefits, including in-work benefits, such as working tax credit, child tax credit, and housing benefit, during any extended period of probationary citizenship leave. Such a pressure will leave the migrant reliant on work-derived income in circumstances where a worker on the same wage but with access to in-work benefits would have access to such benefits in order to alleviate poverty, provide encouragement into work (often low paid), and secure necessary accommodation. 5.193

2. The Green Paper

In respect of the activities that would constitute evidence of active citizenship, the Green Paper identified:[206] 5.194

(a) volunteering with a recognized organization;
(b) employer supported volunteering;
(c) volunteering activity, which may involve short periods overseas, to support the UK's international development objectives;
(d) running or helping to run a playgroup which encourages the different communities to interact;
(e) fund-raising activities for charities or schools;
(f) serving on community bodies, for example as a school governor; and
(g) running or helping run a local sporting team.

[206] Green Paper *The Path to Citizenship: Next Steps in Reforming the Immigration System* (February 2008), p 30.

5.195 The Green Paper proposed that the active citizenship of an applicant could be confirmed by a referee who would be subject to the same penalties for making a false declaration as the two referees required in current applications for citizenship.[207]

3. Commentary

5.196 The activity condition has caused considerable concern to interested parties, with criticism focusing on its potentially discriminatory effect as between nationals and non-nationals, the difficulties faced by vulnerable persons in fulfilling the requirement, and the potential breaches of rights found in international treaties.[208] In a memorandum submitted to the Joint Committee on Human Rights, HSMP Forum noted:

> Migrants will feel being forced to do voluntary work and hence will not contribute whole heartedly. It also undermines the true essence of philanthropic aim of the voluntary work. It would make voluntary work look like a barter system and would reflect it rather in a commercial sense.[209]

5.197 In evidence to the Home Affairs Committee, Liberty addressed a deficiency in the type of volunteering proposed and questioned the impact of volunteering on this scale:

> This type of volunteering will necessarily ignore the ways in which many migrants already volunteer their services to the community, for example with informal childcare arrangements or teaching English . . .
>
> . . . Liberty has serious reservations about the impact on the voluntary sector who, as far as we are aware, have not asked for the creation of large numbers of potential 'volunteers'. It is unclear from clause 39 how the Government intends or expects to regulate volunteering on this scale. By creating unprecedented levels of supply, there is inevitably a danger that those seeking to volunteer may be exploited as an industry of 'volunteering opportunities' is created. [210]

5.198 In a supplementary memorandum also submitted to the Home Affairs Committee, the Joint Council for the Welfare of Immigrants (JCWI) identified who may potentially struggle with an activity condition:

(a) Migrants with health problems (including mental health problems).
(b) Migrants with disabilities.
(c) Migrants with learning difficulties.
(d) Elderly migrants.

---

[207] Ibid, p 30.

[208] In the JCHR Legislative Scrutiny: Borders, Citizenship and Immigration Bill, 9th Report (2008–09) HL Paper 62 HC 375, see the memoranda submitted by JCWI Ev 65–71; Migrants' Rights Network Ev 103–6 and the Northern Ireland Human Rights Commission Ev 117–29.

[209] JCHR Legislative Scrutiny: Borders, Citizenship and Immigration Bill, 9th Report (2008–09) HL Paper 62 HC 375, Ev 26.

[210] HC Home Affairs Committee 5th Report (2008–09) HC 425, Ev 186.

(e) Migrants with personality disorders.
(f) Migrants who work long hours.
(g) Migrants who undertake shift work.
(h) Migrants on low incomes.
(i) Single parents and other migrants with caring responsibilities.
(j) Female migrants who for 'cultural reasons' are 'prohibited' by their spouses and families from participating in public domains.[211]

The Home Affairs Committee recommended that: 5.199

45 . . . the prescribed activities should recognise the range of forms of volunteering already undertaken in communities, and should count existing informal volunteering arrangements towards the requirement, rather than imposing additional burdens.[212]

The Joint Committee on Human Rights expressed its concern that: 5.200

1.49 . . . the proposed community activity requirement may have a discriminatory effect on groups who are unable to undertake such activity for various reasons, such as physical or mental disability, caring responsibilities, or being in full time work. We are not reassured by the power to make regulations which treat specified types of persons as having fulfilled the activity condition even though they have not. We recommend that the exemptions are included on the face of the bill. Failing that, we recommend that the Government publish the regulations in draft, during the passage of the Bill, to enable Parliament to scrutinise them properly for any possible discriminatory effect.[213]

4. The Justification Offered by the Government

In a letter of 23 February 2009 to the Chairman of the Committee, Lord West of Spithead, Parliamentary Under-Secretary of State, Home Office, noted that the activity condition was not a compulsory requirement and those migrants who are unwilling to undertake any form of activity can choose not to do so, albeit it would take them two years longer to qualify for citizenship. He further stated that: 5.201

. . . active citizenship will be designed so that migrants, even where they have significant commitments (eg work or family related), will be able to fulfil the requirements. That is why we believe it is right that people should be able to demonstrate active citizenship at any point in their journey. This will allow migrants to plan activities better in line with work and family commitments. We will also ensure that we permit a wide range of activities to ensure migrants can utilise their particular skills and interests . . .[214]

In addition, Phil Woolas MP, Minister of State, Home Office, stated that the Government did not believe that it was appropriate to specify exceptions to the 5.202

[211] Ibid, Ev 193.
[212] Ibid, p 15.
[213] JCHR Legislative Scrutiny: Borders, Citizenship and Immigration Bill, 9th Report (2008–09) HL Paper 62 HC 375, p 14.
[214] JCHR Legislative Scrutiny: Borders, Citizenship and Immigration Bill, 9th Report (2008–09) HL Paper 62 HC 375, Ev 5.

activity condition on the face of the Bill as the provisions were detailed, complex, and may change with time. He agreed that Parliament should be able to scrutinise any exemptions to be set out in regulations and that the affirmative resolution procedure would cater for this. The Government was developing its operation of the activity condition through a design group which included representatives of third sector organizations and local authorities. He considered it would be premature to publish draft regulations until the work of the design group is completed.[215] He later confirmed that he did not believe there were any equality and human rights implications in the proposal for an activity condition.[216]

5. The Design Group

5.203 The content and regulation of the activity condition is the subject of work by a Design Group, set up by the Home Office. The group includes representatives from the voluntary sector and local government. No final scheme has been devised but the thinking of the group is clear from a series of documents laid in the House of Lords' library. The group proposes that:[217]

(a) the burden of demonstrating active citizenship (of a maximum of 50 hours activity) will fall on the applicant with a role for a referee and a process to verify the status of the organization with whom the activity took place;

(b) there will be penalties for applicants and referees who act inappropriately, the BNA 1981, s 46, making it a criminal offence to make a statement known to be false in a material particular or recklessly to make a statement false in a material particular, for the purposes of procuring anything to be done or not to be done under the BNA 1981;

(c) the Nationality Checking Service (NCS) will be used to verify active citizenship;

(d) the verification regime will vary as between registered charities (taken at face value) and non-registered charities and other organizations (requiring an additional reference);

(e) activities that might count include those advancing education; health, social, and community welfare, heritage, arts, culture, sport, the natural environment; those which benefit children, young people, the elderly, the disabled, or other vulnerable groups; those which involve mentoring or befriending; volunteering with a recognized organization such as a registered charity or constituted group; employer supported volunteering, serving on a community body, or

[215] JCHR Government replies to the Second, Fourth, Eighth, Ninth and Twelfth Reports of Session 2008–09, 17th Report (2008–09) HL Paper 104 HC 592, Written Evidence p 7.

[216] PBC Deb 4th Sitting 11 June 2009 c119.

[217] Document made available to the House to illustrate the Government's emerging thinking on active citizenship—4 June 2009.

activities which advance social justice and promote democratic and political engagement;

(f) the type of activities which might count includes volunteering at a hospital, health related community education project, local school, local museum, lunch club for the elderly, soup kitchen for the homeless, or the Red Cross; undertaking conservation work; taking part in a local environment improvement project; helping vulnerable groups access services; formally mentoring a newly arrived refugee; serving as a school governor or on a community organization; canvassing for a political party; trade union activities; or volunteering for a social enterprise (paid employment or internships will not count).

I. ACCESS TO BENEFITS

1. Introduction

5.204 It is the intention of the Government to prohibit persons with probationary citizenship leave from access to non-contributory benefits and certain other forms of social assistance. The prohibition is intended to apply to those on the 'work' and 'family' route to citizenship. It is not to apply to those on the 'protection' route. Thus the prohibition is not to apply to those recognized as having Refugee Status, or those granted Humanitarian Protection or Discretionary Leave.[218]

5.205 There is no intention to restrict access to national insurance contribution-based benefits for any person subject to immigration control with any form of leave to enter or remain. Such benefits are paid to those who have made the required contributions.

2. The Green Paper

5.206 The Green Paper contemplated prohibiting probationary citizens on the work route and the family route from access to benefits and housing and restricting access to further and higher education to the 'home rate' (see para **5.29** above). However, probationary citizens were to have access to English for speakers of other languages (ESOL) further education courses at the same 'home rate' as British citizens in order to support the path to British citizenship or permanent residence and contribute to community cohesion. Higher education and other further education at the 'home rate' were only to be available to those who had become British citizens or permanent residents.[219] In a letter of 19 February 2009 from Lord West of Spithead,

[218] JCHR Legislative Scrutiny: Borders, Citizenship and Immigration Bill, 9th Report (2008–09) HL Paper 62 HC 375, Ev 5–6, per Letter from Lord West of Spithead, Parliamentary Under-Secretary of State, Home Office, of 23 February 2009 to the Chairman of the JCHR.

[219] Green Paper *The Path to Citizenship: Next Steps in Reforming the Immigration System* (February 2008), p 34, paras 196–7.

Parliamentary Under-Secretary of State, Home Office, to Lord Avebury (Liberal Democrat) it was made clear that all further education was to continue to be made available to those under eighteen at the 'home rate'.

3. The Statutory Framework

5.207 Presently, by Immigration and Asylum Act 1999, s 115, persons subject to immigration control are prohibited from entitlement to income-based jobseekers' allowance, income related employment and support allowance, attendance allowance, state pension credit, severe disablement allowance, disability living allowance, carer's allowance, income support, a social fund payment, a health in pregnancy grant, child benefit, housing benefit, or council tax benefit. There is an equivalent prohibition on access to working tax credit and child tax credit under Tax Credits Act 2002, s 42. 'Persons subject to immigration control' are defined for this purpose by Immigration and Asylum Act 1999, s 115(9). The definition does not embrace all those persons who are subject to immigration control for immigration purposes under the Immigration Act 1971, ss 1–3.[220]

5.208 The ability of persons subject to immigration control[221] to access permanent social housing is regulated by Housing Act 1996, s 160A, and to secure homelessness assistance by Housing Act 1996, s 185. Only certain classes of persons subject to immigration control are eligible for permanent social housing or homelessness assistance.[222]

5.209 Persons with probationary citizenship leave are persons subject to immigration control in that they are persons with limited leave to enter or remain in the United Kingdom where such leave is of a description identified in the Immigration Rules as probationary citizenship leave (see para **5.71** above). The Government did not have to introduce provisions by the BCIA 2009 to prohibit persons with probationary citizenship leave from access to non-contributory benefits and certain other forms of social assistance as such an objective may be carried into effect through the existing statutory machinery set out above in para **5.207**.

[220] See also the Social Security (Immigration and Asylum) Consequential Amendment Regulations 2000, SI 2000/636 for the subordinate regulations made under the Immigration and Asylum Act 1999, s 115(3) and (4), and the Tax Credit (Immigration) Regulations 2003, SI 2003/653.

[221] 'Person subject to immigration control' is defined for this purpose by the Asylum and Immigration Act 1996, s 13(2). This definition is broader than that found in the Immigration and Asylum Act 1999, s 115.

[222] See the Allocation of Housing and Homelessness (Eligibility) (England) Regulations 2006, SI 2006/1296, the Allocation of Housing (Wales) Regulations 2003, (W 36) SI 2003/239, and the Homelessness (Wales) Regulations 2006, (W 227) SI 2006/2646.

4. Commentary

The Joint Committee on Human Rights considered that the denial of certain emergency benefits on the ground of nationality may require justification under Article 14 of the ECHR (prohibition of discrimination) in conjunction with Article 1 Protocol 1 of the ECHR (protection of property) and sought further detail and justification for the proposal from the Government.[223] 5.210

Persons with indefinite leave to enter or remain are, subject to certain exceptions, not restricted in their access to non-contributory benefits or access to housing and homelessness assistance under the Housing Act 1996. Through the interpolation of an additional period of limited leave in the form of probationary citizenship leave before British citizenship or permanent residence leave (indefinite leave), the period of time before which those on the 'work' or 'family' route may have access to these benefits and specified forms of social assistance is extended. There is a further period of one to three years without benefits and access to housing for those applying for naturalisation under BNA 1981, s 6(1) or 6(2), and three to five years for those applying for permanent residence. The Joint Committee on Human Rights recorded its concern and asked the Government to reconsider the intention to restrict access for persons on probationary citizenship leave.[224] 5.211

Further, in a supplementary memorandum submitted to the Home Affairs Committee, the Migrants' Rights Network (MRN) recorded the fear that: 5.212

> Migrants who become unemployed or suffer a family breakdown during this period could find themselves supported and at risk of illness, destitution and homelessness with no state support. In the context of a national financial crisis, likely to increase the vulnerability and instability of many migrants in the UK, such restrictions will have an even greater impact.[225]

5. The Justification Offered by the Government

The justification advanced by Phil Woolas MP, Minister of State, Home Office, is that: 5.213

> . . . the effect of the proposals on earned citizenship, although not specifically arising from the clauses in the Bill, will be to delay access to *some* benefits for *some* migrants. However, this is on the basis that those persons have probationary citizenship leave, which is a form of temporary leave, rather than on the basis that they are not British citizens; permanent residents have no such restrictions on their access to benefits. Furthermore, we believe that any discrimination in access to benefits is justifiable. It is a long standing policy position that migrants who come here to work, or as family members of British citizens or permanent residents, should be able to support themselves and should not be a burden to the state.

[223] JCHR Legislative Scrutiny: Borders, Citizenship and Immigration Bill, 9th Report (2008–09) HL Paper 62 HC 375, p 12, paras 1.38–1.39.

[224] Ibid, p 13, para 1.43.

[225] HC Home Affairs Committee 5th Report (2008–09) HC 425, Ev 182.

There are exceptions to this general restriction on access to non-contributory benefits for those with temporary residence leave and probationary citizenship leave, for example, refugees and people with specific emergency needs.[226]

5.214 In the Impact Assessment of the Earned Citizenship Proposals in the Bill, the UK Border Agency noted that in delaying access to benefits there was a risk of increased applications to local authorities for support under the National Assistance Act 1948 and the Children Act 1989. The Assessment noted that this would be mitigated by the removal of migrants who no longer qualify to stay.[227] In terms of those affected the Assessment stated:

> 39. The change in architecture implies that the group of migrants affected are those who would currently claim benefits as Settled migrants (with ILR) but now will need to wait an additional 1 to 3 years as Probationary Citizens if attempting to become a British Citizen or a minimum of 3 or 5 years for those wanting to apply for permanent residence.[228]

J. COMPATIBILITY WITH THE REFUGEE CONVENTION

1. Introduction

5.215 There is concern about the compatibility of the policy proposals and the contents of the BCIA 2009 with Articles 31 and 34 the Refugee Convention.[229]

2. Article 31 of the Refuge Convention

5.216 Article 31(1) of the Refugee Convention provides:

> Article 31
>
> REFUGEES UNLAWFULLY IN THE COUNTRY OF REFUGE
>
> 1. The Contracting States shall not impose penalties, on account of their illegal entry or presence, on refugees who, coming directly from a territory where their life or freedom was threatened in the sense of article 1, enter or are present in their territory without authorization, provided they present themselves without delay to the authorities and show good cause for their illegal entry or presence.

5.217 Article 31 of the Refugee Convention prohibits the imposition of penalties on refugees on account of their illegal entry or presence.

---

226 JCHR Government replies to the Second, Fourth, Eighth, Ninth and Twelfth Reports of Session 2008–09, 17th Report (2008–09) HL Paper 104 HC 592, Written Evidence pp 6–7.

227 Impact Assessment of Earned Citizenship Proposals, Borders Citizenship and Immigration Bill, version 1.0, 15 January 2009, para 36.

228 Ibid, para 39.

229 Geneva, 28 July 1951; UNTS 2545 (1954) and Protocol Relating to the Status of Refugees of 31 January 1967; UNTS 8791 (1967).

In a memorandum submitted to the Joint Committee on Human Rights, commenting on the Draft (Partial) Immigration and Citizenship Bill, the United Nations High Commission for Refugees (UNCHR) stated: 5.218

16. UNHCR is concerned that the provisions of the Draft Bill do not make it sufficiently clear that persons who come to the UK illegally and who are in need of international protection should not be penalised.[612] In light of this, UNHCR is concerned that as part of the requirements for naturalisation it is required that the applicant was not at any time in the qualifying period in the UK in breach of the immigration laws . . .[230]

Further, the Joint Committee on Human Rights noted the requirement not to be in breach of immigration laws during the qualifying period when applying for naturalisation. The Committee agreed with the UNHCR that penalization for illegal entry may prolong the period before which refugees and persons with humanitarian protection may apply for naturalisation. It recommended an amendment to the Bill to ensure that penalization for illegal entry did not affect the qualifying period for such persons.[231] 5.219

3. Article 34 of the Refugee Convention

Article 34 of the Refugee Convention provides: 5.220

Article 34

NATURALIZATION

The Contracting States shall as far as possible facilitate the assimilation and naturalization of refugees. They shall in particular make every effort to expedite naturalization proceedings and to reduce as far as possible the charges and costs of such proceedings.

In a memorandum submitted to the Joint Committee on Human Rights, commenting on the Draft (Partial) Immigration and Citizenship Bill, the United Nations High Commission for Refugees (UNCHR) stated: 5.221

13. UNHCR is of the view that the proposed route to citizenship complicates, rather than simplifies, the immigration system by requiring migrants and refugees to pass through an additional stage of 'probationary citizenship'. There is a real risk that the complexity of the process and the fees involved will make the integration process longer and more expensive for refugees, contrary to Article 34 of the 1951 Refugee Convention which requires that States 'expedite naturalization proceedings' and 'reduce as far as possible the costs and charges of such proceedings'.

14. UNHCR urges the UK Home Office to consider making exceptions for refugees who are unable to participate, or are limited in the manner in which they are able to participate in

[230] JCHR Legislative Scrutiny: Borders, Citizenship and Immigration Bill, 9th Report (2008–09) HL Paper 62 HC 375, Ev 154.

[231] JCHR Legislative Scrutiny: Borders, Citizenship and Immigration Bill, 9th Report (2008–09) HL Paper 62 HC 375, p 16, paras 1.56–1.57.

community activities. In this regard it should be borne in mind that refugees may have faced specific forms of persecution in the past and the association with community activities may have an unintended impact on their emotional and physical well being. Although this 'activity condition' is not mandatory, it appears to serve as a form of indirect penalty for not participating in the community activities. In the circumstances described above, in UNHCR's view, it would not be fair to expect the individuals concerned to spend three years as probationary citizens, increasing the total period of time before they become eligible for citizenship to eight years should they be unable, for reasons of their past persecution experience, to participate in community activities.[232]

5.222 In a later memorandum submitted to the Home Affairs Committee, UNHCR stated:

22. UNHCR considers that, as a matter of best practice, the required period of residence in order to be eligible for naturalisation should not exceed 5 years for refugees. This is in order to restore an effective nationality to refugees and those with humanitarian protection and promote their full integration into society. Further, UNHCR believes that a cumulative period of the initial 5 years should include periods spent in the country whilst asylum applications are under consideration.[233]

5.223 The Joint Committee on Human Rights noted that the BCIA 2009 requires refugees and persons with humanitarian protection to have to pass though a qualifying period of eight years before being eligible to apply for naturalisation. Although this could be reduced to six years if the activity condition is satisfied, the Committee noted that this was a requirement that refugees would find difficult to fulfil on account of having faced persecution or ill-treatment in the past. The provisions could make it more difficult for such persons to naturalise as a British citizen, contrary to Article 34 of the Refugee Convention.[234]

5.224 The Home Affairs Committee took the view that:

57 . . . The Government should make public its intentions for the operation of the discretionary power, and in addition should make an explicit exemption for certain abused groups, including refugees, victims of domestic violence and human trafficking.[235]

5.225 In addition, it stated that:

58 . . . We welcome the Government's amendments at Report stage in the Lords which introduce a discretionary power to waive the requirement to have had a qualifying immigration status for whole of the qualifying period, introduced in response to concerns about refugees. However, we recommend that the Government should set out on the face of the Bill that

[232] JCHR Legislative Scrutiny: Borders, Citizenship and Immigration Bill, 9th Report (2008–09) HL Paper 62 HC 375, Ev 153–4.

[233] HC Home Affairs Committee 5th Report (2008–09) HC 425, Ev 158.

[234] JCHR Legislative Scrutiny: Borders, Citizenship and Immigration Bill, 9th Report (2008–09) HL Paper 62 HC 375, pp 15–16, paras 1.53–1.55.

[235] HC Home Affairs Committee 5th Report (2008–09) HC 425, p 17.

this discretion will apply to refugees, unless there are exceptional circumstances why it should not.[236]

4. The Justification Offered by the Government

The Government did not consider that the citizenship provisions were incompatible with either Article 31 or Article 34 of the Refugee Convention as Phil Woolas MP, Minister of State, Home Office, made clear in written evidence to the Joint Committee on Human Rights.[237] He stated that the citizenship provisions do not penalize unlawful entry or presence and do not make the route to naturalisation unduly onerous. He said the requirement not to be in breach of immigration laws referred to the correct sort of status and not to the commission of offences and that amendments to the Bill had introduced a discretion to waive the requirement to have a qualifying immigration status for the whole of the qualifying period in relation to applications for naturalisation. He stated that: 5.226

In the case of refugees, we would usually expect to exercise that discretion where undue delay had occurred in determining an asylum application and where this delay was not attributable to the applicant.[238]

At the Committee Stage of the Bill, Lord Brett, Government Whip, Government Spokesman for the Home Office, stated that: 5.227

. . . we do not propose to go as far as permitting any time spent in detention, or on temporary admission, or temporary release where that is followed by a grant of qualifying leave, or any time spent pending an application for leave to remain in connection with an asylum, human rights or humanitarian protection claim, to count towards the qualifying period. This is in part because, in asylum cases, a decision is based on the prevailing circumstances at the time the case is considered—some 60 per cent of cases are now dealt with in a six-month period—in addition to taking into account the facts of the claim when originally made. For example, the fact that a person is recognised as a refugee does not always mean that he was so from the start. Events in the country of origin, fresh evidence or case law, or a finding on appeal could justify recognition after the initial application was made.[239]

---

236 Ibid, pp 17–18.

237 JCHR Government replies to the Second, Fourth, Eighth, Ninth and Twelfth Reports of Session 2008–09, 17th Report (2008–09) HL Paper 104 HC 592, Written Evidence pp 8–9.

238 Ibid, p 9.

239 HL Comm Deb 2 March 2009 vol 708, c537. See also the letter of Lord Brett to Lord Avebury (Liberal Democrat) of 6 April 2009 in respect of the exercise of discretion in compassionate circumstances.

6

ACQUISITION OF BRITISH CITIZENSHIP BY BIRTH AND REGISTRATION, AND OTHER MATTERS

A. INTRODUCTION

6.01 Apart from the modifications made to the provisions for naturalisation as a British citizen in the British Nationality Act 1981 (BNA 1981), the Borders, Citizenship and Immigration Act 2009 (BCIA 2009), Part 2, makes other amendments to British nationality law, including the introduction of several new provisions in respect of the acquisition of British citizenship (other than by naturalisation). These provisions are largely effected through modifications to the BNA 1981. They are considered separately below. Some were brought forward in the initial Bill as originally introduced in the House of Lords.[1] Other provisions were accepted as

[1] Borders, Citizenship and Immigration Bill [HL] HL Bill 15.

amendments by the Government following sustained lobbying by Opposition peers, with Lord Avebury (Liberal Democrat) in the vanguard.

The BCIA 2009 received Royal Assent on 21 July 2009. The provisions in Part 2 (Citizenship) come into force on such day as the Secretary of State may appoint by order[2] (see paras **5.55–5.56**). 6.02

As of August 2009, the Government intends to commence the provisions of Part 2, other than those that relate to naturalisation, in January 2010. 6.03

There are no express transitional arrangements for the provisions referred to in this chapter, other than in relation to the modification to BNA 1981, s 4C, considered at paras **6.50** and **6.54** below. 6.04

B. CHILDREN BORN IN THE UK TO MEMBERS OF THE ARMED FORCES

1. Introduction

The BCIA 2009, s 42, makes amendments to the BNA 1981 to provide a statutory basis for the acquisition of British citizenship by birth in the United Kingdom for the children of members of the armed forces. 6.05

2. Automatic Acquisition

Prior to the amendments made to the BNA 1981 by the BCIA 2009, children born in the UK to members of the armed forces who were not British citizens or otherwise settled in the UK, automatically acquired British citizenship under BNA 1981, s 1(1), because the parent serving in the armed forces was *treated as* settled in the UK.[3] At the Committee Stage of the Bill in the House of Lords, Lord Brett, Government Whip, Government Spokesman for the Home Office, stated: 6.06

> . . . Those serving in the British Armed Forces are exempt from immigration control under Section 8(4)(a) of the Immigration Act 1971 and have, as a matter of policy, been treated as settled for nationality purposes since commencement of the British Nationality Act 1981. This means that any child born in this country today will be eligible for British citizenship under either Section 1(1) or Section 1(3) of the 1981 Act, depending on whether the parent is in our Armed Forces when the child is born, or enlists later. We will continue to apply this policy in practice until Clause 40 [now section 42] has commenced, which means that there should be no children missing out on British citizenship because of their birth date.[4]

---

2 Ibid, s 58(2).

3 See BNA 1981, s 50(2)–(4); see also Nationality Instructions, Chapter 6, Annex F, para 30.

4 HL Comm Deb 2 March 2009 vol 708 c596.

6.07 The new BNA 1981, s 1(1A),[5] provides that a person born in the United Kingdom or a qualifying territory on or after the relevant day shall be a British citizen if at the time of the birth his father or mother is a member of the armed forces.

6.08 This new provision removes the need (where applicable) to treat as settled the parent who is a member of the armed forces, in order that there be automatic acquisition of British citizenship by the child.

6.09 A qualifying territory is defined in BNA, s 50(1), as a British overseas territory other than the Sovereign Base Areas of Akrotiri and Dhekelia. The other remaining British overseas territories are Anguilla; Bermuda; British Antarctic Territory; British Indian Ocean Territory; Cayman Islands; Falkland Islands; Gibraltar; Montserrat; Pitcairn, Henderson, Ducie and Oeno Islands; St Helena and Dependencies; South Georgia and the South Sandwich Islands; Turks and Caicos Islands; and Virgin Islands.[6]

6.10 For the definition of a member of the armed forces, see paras **5.101–5.102**.

6.11 The relevant day for the purposes of BNA 1981, s 1(1A) (see para **6.07** above) or s 1(3A) (see para **6.14** below), is the day appointed for the commencement of BCIA 2009, s 42.[7]

3. Acquisition by Registration

6.12 Three further consequential amendments are made to complete the aim of the provisions to provide for the acquisition of British citizenship by birth in the United Kingdom for the children of members of the armed forces. Firstly, a further amendment is made to BNA 1981, s 1(3),[8] so that a person born in the United Kingdom who is not a British citizen by virtue of BNA 1981, s 1(1A) (see para **6.07** above), is entitled to be registered as a British citizen if, while he is a minor, his father or mother becomes a British citizen or becomes settled in the United Kingdom, and an application is made for his registration as a British citizen.

6.13 Secondly, a further amendment is made to BNA 1981, s 1(4),[9] so that a *person* (ie not only a minor) born in the United Kingdom who is not a British citizen by virtue of BNA 1981, s 1(1A) (see para **6.07** above), is entitled, on an application for his registration as a British citizen made at any time after he has attained the age of 10 years, to be registered if, as regards each of the first 10 years of that person's life, the number of days on which he was absent from the United Kingdom in that year does not exceed 90.

6.14 Thirdly, by BNA 1981, s 1(3A),[10] new provision is made for a person born in the United Kingdom on or after the relevant day who is not a British citizen by

---

[5] Inserted by BCIA 2009, s 42(2).
[6] BNA 1981, Sch 6.
[7] Ibid, s 1(9), as inserted by BCIA 2009, s 42(6).
[8] Inserted by BCIA 2009, s 42(3).
[9] Ibid, s 42(5).
[10] Ibid, s 42(4).

automatic acquisition by virtue of BNA 1981, s 1(1) (birth in the UK or qualifying territory to a father or mother who British citizen or settled in the UK or that territory), s 1(1A) (see para **6.07** above), or s 1(2) (a newborn infant found abandoned in the UK or a qualifying territory) to be entitled to be registered as a British citizen if, while he is a minor:

(a) his father or mother becomes a member of the armed forces; and
(b) an application is made for his registration.

4. The Good Character Test

Before granting an application for registration the Secretary of State must be satisfied that an adult or young person is of good character, where the application for registration as a British citizen is made under BNA 1981, s 1(3), 1(3A), or 1(4).[11] An adult or young person means a person who has attained the age of 10 at the time when the application is made.[12] 6.15

C. CHILDREN BORN OUTSIDE THE UK TO MEMBERS OF THE ARMED FORCES

1. Introduction

In the Green Paper *The Nation's Commitment: Cross-Government Support to our Armed Forces, their Families and Veterans* (July 2008) the Government stated that the UK Borders Agency would:[13] 6.16

e. Allow children born outside the UK to F&C [Foreign and Commonwealth] Service personnel on operations or postings overseas to be able to acquire British citizenship where this has the consent of both parents.

BCIA 2009, s 46, inserts s 4D into the BNA 1981 to provide for the acquisition of British citizenship by registration by children born outside the UK to members of the armed forces *serving outside* the UK (but not those *serving in* the UK). 6.17

At the Committee Stage of the Bill in the House of Lords, Lord Brett, Government Whip, Government Spokesman for the Home Office, stated: 6.18

. . . This is principally to ensure that, as has historically been the case, the mother of the child does not need to travel to the UK when heavily pregnant in order to ensure that the child acquires British citizenship automatically at birth as a child born to a parent who is settled for nationality purposes in the UK or qualifying territories. Such a mother will instead be able to

[11] BNA 1981, s 41A(1), inserted by BCIA 2009, s 47(1).
[12] Ibid, s 41A(5), inserted by BCIA 2009, s 47(1).
[13] Cm 7424, para 2.43.

give birth to her child overseas and the child can be registered as a British citizen from abroad.[14]

6.19 Prior to commencement of BNA 1981, s 4D, children born abroad to members of the armed forces (not satisfying any other provision for registration, eg BNA 1981, s 3(2) or 3(5)) may make an application for registration at discretion as a British citizen while a minor under BNA 1981, s 3(1), although the discretion is exercised sparingly.[15]

6.20 In a letter of 20 March 2009 to Lord Avebury (Liberal Democrat), Lord Brett, Government Whip, Government Spokesman for the Home Office, stated:

> In practice UKBA do currently register children born overseas into armed forces families as British citizens (as a matter of policy this is done when the family return to live in the UK—we will continue to do this for those born overseas before commencement of clause 42 [now section 46).

2. The New Provision

6.21 A *person* (ie not only a minor) born outside the United Kingdom and the qualifying territories on or after the relevant day is entitled to be registered as a British citizen if:[16]

(a) an application is made for the person's registration under BNA 1981, s 4D;
(b) at the time of the person's birth, his father or mother was a member of the armed forces and serving outside the United Kingdom and the qualifying territories; and
(c) if the person is a minor on the date of the application, the consent of his father and mother to his registration has been signified in the prescribed manner. Where the person's father or mother has died on or before the date of the application, the reference to his father and mother is to be read as a reference to either of them.

6.22 There is a discretion conferred so that the Secretary of State may, in the special circumstances of a particular case, waive the need where a person is a minor on the date of the application, for the consent of his father and mother to his registration to be signified in the prescribed manner.[17]

6.23 For the definition of qualifying territory, see para **6.09** above.

6.24 For the definition of a member of the armed forces, see paras **5.101–5.102**.

6.25 The relevant day for the purposes of BNA 1981, s 4D, is the day appointed for the commencement of BCIA 2009, s 46.[18]

---

[14] HL Deb Comm 4 March 2009 vol 708 c748.
[15] Nationality Instructions, Chapter 9, eg para 9.17.5.
[16] BNA 1981, s 4D(1)–(4), as inserted by BCIA 2009, s 46.
[17] Ibid, s 4D(5), as inserted by BCAI 2009, s 46.
[18] Ibid, s 4D(6), as inserted by BCIA 2009, s 46.

The power to prescribe the manner of consent of a person's mother and/or father to their child's registration is conferred upon the Secretary of State. The power is exercisable by regulations made by statutory instrument under the negative resolution procedure.[19] By BNA 1981, s 50(1), 'prescribed' means prescribed by regulations made under BNA 1981, s 41. There is a similar power to prescribe the manner of parental consent in cases of application for registration as a British citizen under BNA 1981, s 3(5).[20] 6.26

3. The Good Character Test

There is a requirement for the Secretary of State to be satisfied that an adult or young person is of good character, where an application for registration as a British citizen is made under BNA 1981, s 4D.[21] An adult or young person means a person who has attained the age of 10 at the time when the application is made.[22] 6.27

D. THE REGISTRATION OF MINORS

1. Introduction

BCIA 2009, s 43, amends BNA 1981, s 3, by removing the requirement for a s 3(2) registration application to be made within 12 months of birth and permitting such an application at any time while the child is a minor. 6.28

As a consequential amendment, the discretion found in BNA 1981, s 3(4), to permit an application to be made within six years of birth, is omitted.[23] 6.29

At the Report Stage of the Bill in the House of Lords, Lord Brett, Government Whip, Government Spokesman for the Home Office, stated: 6.30

> . . . The Government accept that, in view of the changing employment and residence patterns over time, the 12-month requirement set out in 1981 is now too stringent . . .[24]

Section 3(2) of the 1981 Act caters for children born outside the UK and the qualifying territories, where at least one parent is a British citizen but *by descent* only, thus inhibiting the further automatic transmission of citizenship to the child. It gives a minor an entitlement to register as a British citizen. Two criteria in particular are worthy of note. Firstly, the parent who is a British citizen by descent at the time of the birth must have a father or mother (ie a person who would be a grandparent of the child) who was a British citizen *otherwise than by descent* at the time of his or her 6.31

---

[19] Ibid, s 41(1)(a).

[20] HL Delegated Powers and Regulatory Reform Committee 3rd Report (2008–09) HL Paper 29, Appendix 1, p 20.

[21] BNA 1981, s 41A(1), as inserted by BCIA 2009, s 47(1).

[22] Ibid, s 41A(5), inserted by BCIA 2009, s 47(1).

[23] BCIA 2009, s 43(3).

[24] HL Deb 1 April 2009 vol 709 c1082.

birth or who became a British citizen *otherwise than by descent* on 1 January 1983 (or would have done so but for his or her death). Secondly, other than where the person is born stateless, the parent must have been present in the UK or a qualifying territory for the requisite time (three years subject to absences not exceeding 270 days), ending not later than the date of the birth.

6.32 The provision for registration as a British citizen under BNA 1981, s 3(2), should be contrasted but not confused with the separate provision for registration as a British citizen as a minor under BNA 1981, s 3(5), where there is a requirement for the child and his or her parents to be present in the UK or a qualifying territory for the requisite time *following* birth.

2. The Amended Provision

6.33 Following amendment, BNA 1981, s 3(2)–(3), provides:

3 Acquisition by registration: minors

(2) A person born outside the United Kingdom and the qualifying territories shall be entitled, on an application for his registration as a British citizen made while he is a minor, to be registered as such a citizen if the requirements specified in subsection (3) or, in the case of a person born stateless, the requirements specified in paragraphs (a) and (b) of that subsection, are fulfilled in the case of either that person's father or his mother ('the parent in question').

(3) The requirements referred to in subsection (2) are—
- (a) that the parent in question was a British citizen by descent at the time of the birth; and
- (b) that the father or mother of the parent in question—
  - (i) was a British citizen otherwise than by descent at the time of the birth of the parent in question; or
  - (ii) became a British citizen otherwise than by descent at commencement, or would have become such a citizen otherwise than by descent at commencement but for his or her death; and
- (c) that, as regards some period of three years ending with a date not later than the date of the birth—
  - (i) the parent in question was in the United Kingdom or a qualifying territory at the beginning of that period; and
  - (ii) the number of days on which the parent in question was absent from the United Kingdom and the qualifying territories in that period does not exceed 270.

6.34 For the definition of qualifying territory, see para **6.09** above.

6.35 For guidance on the consideration given to applications for registration under this provision, see the Nationality Instructions, Chapter 10.

3. The Good Character Test

Where an application for registration as a British citizen is made under BNA 1981, s 3(2) or (5), the Secretary of State must be satisfied that an adult or young person is of good character.[25] An adult or young person means a person who has attained the age of 10 at the time when the application is made.[26] 6.36

E. THE REGISTRATION OF BRITISH NATIONALS (OVERSEAS) WITHOUT OTHER CITIZENSHIP

1. Introduction

BCIA 2009, s 44, amends BNA 1981, s 4B, to allow British Nationals (Overseas) (BN(O)s) to register by entitlement as British citizens. Prior to amendment, registration under this provision was only available to British Overseas citizens (BOCs), British subjects (BSs), and British protected persons (BPPs). 6.37

Lord Avebury (Liberal Democrat), who had pressed for this change in debates on previous Bills, introduced an amendment to insert British Nationals (Overseas) into BNA 1981, s 4B, at the Committee Stage of the Bill in the House of Lords.[27] Following a meeting between Lord Avebury, accompanied by representatives of the Immigration Law Practitioners' Association (ILPA), and UK Border Agency officials, a letter of 20 March 2009 from Lord Brett, Government Whip, Government Spokesman for the Home Office, to Lord Avebury indicated that the Government were persuaded to move an amendment to effect the inclusion and this was done.[28] 6.38

In a letter of 19 March 2009 to Baroness Hanham (Conservative), Lord West of Spithead, Parliamentary Under-Secretary of State, Home Office, stated: 6.39

> Section 4B of the British Nationality Act 1981 (which was inserted by the Nationality, Immigration and Asylum Act 2002) . . . was not extended to those who have British National (Overseas) status when introduced in 2002 because it was felt that this group of persons was sufficiently dealt with by the British Nationality (Hong Kong) Act 1997 and that such persons, having the equivalent of Indefinite Leave to Remain in Hong Kong, did not need to benefit from the new provision. However, following pressure in the Lords in the Borders, Citizenship and Immigration Bill we wish to change this approach . . .

---

25 BNA 1981, s 41A(1), inserted by BCIA 2009, s 47(1).

26 Ibid, s 41A(5), inserted by BCIA 2009, s 47(1).

27 HL Comm Deb 2 March 2009 c597ff, amendment 90.

28 HL Deb 1 April 2009 vol 709 c1085.

2. British Nationals (Overseas)

6.40 BN(O)s do not, by virtue of that status, have the right of abode in the United Kingdom;[29] that is, as BN(O)s they have no right to live in and to come and go into and from the UK.[30]

6.41 BN(O) status was created[31] as part of the arrangements for the cessation on 1 July 1997 of British rule in Hong Kong and the loss of British Dependent Territories citizenship held by virtue of a connection with Hong Kong. BN(O) status was available to any Hong Kong British Dependent Territories citizen (BDTC—now re-branded British overseas territories citizen, or BOTC) who wished to retain a British status and corresponding British passport after British sovereignty ended on 1 July 1997. Generally BN(O) status could only be obtained on an application made before that date.

6.42 BDTCs who lost that status on 1 July 1997 (because they failed to register as BN(O)s) and who were otherwise stateless became BOCs by operation of law on that date,[32] although that status also does not confer the right of abode in the United Kingdom.

6.43 The majority of Hong Kong BDTCs were ethnically Chinese and, therefore, generally regarded by China as Chinese nationals. Broadly speaking, non-Chinese ethnic minorities who were otherwise stateless either became BN(O)s on an application made before 1 July 1997 or, by default, automatically became BOCs on that date. Under s 4B of the BNA 1981, stateless BOCs became entitled to register as British citizens, but not so stateless BN(O)s (see para **6.45** below).

6.44 Some of Hong Kong's stateless (ie non-Chinese ethnic minority) BN(O)s were able, subject to satisfaction of an ordinary residence test with respect to Hong Kong, to apply for registration as British citizens under British Nationality (Hong Kong) Act 1997, s 1. However not all of them are able to meet the ordinary residence test, and thus they remained, for practical purposes, stateless. BN(O) status has never, per se, conferred the functional benefits of a nationality permitting a person to live, enter into, and depart from, the country of their nationality.

3. BN(O)s and the British Nationality Act 1981, s 4B

6.45 As originally enacted BNA 1981, s 4B,[33] catered for other classes of 'British nationals' but not for BN(O)s. Thus, although it was a measure designed to alleviate the de facto or functional statelessness of certain classes of British nationals, it did not assist BN(O)s. The amendments made by BCIA 2009, s 44, rectify this omission.

---

29 See Immigration Act, 1971, s 2.

30 Ibid, s 1.

31 Hong Kong Act 1997, s 2(2), Sch, para 2, and Hong Kong (British Nationality) Order 1986, SI 1986/948, art 4.

32 Hong Kong (British Nationality) Order 1986, SI 1986/948, art 6.

33 Inserted into the BNA 1981 by the Nationality, Immigration and Asylum Act 2002, s 12.

As originally enacted, BNA 1981, s 4B, was a step taken following the abolition of the special voucher scheme on 5 March 2002. This scheme had enabled certain heads of households and their families, who were BOCs, BSs, and BPPs (who, as such, had no right of abode in the UK) to apply for a voucher to enter the UK to settle on a quota basis. The beneficiaries were mainly British East African Asians, most of whom as citizens of the United Kingdom and Colonies (CUKCs) had been stripped of their right to enter the UK without restriction by the Commonwealth Immigrants Act 1968. Following the abolition of the special voucher scheme, the BNA 1981, s 4B provision was enacted as an alternative arrangement, by Nationality, Immigration and Asylum Act 2002, s 12. The amendments now made by the BCIA 2009, extend the reach of BNA 1981, s 4B, to address the problems faced by BN(O)s who hold no other nationality or citizenship. 6.46

4. The Amended Provision

Following amendment, BNA 1981, s 4B, provides:[34] 6.47

4B Acquisition by registration: certain persons without other citizenship

(1) This section applies to a person who has the status of—
 (a) British Overseas citizen,
 (b) British subject under this Act,
 (c) British protected person, or
 (d) British National (Overseas).
(2) A person to whom this section applies shall be entitled to be registered as a British citizen if—
 (a) he applies for registration under this section,
 (b) the Secretary of State is satisfied that the person does not have, apart from the status mentioned in subsection (1), any citizenship or nationality, and
 (c) the Secretary of State is satisfied that the person has not after the relevant day renounced, voluntarily relinquished or lost through action or inaction any citizenship or nationality.
(3) For the purposes of subsection (2)(c), the 'relevant day' means—
 (a) in the case of a person to whom this section applies by virtue of subsection (1)(d) only, 19th March 2009, and
 (b) in any other case, 4th July 2002.

As a result of the amendment, British Nationals (Overseas) become entitled to register as British citizens, on application, where they satisfy the Secretary of State: 6.48

(a) that they hold no other citizenship or nationality (other than that of BN(O)); and
(b) that they have not renounced, voluntarily relinquished, or lost through action or inaction any citizenship or nationality after 19 March 2009, the latter being the date that the amendment was announced.

[34] As amended by BCIA 2009, s 44.

6.49 For guidance on the consideration of applications for registration under this provision, see the Nationality Instructions, Chapter 12 and Annex D of the same. For further information on British Nationals (Overseas), see the Nationality Instructions, Chapters 50–53.

F. DESCENT THROUGH THE FEMALE LINE: REGISTRATION UNDER S 4C OF THE BRITISH NATIONALITY ACT 1981

1. Introduction

6.50 BNA 1981, s 4C, provides a route to registration as a British citizen for persons who, but for a woman's inability prior to 1 January 1983 to transmit citizenship by descent, would have automatically become British citizens on 1 January 1983. The idea was, and remains, to offer British citizenship to those who, through reliance on a parent, would have been reclassified as British citizens under the BNA 1981 save only for the fact that the parent in question was a mother and not a father. The original provision (inserted into the BNA 1981 by the Nationality, Immigration and Asylum Act 2002 (NIAA 2002)) applied only to those born after 7 February 1961 (for reasons explained below). The BCIA 2009 amendment effectively removes that restriction but the Government also took the opportunity to redraft much of the text, realizing that the original wording was inadequate. (A person will have been reclassified as a British citizen on 1 January 1983 if immediately prior to that date he was a CUKC with the right of abode in the UK. The original wording's inadequacy was that it applied only where, but for the discrimination against women, the applicant would have become a CUKC *by descent under British Nationality Act 1948 (BNA 1948), s 5*, but there were other means whereby it was possible to become a CUKC. The new wording seeks to identify those other means and include them in addition to the s 5 route.)

6.51 The original discrimination was that prior to 1 January 1983, citizenship of the United Kingdom and Colonies was transmissible by descent from a father but not from a mother: BNA 1948, s 5 (see para **6.57** below). Persons who were descended from a CUKC father and who held the right of abode on 31 December 1982 became British citizens on 1 January 1983.[35] Persons descended from a CUKC mother were excluded from this reclassification. The impact was discriminatory by reference to gender. BNA 1981, s 4C, was a measure to alleviate this outcome by providing a route to registration for certain persons who had been disadvantaged by this discriminatory exclusion.

[35] BNA 1981, s 11(1).

On 31 March 2008,[36] the House of Commons considered an individual case of hardship resulting from the 7 February 1961 cut-off date restriction. Liam Byrne MP, Minister of State, Home Office, gave a commitment to bring forward a legislative remedy.[37] That commitment was reiterated in *Making Change Stick*[38] and effect given to it in the BCIA 2009. 6.52

BCIA 2009, s 45, amends BNA 1981, s 4C, as already mentioned. However, although on the one hand a wider class of persons is brought within the provision, on the other hand a particular statutory assumption is introduced, which may exclude certain persons hitherto arguably included. BNA 1981, s 4C, with its old and new wording indicated, is set out at the end of this section (see para **6.93** below). 6.53

In respect of transitional arrangements, on commencement of BCIA 2009, s 45, the order commencing BCIA 2009, s 45, may, in particular, provide that s 45 is to apply to an application made, but not determined, under BNA 1981, s 4C, prior to commencement.[39] 6.54

For guidance on the consideration of applications for registration under BNA 1981, s 4C, see the Nationality Instructions, Chapter 7. 6.55

2. Section 4C of the British Nationality Act 1981, Prior to Amendment by the BCIA 2009

Prior to amendment, BNA 1981, s 4C, provided that a person was entitled to be registered as a British citizen if he applied for such registration and satisfied three conditions: 6.56

(a) First Condition: the applicant was born after 7 February 1961 and before 1 January 1983;
(b) Second Condition: the applicant would at some time before 1 January 1983 have become a CUKC by virtue of BNA 1948, s 5 (see para **6.57** below), if it had provided for citizenship by descent from a mother in the same terms as it provided for citizenship by descent from a father; and
(c) Third Condition: immediately before 1 January 1983 the applicant would have had the right of abode in the United Kingdom by virtue of the Immigration Act 1971, s 2, had he become a CUKC by virtue of meeting the second condition.

To make sense of the Second Condition in BNA 1981, s 4C, it is necessary to have BNA 1948, s 5, in mind. The latter, as in force from 1 January 1949 to 6.57

[36] HC Deb 31 March 2008 vol 474 cc601–6.
[37] Ibid, c605.
[38] UK Border Agency (14 July 2008), p 7.
[39] BCIA 2009, s 58(14).

31 December 1982, provided for automatic acquisition of citizenship by descent in the male line:

5.—(1) Subject to the provisions of this section, a person born after the commencement of this Act shall be a citizen of the United Kingdom and Colonies by descent if his father is a citizen of the United Kingdom and Colonies at the time of the birth:

Provided that if the father of such a person is a citizen of the United Kingdom and Colonies by descent only, that person shall not be a citizen of the United Kingdom and Colonies by virtue of this section unless—

(*a*) that person is born or his father was born in a protectorate, protected state, mandated territory or trust territory or any place in a foreign country where by treaty, capitulation, grant, usage, sufferance, or other lawful means, His Majesty then has or had jurisdiction over British subjects; or

(*b*) that person's birth having occurred in a place in a foreign country other than a place such as is mentioned in the last foregoing paragraph, the birth is registered at a United Kingdom consulate within one year of its occurrence, or, with the permission of the Secretary of State, later; or

(*c*) that person's father is, at the time of the birth, in Crown service under His Majesty's government in the United Kingdom; or

(*d*) that person is born in any country mentioned in subsection (3) of section one of this Act in which a citizenship law has then taken effect and does not become a citizen thereof on birth.

(2) If the Secretary of State so directs, a birth shall be deemed for the purposes of this section to have been registered with his permission notwithstanding that his permission was not obtained before the registration.

6.58 To make sense of the Third Condition in BNA 1981, s 4C, it is necessary to have in mind Immigration Act 1971, s 2, as in force immediately prior to 1 January 1983. This provision is contained in Annex 2 to this Guide.

3. The Amendments in Outline

6.59 Following amendment, BNA 1981, s 4C, has been renovated so that:

(a) First Condition: the requirement to be born after 7 February 1961 has been removed;
(b) Second Condition: a new and complex Second Condition has been substituted;
(c) Third Condition: remains the same; and
(d) A modification to the treatment of BNA 1948, s 5, has been added.

4. The Amended First Condition

6.60 BCIA 2009, s 45(2), removes the requirement to be born after 7 February 1961 from BNA 1981, s 4C(2). As a result persons born on or before that date may apply for registration.

The requirement to be born before 1 January 1983 remains. Persons born on and after that date are catered for by BNA 1981, s 2. 6.61

The original requirement to be born after 7 February 1961 was an echo of an earlier policy introduced on 7 February 1979, prior to the introduction of BNA 1981, s 4C; a policy whose beneficiaries were, prima facie eligible to benefit as minors for discretionary registration. 6.62

As minors born on and after 1 January 1983 are catered for by BNA 1981, s 2, the policy ceased to be of benefit eighteen years after 31 December 1982. However, many potential beneficiaries had not taken advantage of it when it ceased to be of practical benefit and so BNA 1981, s 4C, was enacted by the Nationality, Immigration and Asylum Act 2002, s 13, to provide a route to registration as a British citizen for such persons. 6.63

The justification for the requirement to be born after 7 February 1961 was that this was consistent with the original policy, which was to benefit minors on the day it was introduced (7 February 1979)—only those born after 7 February 1961 were under 18 years of age on 7 February 1979. However, the purpose of the original policy was to remove a discriminatory effect (on grounds of gender) of BNA 1948, s 5. The policy (and indeed BNA 1981, s 4C, as enacted) was but an imperfect solution to this as those born on or before 7 February 1961 still suffered from the discriminatory effect. The omission of the requirement to be born after 7 February 1961 extends the benefit of BNA 1981, s 4C, to those born earlier. 6.64

5. The Substituted Second Condition

(a) *Outline of the Second Condition*

The substituted Second Condition provides for a number of ways by which it may be satisfied. It sets out a complicated structure through which an applicant must pass in order to be successful. The Second Condition: 6.65

(a) introduces two assumptions (Assumption A and Assumption B) that are to apply;
(b) prohibits a further assumption being made; and
(c) adds in addition to the route via BNA 1948, s 5, further routes by which a person may have acquired CUKC by descent, *had it flowed through the female line as well as the male.*

(b) *Assumption A*

Assumption A concerns those falling within the scope of the BNA 1948. It provides for references to a father to be read as references to a mother and for a reading of citizenship by descent as occurring in the female line. 6.66

6.67 Assumption A is set out in BNA 1981, s 4C(3A).[40] The assumption is that:

(a) BNA 1948, s 5, s 12(2), or Sch 3, para 3 (as the case may be) provided for citizenship by descent from a mother in the same terms as it provided for citizenship by descent from a father; and

(b) references in that provision to a father were references to the applicant's mother.

6.68 To make sense of Assumption A, it is necessary to have BNA 1948, s 5, in mind. It has been set out above at para **6.57**.

6.69 To make sense of Assumption A, it is also necessary to have in mind BNA 1948, s 12(1)–(2) as in force 1 January 1949 to 31 December 1982. It provided:

> (1) A person who was a British subject immediately before the date of the commencement of this Act shall on that date become a citizen of the United Kingdom and Colonies if he possesses any of the following qualifications, that is to say—
>
> *(a)* that he was born within the territories comprised at the commencement of this Act in the United Kingdom and Colonies, and would have been such a citizen if section four of this Act had been in force at the time of his birth;
>
> *(b)* that he is a person naturalised in the United Kingdom and Colonies;
>
> *(c)* that he became a British subject by reason of the annexation of any territory included at the commencement of this Act in the United Kingdom and Colonies.
>
> (2) A person who was a British subject immediately before the date of the commencement of this Act shall on that date become a citizen of the United Kingdom and Colonies if at the time of his birth his father was a British subject and possessed any of the qualifications specified in the last foregoing subsection.

6.70 To make sense of Assumption A, it is also necessary to have in mind BNA 1948, Sch 3, para 3, in force 1 January 1949 to 31 December 1982. It provided:

> 3. If while a male person remains a British subject without citizenship by virtue of section thirteen of this Act a child is born to him, the child shall, unless the child has previously become a citizen of the United Kingdom and Colonies, or of any country mentioned in subsection (3) of section one of this Act or of Eire, become a citizen of the United Kingdom and Colonies if and when the father becomes, or would but for his death have become, such a citizen; and a male person who becomes a citizen of the United Kingdom and Colonies by virtue of this paragraph shall be deemed for the purposes of the proviso to subsection (1) of section five of this Act to be a citizen thereof by descent only. [Added by Pakistan Act 1973, s 1(2), Sch 1: Provided that this paragraph shall not apply where the father was at commencement of the Act potentially a citizen of Pakistan and becomes a citizen of the United Kingdom and Colonies by registration at a time when the child is a citizen of Pakistan.]

6.71 Unfortunately, BNA 1948, Sch 3, para 3, begs further citation of the statutory provisions cited within it. However, for present purposes some information on British subjects without citizenship under BNA 1948, s 13, may be gleaned from the Nationality Instructions, Chapter 43 and its Annexes A, B, and C. A list of countries

---

[40] Inserted by BCIA 2009, s 45(3).

mentioned in BNA 1948, s 1(3), can be found in the Nationality Instructions, Volume 2, Section 2, 'Commonwealth countries'.[41]

(c) *Assumption B*

Assumption B concerns the scope of British nationality law as it existed prior to 1 January 1949, but for the purposes of the BNA 1948. In other words, Assumption B is an assumption made about a person's treatment under the pre-1949 law, for the purpose of calculating that person's re-classification on 1 January 1949 under the BNA 1948. Assumption B provides for references to a father to be read as references to a mother and for a reading of a nationality status by descent as occurring in the female line. 6.72

Assumption B is set out in BNA 1981, s 4C(3B).[42] It is that: 6.73

(a) a provision of the law at some time before 1 January 1949 which provided for a nationality status to be acquired by descent from a father, provided in the same terms for its acquisition by descent from a mother; and
(b) references in that provision to a father were references to the applicant's mother.

(d) *The Prohibition of Assumptions for the Purposes of BCIA 2009, s 4C(3C)(b), (3D)*

Prior to the amendments made by the BCIA 2009 to section 4C of the BNA 1981, the Second Condition was perhaps open to being interpreted so that all children of female CUKCs otherwise than by descent *and by descent* were beneficiaries. This is because it might have been argued that an assumption was built in that a CUKC mother by descent *would have* registered her child at a British consulate. Such an interpretation is not, in any event, accepted by the UK Border Agency, who require evidence of a consular birth certificate.[43] However, the amendments made by the BCIA 2009 to BNA 1981, s 4C, put the matter beyond doubt and preclude such an interpretation. The amendments to which we refer here are not just those inserted as the new s 4C(3C)(b) and s 4C(3D), but also s 4C(5), discussed at para **6.87** below. 6.74

For the purposes of Assumption B a nationality status is acquired by a person by descent where its acquisition:[44] 6.75

(a) depends, amongst other things, on the nationality status of one or both of that person's parents; and
(b) *does not depend* upon an application being made for that person's registration as a person who has the status in question.

[41] See also L Fransman, *British Nationality Law* (2nd edn, London: Butterworths, 1998) 7.5–7.6.
[42] Inserted by BCIA 2009, s 45(3).
[43] Nationality Instructions, Chapter 7, para 7.3.3.
[44] BNA 1981, s 4C(3C), as inserted by BCIA 2009, s 45.

6.76 At the Committee Stage in the House of Lords, Lord Brett, Government Whip, Government Spokesman for the Home Office, stated:

> . . . new Section 4C(3C) is intended to ensure that Section 4C covers only provisions that are about a child automatically acquiring British nationality from their parent, rather than any provision where the acquisition would have required an application to be made by that parent. This is because we cannot now be sure whether such an application would have been submitted and, even if it had been, whether that application would have been successful. Therefore, this subsection provides that an applicant for registration under Section 4C can rely only on those provisions that depend on the nationality of one or both of their parents and does not depend on an application being made for registration as a person who holds that status.[45]

6.77 For the purposes of considering the routes by which a person may have become a CUKC by descent, *had it flowed through the female line as well as the male* (see para **6.82** below), it is not to be assumed that any registration or other requirement necessary to give effect to the provisions mentioned in any of the routes to registration or in Assumption B (see para **6.72** above), were met.[46]

6.78 Thus, where a registration of birth or other requirement depended on human agency (as opposed to occurring by operation of law), it must not be assumed that this requirement was met for the purposes of considering whether the Second Condition is satisfied (see para **6.65** above).

6.79 Prior to 1 January 1983, children born to a male CUKC *by descent* did not, as a general rule, automatically become CUKCs by descent themselves: BNA 1948, s 5. However, on these facts, where the birth occurred in a foreign country and was registered at a British consulate within a year (or later with permission of the Secretary of State), the child automatically became a CUKC by descent notwithstanding the general rule: see BNA 1948, s 5(1), proviso, para (b). Under the pre-1949 statutes similar provisions obtained for the transmission of British subject status by descent, save for the additional requirement for the child to declare an intention to remain British on reaching the age of majority.

6.80 In a letter of 20 March 2009 to Lord Avebury (Liberal Democrat), Lord Brett, Government Whip, Government Spokesman for the Home Office, stated:

> . . . It has been suggested that mothers unable to transmit their citizenship status under the British Nationality Act 1948 may not have taken action, such as consular registration of their child born overseas, because they would divine no practical benefit from doing so. However, some women who gave birth to children in such circumstances did in fact consularly register their child: that child would now be caught by the parameters of section 4C . . .

6.81 At the Committee Stage in the House of Lords, Lord Brett stated:

> New Section 4C(3D) provides that it will not be assumed that any registration or other requirements have been met. There are a number of provisions that enable someone to

[45] HL Deb 2 March 2009 vol 708 c608.

[46] BNA 1981, s 4C(3D), as inserted by BCIA 2009, s 45.

acquire British nationality if certain requirements are met. For example, Section 5(1)(b) of the British Nationality Act 1948 states that a child born overseas would have been a CUKC if their birth was registered at a British consulate within a year. According to new Section 4C(3D) we will not assume that any such requirement would have been met, had previous nationality law provided for descent from a mother in the same way as a father . . .

(e) *The Routes by which a Person may have Become a CUKC by Descent, had it Flowed through the Female Line as well as the Male*

There are now several routes to satisfaction of the Second Condition, in addition to that arising by virtue of BNA 1948, s 5, the latter being the sole route available under BNA 1981, s 4C, prior to amendment by the BCIA 2009. 6.82

The modified Second Condition is that the applicant would at some time before 1 January 1983 have become a CUKC:[47] 6.83

(a) under BNA 1948, s 5 (see para **6.57** above) or Sch 3, para 3 (see para **6.70** above), *if* Assumption A had applied;
(b) under BNA 1948, s 12(3), (4), or (5) (see para **6.84** below), *if* Assumption B had applied and as a result of its application the applicant would have been a British subject immediately before 1 January 1949; or
(c) under BNA 1948, s 12(2) (see para **6.69** above), *if* one or both of the following had applied:
    (i) Assumption A had applied;
    (ii) Assumption B had applied and as a result of its application the applicant would have been a British subject immediately before 1 January 1949.

To make sense of the Second Condition, it is necessary to have in mind BNA 1948, s 12(3)–(5), in force from 1 January 1949 to 31 December 1982. These subsections provided: 6.84

(3) A person who was a British subject immediately before the date of the commencement of this Act shall on that date become a citizen of the United Kingdom and Colonies if he was born within the territory comprised at the commencement of this Act in a protectorate, protected state or United Kingdom trust territory.
(4) A person who was a British subject immediately before the date of the commencement of this Act and does not become a citizen of the United Kingdom and Colonies by virtue of any of the foregoing provisions of this section shall on that date become such a citizen unless—
    (a) he is then a citizen of any country mentioned in subsection (3) of section one of this Act under a citizenship law having effect in that country, or a citizen of Eire; or
    (b) he is then potentially a citizen of any country mentioned in subsection (3) of section one of this Act.
(5) A woman who was a British subject immediately before the date of the commencement of this Act and has before that date been married to a person who becomes, or would but for his death have become, a citizen of the United Kingdom and Colonies by virtue of

[47] BNA 1981, s 4C(3), as substituted by BCIA 2009, s 45.

> any of the foregoing provisions of this section shall on that date herself become such a citizen.

6.85 To make sense of BNA 1948, s 12(4), the list of countries mentioned in BNA 1948, s 1(3), can be found in the Nationality Instructions, Volume 2, Section 2, 'Commonwealth countries'.[48]

6. The Third Condition Remains the Same

6.86 The Third Condition,[49] that immediately before 1 January 1983 the applicant would have had the right of abode in the United Kingdom by virtue of Immigration Act 1971, s 2, had he become a CUKC by virtue of meeting the Second Condition, remains unaltered by the BCIA 2009. Immigration Act 1971, s 2, as in force immediately prior to 1 January 1983, is contained in Annex 2 to this Guide.[50]

7. The Modification to the Treatment of BNA 1948, s 5

6.87 BCIA 2009, s 45, inserts BNA 1981, s 4C(5), to ensure that for the purposes of the interpretation of BNA 1948, s 5, and the application of Assumption A, an applicant's mother who became a CUKC under specified provisions is treated as a CUKC *by descent* and not otherwise than by descent. This deals directly with a point of interpretation that would otherwise have been in doubt, as explained in para **6.74** above.

6.88 For the purposes of the interpretation of BNA 1948, s 5, in its application of Assumption A to a case of descent from a mother, the reference in the proviso to BNA 1948, s 5(1), to 'a citizen of the United Kingdom and Colonies by descent only' includes a reference to a female person who became a CUKC by virtue of:

(a) BNA 1948, s 12(2) (see para **6.69** above), s 12 (4) (see para **6.84** above), or 12(6) (see para **6.89** below);
(b) BNA 1948, s 13(2) (see para **6.90** below);
(c) BNA 1948, Sch 3, para 3 (see para **6.70** above); or
(d) British Nationality (No 2) Act 1964, s 1(1)(a) or (c) (see para **6.92** below).

6.89 BNA 1948 s 12(6), was in force from 1 January 1949 to 31 December 1982 inclusive and provided:

> (6) If any person of full age and capacity who would have become a citizen of the United Kingdom and Colonies on the date of the commencement of this Act by virtue of subsection (4) of this section but for his citizenship or potential citizenship of any country mentioned in subsection (3) of section one of this Act makes application to the Secretary of State in the prescribed manner *before the first day of January nineteen hundred and fifty*

---

[48] See also L Fransman, *British Nationality Law* (n 41 above) 7.7.

[49] BNA 1981, s 4C(4).

[50] See also the Nationality Instructions, Chapter 7, para 7.3.3.

[Italicised words omitted by British Nationality Act 1958, s 3(1)(a)] for the registration of himself and any of his minor children as citizens of the United Kingdom and Colonies, and on such application satisfies the Secretary of State—

(a) that he is descended in the male line from a person possessing any of the qualifications specified in sub-section (1) of this section; and

(b) that he intends to make his ordinary place of residence within the United Kingdom and Colonies,

then, if it seems to the Secretary of State fitting that that person should by reason of his close connection with the United Kingdom and Colonies become a citizen thereof, the Secretary of State may cause him, and any minor children to whom the application relates, to be registered as such; and that person, and any such minor children as aforesaid, shall thereupon become citizens of the United Kingdom and Colonies.

BNA 1948, s 13(2), provided: 6.90

(2) A person remaining a British subject without citizenship as aforesaid shall become a citizen of the United Kingdom and Colonies on the day on which a citizenship law has taken effect in each of the countries mentioned in subsection (3) of section one of this Act of which he is potentially a citizen, unless he then becomes or has previously become a citizen of any country mentioned in subsection (3) of section one of this Act, or has previously become a citizen of the United Kingdom and Colonies, a citizen of Eire or an alien.

To make sense of BNA 1948, s 13(2), the list of countries mentioned in BNA 1948, s 1(3), can be found in the Nationality Instructions, Volume 2, Section 2, 'Commonwealth countries'.[51] 6.91

British Nationality (No 2) Act 1964, s 1(1)(a), (c), provided: 6.92

1.—(1) A person shall be entitled, on making application to the Secretary of State in the prescribed manner, to be registered as a citizen of the United Kingdom and Colonies if he satisfies the Secretary of State that he is and always has been stateless and—

(a) that his mother was a citizen of the United Kingdom and Colonies at the time when he was born; or

. . .

(c) that he is otherwise qualified for registration under this section by parentage, or by residence and parentage, as mentioned in the Schedule to this Act (which deals with certain transitional cases).

8. The Amended Provision

BNA 1981, s 4C, with the 2009 deletions and insertions shown, respectively, using strikethrough and underlining, reads as follows: 6.93

4C Acquisition by registration: certain persons born ~~between 1961 and~~ <u>before</u> 1983

(1) A person is entitled to be registered as a British citizen if—

(a) he applies for registration under this section, and

(b) he satisfies each of the following conditions.

[51] See also L Fransman, *British Nationality Law* (n 41 above) 7.7.

(2) The first condition is that the applicant was born ~~after 7th February 1961 and~~ before 1st January 1983.

(3) ~~The second condition is that the applicant would at some time before 1st January 1983 have become a citizen of the United Kingdom and Colonies by virtue of section 5 of the British Nationality Act 1948 (c. 56) if that section had provided for citizenship by descent from a mother in the same terms as it provided for citizenship by descent from a father.~~

The second condition is that the applicant would at some time before 1st January 1983 have become a citizen of the United Kingdom and Colonies—

(a) under section 5 of, or paragraph 3 of Schedule 3 to, the 1948 Act if assumption A had applied,

(b) under section 12(3), (4) or (5) of that Act if assumption B had applied and as a result of its application the applicant would have been a British subject immediately before 1st January 1949, or

(c) under section 12(2) of that Act if one or both of the following had applied—

(i) assumption A had applied;

(ii) assumption B had applied and as a result of its application the applicant would have been a British subject immediately before 1st January 1949.

(3A) Assumption A is that—

(a) section 5 or 12(2) of, or paragraph 3 of Schedule 3 to, the 1948 Act (as the case may be) provided for citizenship by descent from a mother in the same terms as it provided for citizenship by descent from a father, and

(b) references in that provision to a father were references to the applicant's mother.

(3B) Assumption B is that—

(a) a provision of the law at some time before 1st January 1949 which provided for a nationality status to be acquired by descent from a father provided in the same terms for its acquisition by descent from a mother, and

(b) references in that provision to a father were references to the applicant's mother.

(3C) For the purposes of subsection (3B), a nationality status is acquired by a person ('P') by descent where its acquisition—

(a) depends, amongst other things, on the nationality status of one or both of P's parents, and

(b) does not depend upon an application being made for P's registration as a person who has the status in question.

(3D) For the purposes of subsection (3), it is not to be assumed that any registration or other requirements of the provisions mentioned in that subsection or in subsection (3B) were met.

(4) The third condition is that immediately before 1st January 1983 the applicant would have had the right of abode in the United Kingdom by virtue of section 2 of the Immigration Act 1971 (c. 77) had he become a citizen of the United Kingdom and Colonies as described in subsection (3) above.

(5) For the purposes of the interpretation of section 5 of the 1948 Act in its application in the case of assumption A to a case of descent from a mother, the reference in the proviso to subsection (1) of that section to 'a citizen of the United Kingdom and Colonies by descent only' includes a reference to a female person who became a citizen of the United Kingdom and Colonies by virtue of—

(a) section 12(2), (4) or (6) only of the 1948 Act,

(b) section 13(2) of that Act,

(c) paragraph 3 of Schedule 3 to that Act, or

(d) section 1(1)(a) or (c) of the British Nationality (No. 2) Act 1964.

G. THE GOOD CHARACTER REQUIREMENT

1. Introduction

Immigration, Asylum and Nationality Act 2006, s 58, introduced a new good character requirement in respect of registration applications by adults and young persons for British citizenship and other forms of 'British nationality'. These requirements have now been taken out of the 2006 Act by the BCIA 2009 and moved to the appropriate sections of the different nationality statutes, namely, BNA 1981, s 41A; Hong Kong (War Wives and Widows) Act 1996, s 1; and British Nationality (Hong Kong) Act 1997, s 1.[52] In addition, consequential amendments are made to the powers providing for the supply of police and Customs information to the Secretary of State in connection with the good character requirement.[53] 6.94

The Government resisted attempts to have the good character requirement omitted for Hong Kong war wives and widows on the grounds that it was disrespectful and insensitive.[54] However, in a letter of 20 March 2009 to Lord Avebury (Liberal Democrat), Lord Brett, Government Whip, Government Spokesman for the Home Office, stated: 6.95

> . . . we have agreed – in the unlikely event that any such problem should arise – to consider the exercise of *discretion* in favour of those Hong Kong Widows who meet the requirements for registration as a British citizen under the Hong Kong (War Wives and Widows) Act 1996.[55]

An adult or young person means a person who has attained the age of 10 at the time when the application is made.[56] 6.96

The good character requirement remains unchanged where the application is for naturalisation as a British citizen under BNA 1981, s 6(1) or (2), or for naturalisation as a British overseas territories citizen under BNA 1981, s 18(1) or (2).[57] 6.97

2. New Requirements to be of Good Character

A good character requirement has been inserted into the provisions for registration under BNA 1981, ss 1(3A) (see para **6.14** above), 3(2) (see para **6.28** above), and 4D (see para **6.16** above) as a result of other amendments to the BNA 1981 made by the BCIA 2009. 6.98

[52] BCIA 2009, s 47(1)–(3), Sch.

[53] Ibid, s 47(4)–(5).

[54] eg HL Deb 1 April 2009 vol 709 cc1093–6.

[55] See also PBC 5th Sitting 16 June 2009 cc139–40, per Phil Woolas MP, Minister of State, Home Office.

[56] BNA 1981, s 41A(5); British Nationality (Hong Kong) Act 1997, s 1(5B); as inserted by BCIA 2009, s 47(1) and (3).

[57] Ibid, Sch 1, paras 1(1)(b), 3(e), 5(1)(b), and 7(e); see also the Nationality Instructions, Chapter 18, Annex D 'The good character requirement'.

3. The Full List of Provisions with a Good Character Requirement

6.99 Following the amendments made by the BCIA 2009, the full list of routes to registration when there is now a good character requirement is as follows:

(a) BNA 1981, s 1(3): registration by entitlement as a British citizen, of a minor born in the UK, where his or her father or mother becomes a British citizen or settled in the UK;

(b) BNA 1981, s 1(3A): registration by entitlement as a British citizen, of a minor born in the UK where his or her father or mother becomes a member of the armed forces;

(c) BNA 1981, s 1(4): registration by entitlement as a British citizen, of a person born in the UK on an application made at any time after he or she has attained the age of 10 years, if, as regards each of the first 10 years of that person's life, the number of days on which he or she has been absent from the United Kingdom in that year does not exceed 90;

(d) BNA 1981, 3(1): registration at discretion as a British citizen, of a minor;

(e) BNA 1981, s 3(2): registration by entitlement as a British citizen, of a minor born outside the United Kingdom;

(f) BNA 1981, s 3(5): registration by entitlement as a British citizen, of a minor born outside the United Kingdom;

(g) BNA 1981, s 4(2): registration by entitlement as a British citizen, of a person who is a British overseas territories citizen, a British National (Overseas), a British Overseas citizen, a British subject under the BNA 1981, or a British protected person;

(h) BNA 1981, s 4(5): registration at discretion as a British citizen, of a person who is a British overseas territories citizen, a British National (Overseas), a British Overseas citizen, a British subject under the BNA 1981, or a British protected person;

(i) BNA 1981, s 4A: registration at discretion as a British citizen, of a British overseas territories citizen;

(j) BNA 1981, s 4C: registration by entitlement as a British citizen, of a person born before 1 January 1983;

(k) BNA 1981, s 4D: registration by entitlement as a British citizen, of a person born outside the UK and the qualifying territories (see para **6.09** above) where that person's father or mother is a member of the armed forces.

(l) BNA 1981, s 5: registration by entitlement as a British citizen, of a British overseas territories citizen who is a UK national for the purposes of the Community Treaties;[58]

[58] See the European Communities Act 1972, s 1.

(m) BNA 1981, s 10(1): registration by entitlement as a British citizen, of a person who has renounced citizenship of the UK and Colonies (CUKC);
(n) BNA 1981, s 10(2): registration at discretion as a British citizen, of a person who has renounced CUKC;
(o) BNA 1981, s 13(1): registration by entitlement as a British citizen, of a person who has renounced British citizenship;
(p) BNA 1981, s 13(3): registration at discretion as a British citizen, of a person who has renounced British citizenship;
(q) BNA 1981, s 15(3): registration by entitlement as a British overseas territories citizen, of a minor born in a British overseas territory where that person's father or mother becomes such a citizen or settled in a British overseas territory;
(r) BNA 1981, s 15(4): registration by entitlement as a British overseas territories citizen, of a person born in a British overseas territory on an application made at any time after he or she has attained the age of 10 years, if, as regards each of the first 10 years of that person's life, the number of days on which he or she was absent from that territory in that year does not exceed 90;
(s) BNA 1981, s 17(1): registration at discretion as a British overseas territories citizen, of a minor;
(t) BNA 1981, s 17(5): registration by entitlement as a British overseas territories citizen, of a minor born outside the British overseas territories;
(u) BNA 1981, s 22(1): registration by entitlement as a British overseas territories citizen, of a person who has renounced CUKC;
(v) BNA 1981, s 22(2): registration at discretion as a British overseas territories citizen, of a person who has renounced CUKC;
(w) BNA 1981, s 24: registration by entitlement and at discretion as a British overseas territories citizen, of a person who has renounced British overseas territories citizenship;
(x) BNA 1981, s 27(1): registration at discretion as a British Overseas citizen, of a minor;
(y) BNA 1981, s 32: registration at discretion as a British subject, of a minor;
(z) Hong Kong (War Wives and Widows) Act 1996, s 1: registration at discretion as a British citizen, of a woman who is a Hong Kong war wife or widow; and
(aa) British Nationality (Hong Kong) Act 1997, s 1: registration by entitlement as a British citizen, of a person who was ordinarily resident in Hong Kong, and would have been stateless but for holding another form of British nationality.

4. The Supply of Police and Customs Information in Connection with the Requirement to be of Good Character

(a) *Introduction*

6.100 BCIA 2009, s 47(4)–(5), makes further consequential amendments in the light of the reassignment of the mandatory good character requirement, to provide for the purposes for which police information and Revenue and Customs information may be sought by the Secretary of State.

(b) *Police Information Pre-amendment*

6.101 In respect of the use of police information for nationality purposes, prior to amendment by the BCIA 2009, Nationality, Immigration and Asylum Act 2002, s 131, provides that information may be supplied to the Secretary of State under Immigration and Asylum Act 1999, s 20, for use for the purpose of:

(a) determining whether an applicant for naturalisation under the BNA 1981 is of good character;
(b) determining whether an applicant for registration under a provision specified in the Immigration, Asylum and Nationality Act 2006, s 58(1), is of good character; and
(c) determining whether to make an order for deprivation of citizenship status under BNA 1981, s 40.

6.102 Information may be supplied to the Secretary of State where held by:[59]

(a) a chief officer of police;
(b) the Serious Organised Crime Agency;
(c) a person with whom the Secretary of State has made a contract or other arrangements under the Immigration and Asylum Act 1999, ss 95 and 98, (asylum support powers) or a sub-contractor of such a person; and
(d) other persons for other unrelated specified purposes.

(c) *Police Information Post-amendment*

6.103 Following amendments made by the BCIA 2009, the provision made for the supply of police information in respect of the good character requirement *for the specified registration provisions* is substituted, so that it tracks the re-assigned good character requirements for the specified registration provisions. Thus, police information may be supplied to the Secretary of State for use for the purpose of:[60]

1. determining whether an applicant for registration, for the purposes of an application referred to in BNA 1981, s 41A, is of good character;

---

[59] Immigration and Asylum Act 1999, s 20; Immigration (Supply of Information to the Secretary of State for Immigration Purposes) Order 2008, SI 2008/2077.

[60] Nationality, Immigration and Asylum Act 2002, s 131(b)–(bb), as substituted and inserted by BCIA 2009, s 47(4).

2. determining whether an applicant for registration, for the purposes of an application under Hong Kong (War Wives and Widows) Act 1996, s 1, is of good character; and
3. determining whether an applicant for registration, for the purposes of an application under British Nationality (Hong Kong) Act 1997, s 1, is of good character.

(d) *Revenue and Customs Information Pre-amendment*

In respect of the use of Revenue and Customs information for nationality purposes, prior to amendment by the BCIA 2009, UK Borders Act 2007, s 40, provides that Her Majesty's Revenue and Customs (HMRC) and the Revenue and Customs Prosecutions Office (the RCPO) could each supply the Secretary of State with information for use for the purpose of: 6.104

(a) determining whether an applicant for naturalisation under the BNA 1981 is of good character;
(b) determining whether an applicant for registration under a provision specified in the Immigration, Asylum and Nationality Act 2006, s 58(1), is of good character;
(c) determining whether to make an order for deprivation of citizenship status under BNA 1981, s 40; and
(d) doing anything else in connection with the exercise of immigration and nationality functions.

'Immigration and nationality functions' are defined to mean functions exercisable by virtue of:[61] 6.105

(a) the Immigration Acts;[62]
(b) the BNA 1981;
(c) the Hong Kong Act 1985;
(d) the Hong Kong (War Wives and Widows) Act 1996; and
(e) the British Nationality (Hong Kong) Act 1997.

(e) *Revenue and Customs Information Post-amendment*

Following amendments made by the BCIA 2009, the provision made in respect of the good character requirement *for the specified registration provisions* is substituted, so that it tracks the re-assigned good character requirements for the specified registration provisions. Thus, Revenue and Customs information may be supplied to the Secretary of State for use for the purpose of:[63] 6.106

1. determining whether an applicant for registration, for the purposes of an application referred to in BNA 1981, s 41A, is of good character;

[61] UK Borders Act 2007, s 40(4).

[62] Ibid, s 61(2).

[63] Ibid, s 40(1)(h)–(hb), as substituted and inserted by BCIA 2009, s 47(5).

2. determining whether an applicant for registration, for the purposes of an application under Hong Kong (War Wives and Widows) Act 1996, s 1, is of good character; and
3. determining whether an applicant for registration, for the purposes of an application under British Nationality (Hong Kong) Act 1997, s 1, is of good character.

H. MISCELLANEOUS PROVISIONS

6.107 BCIA 2009, s 15, makes provision for the prohibition on disclosure of personal customs information, to a relevant official or a Minister of the Crown, see Chapter 3. However, there is an exception to the prohibition on disclosure where it is made for the purpose of a function relating to nationality, see BCIA 2009, s 16(3)(b). In addition, the duty to share information relating to the passengers, crew, and freight of ships and aircraft under Immigration, Asylum and Nationality Act 2006, s 36, now extends expressly to the Secretary of State insofar as he or she has functions relating to nationality, following the renovation of s 36 by BCIA 2009, s 21 (see Chapter 3).

6.108 By BCIA 2009, s 27, Her Majesty's Revenue and Customs (HMRC) may make facilities and services available to any person by whom functions relating to nationality are exercisable for the purposes of the exercise of those functions, see Chapter 4.

6.109 In respect of children, BCIA 2009, s 34, renovates UK Borders Act 2007, s 21 (code of practice for keeping children safe from harm), although, as before, immigration officers and officials of the Secretary of State exercising nationality functions, among others, fall within its scope, see Chapter 4. The duties that are planned to replace the obligation found in UK Borders Act 2007, s 21, are the duties to safeguard and promote the welfare of children contained in BCIA 2009, s 55 (see Chapter 9). The duties created by that provision are applicable to any function of the Secretary of State in relation to, inter alia, nationality.

7
IMMIGRATION POWERS

A. INTRODUCTION

7.01 The immigration provisions in Part 3 of the Borders, Citizenship and Immigration Act 2009 (BCIA 2009) provide for three matters. Firstly, BCIA 2009, s 50, introduces a new power to attach a condition restricting the studies of a migrant who has limited leave to enter or remain in the United Kingdom. Secondly, BCIA 2009, s 51, extends existing powers to take fingerprints under Immigration and Asylum Act 1999, s 141, so as to include 'foreign criminals' subject to the automatic deportation provisions in the UK Borders Act 2007, ss 32–39. Thirdly, BCIA 2009, s 52, extends the powers of detention contained within UK Borders Act 2007, ss 1–4 to designated immigration officers in Scotland, with the effect that a designated immigration officer there may detain, at a port in Scotland, an individual who he thinks to be subject to a warrant for arrest. In respect of BCIA 2009, s 52, the Sewel Convention provides that the United Kingdom Parliament does not normally legislate with regard to devolved matters (including police powers) in Scotland without the consent of the Scottish Parliament. The necessary legislative consent motion in relation to BCIA 2009, s 52, was passed by the Scottish Parliament on 19 March 2009.[1]

7.02 BCIA 2009, ss 50–52, extend, as material, to England and Wales, Scotland and Northern Ireland.[2] Save in relation to amendments made by BCIA 2009, s 52 (detention at ports in Scotland), an amendment, modification, or repeal by the Act has the same effect as the enactment or relevant part of the enactment to which

[1] SP OR 19. March 2009 c16064-73 and c16086-8.
[2] BCIA 2009, s 51(1).

it relates (ignoring the extent by virtue of an Order in Council made under any of the Immigration Acts).[3]

7.03 By Order in Council, Her Majesty may provide for the provisions of Part 3 of the BCIA 2009 to extend, with or without modifications to any of the Channel Islands or to the Isle of Man.[4] However this does not apply where a provision is extended to a place by virtue of the provisions for an amendment, modification, or repeal, referred to in para **7.02** above.[5]

7.04 BCIA 2009, s 50 (restriction on studies), came into force on the day the Act received Royal Assent (21 July 2009).[6] BCIA 2009, s 51 (fingerprinting of foreign criminals), and s 52 (detention at ports in Scotland), come into force on such day as the Secretary of State may by order appoint.[7] A commencement order must be made by statutory instrument.[8] No order may be made commencing BCIA 2009, s 52, unless the Secretary of State has consulted the Scottish Ministers.[9] In a letter of 18 March 2009 to Kenny MacAskill MSP, Cabinet Secretary for Justice, Scottish Government, Phil Woolas MP, Minister of State, Home Office stated that the provision would not be commenced before the Police Complaints Commissioner for Scotland's remit over immigration officers is secured. In the same letter he stated that provision would be made for the Commissioner to exercise his role in relation to UK Border Agency customs officers operating in Scotland and that provision may also be made to allow for future oversight of contractors in relation to enforcement functions, in case contractors are given enforcement functions.

B. THE RESTRICTION ON STUDIES

1. Background

7.05 One of the current United Kingdom Government's key policy innovations has been the development of 'managed migration'—the idea that migration, if accompanied by strong enforcement and management techniques, can be used as a 'positive economic asset that contributes to macro-economic health'.[10]

7.06 International students, whose tuition fees contributed to the British economy some £2.5 billion in tuition fees alone in one year,[11] and who also supplement both the low skilled labour pool during their studies, and the very high skilled pool

---

[3] Ibid, s 57(3)–(4): see also UK Borders Act 2007, s 61(2) for the definition of 'the Immigration Acts'.

[4] BCIA 2009, s 57(5).

[5] Ibid, s 57(6).

[6] Ibid, s 58(3)(a).

[7] Ibid, s 58(3)(b).

[8] Ibid, s 58(7).

[9] Ibid, s 58(15).

[10] See the White Paper *Secure Borders, Safe Havens: Integration with Diversity in Modern Britain* Cm 5387 and W Somerville, *Immigration under New Labour* (Bristol: Policy Press, 2007) p 22.

[11] HL Comm 4 March 2009 vol 708 c779.

following completion of their studies,[12] have been actively courted by the Government.[13] This has led to a considerable expansion in the numbers of international students studying in the UK.[14]

The expansion in international student numbers has brought to the fore two interlinked concerns about the enforcement of immigration control. Firstly, there has been concern about the ability to track and control the movements of foreign students through the immigration system once they negotiate entry into the UK. Secondly, there has been concern about the expansion of education providers who are not bona fide (so-called 'bogus colleges') who have sought to profit from the international education market.[15] 7.07

These concerns were elaborated upon by Lord West of Spithead, Parliamentary Under-Secretary of State, Home Office, during the Second Reading of the Bill in the House of Lords: 7.08

> . . . At the moment students come here, go to an institution, move after a few months and then disappear. In future, we want to ensure that there is a responsibility on both the educational institution and the student to inform us that they will move to another course at another educational institution, which must be properly sponsored and registered. That is to ensure that we do not have a loophole, which has caused considerable problems in the past. . .
>
> . . . we do not think it appropriate for him or her to come here and then say after months 'I am moving to the school of guerrilla warfare in northern so-and-so'. We want them to go to properly recognised educational establishments . . .[16]

The Government's response to these concerns has hitherto lain in the introduction of a new licensing system under the Points-Based System (PBS), requiring all education providers to obtain a licence[17] for the purpose of teaching students from outside the European Economic Area (EEA) together with a requirement that these education providers assume certain immigration related obligations to the UK Border Agency. 7.09

Tier 4 (Students) of the PBS operates within the Immigration Rules,[18] paras 245ZT–245ZZD, Appendix A paras 113–125, and Appendix C paras 10–18, which provide the framework for the grant of leave to enter or remain under the rules as a student. Further provision is also made for student visitors at paragraphs 56K–56M of the Immigration Rules. Prior to the introduction of Tier 4 of the PBS on 7.10

[12] W Somerville, *Immigration under New Labour* (n 10 above) p 36.

[13] This was formalized in two Prime Minister's Initiatives for International Education (PMI): the first PMI in 1999 and PMI2 in April 2006.

[14] W Somerville, *Immigration under New Labour* (n 10 above) p 36.

[15] HL Comm 4 March 2009 vol 708 c777.

[16] HL Deb 11 February vol 707 c1132.

[17] See *Sponsoring Students under the Points-Based System for Immigration*; *Points-Based System: Guidance for Employers and Sponsors*; and *Guidance for Sponsor applications—Tier 2, Tier 4 and Tier 5 of the Points Based System*; all on UK Border Agency website: <http://www.ukba.homeoffice.gov.uk>.

[18] HC 395 of 1993–94, as amended.

31 March 2009, Part 3 of the Immigration Rules contained the rules in respect of students seeking leave to enter or remain in the United Kingdom. Several paragraphs of this Part remain part of the Immigration Rules, notwithstanding the introduction of Tier 4 of the PBS. Regard should also be had to leave outside the Immigration Rules (LOTR) on a study related basis.[19]

7.11 For the Government, a continuing weakness of the system of immigration control in respect of students lay in the limited ability in law to control the movement of students after they secure entry to the United Kingdom in their capacity as students. In *G Omerenma Obed and others v Secretary of State for the Home Department*[20] the Court of Appeal noted that Immigration Act 1971, s 3, (see para **7.16** below) made general provision for the regulation and control of persons requiring leave to enter or remain but it did not give the Secretary of State, with one arguable exception that was unnecessary to decide, authority to impose upon a student a condition *as to which course he studied.*

7.12 The provisions introduced by BCIA 2009, s 50, seek to address the perceived shortcomings in Immigration Act 1971, s 3, and to address the policy concerns identified above, through the creation of a power to impose a condition restricting the studies of persons subject to immigration control as a condition of the grant of limited leave to enter or remain in the United Kingdom. This power is reinforced through the use of existing powers of enforcement, connected to s 3 (see para **7.18** below).

7.13 As Phil Woolas MP, Minister of State, Home Office explained:

> Under the new system, a student cannot come into the country on a visa for study at a sponsored institution, and then transfer to a non-sponsored institution, because that is not allowed. The [section] states that, if a student wants to transfer to another sponsored institution, they can, but they must first seek permission. That will enable the UK Border Agency and the institution concerned to ensure that we can properly monitor whether the fact, or otherwise, regarding the purpose of the visa—that is, study—is being adhered to, because the abuse of the system in the past has been, partly, that students came in, started at college and then disappeared, and in some cases no check was made.[21]

2. The General Provisions for Immigration Regulation and Control Prior to Amendment by the BCIA 2009

7.14 The following persons do not require leave to enter or remain in the United Kingdom:

(a) British citizens, and Commonwealth citizens with the right of abode; [22]

---

[19] Immigration Directorate Instructions, Chapter 1, Section 14.

[20] [2008] EWCA Civ 747 (1 July 2008) [6]–[7].

[21] PBC Deb 6th Sitting 16 June 2009 c174.

[22] Immigration Act 1971, ss 1, 3(1), 2(1)(b), 2(2).

(b) persons arriving on a local journey from Ireland, the Channel Islands, or the Isle of Man (the Common Travel Area);[23]
(c) persons exempt from control including seamen, aircrews, diplomats, and members of certain armed forces;[24]
(d) persons not required to obtain leave to enter or remain by virtue of an enforceable Community right or under a provision made under European Communities Act 1972, s 2(2);[25] and
(e) prisoners brought to the UK to give evidence in drug trafficking cases.[26]

Other persons shall not enter the United Kingdom unless given leave to do so in accordance with the provisions of, or made under, the Immigration Act 1971.[27] Such persons are persons subject to immigration control who require leave to enter or remain in the United Kingdom. By Immigration Act, s 3(1)(b), leave to enter or remain in the UK may be given for a limited or indefinite period. 7.15

By Immigration Act 1971, s 3(1)(c), where a person is given *limited* leave to enter or remain in the United Kingdom,[28] that leave may be given subject to any or all of the following conditions: 7.16

(a) a condition restricting his employment or occupation in the United Kingdom;
(b) a condition requiring him to maintain and accommodate himself and any dependants without recourse to public funds;
(c) a condition requiring him to register with the police;
(d) a condition requiring him to report to an immigration officer or the Secretary of State; and
(e) a condition about residence.

Any conditions imposed under Immigration Act 1971, s 3, are quite distinct from the requirements to be satisfied under the Immigration Rules, although there is some overlap in content; the former arise under primary legislation and have connected criminal sanctions and enforcement powers, whereas the latter (albeit arising in the context of the Immigration Act 1971) are rules made as part of the practice to be followed in the administration of the Immigration Act 1971. 7.17

Failure to observe conditions attached to limited leave to enter or remain has four principal effects: 7.18

(a) it renders the person liable to administrative removal;[29]
(b) it renders the person liable to prosecution for a criminal offence where he knowingly fails to observe a condition of leave (together with engaging the

[23] Ibid, s 1(3), 9, and s 11(4); see also the Immigration (Control of Entry through Republic of Ireland) Order 1972, SI 1972/1610 and the Immigration Rules HC 395 of 1993–94 as amended, para 15.
[24] Immigration Act 1971, s 8.
[25] Immigration Act 1988, s 7.
[26] Criminal Justice (International Co-operation) Act 1990, s 6(6).
[27] Immigration Act 1971, s 3(1)(a).
[28] Ibid, s 3(1)(b).
[29] Immigration and Asylum Act 1999, s 10(1)(a).

connected criminal justice powers or arrest, entry and search found in the Immigration Act 1971);[30]

(c) it constitutes a ground on which leave to remain in the United Kingdom should normally be refused and on which leave to enter or remain may be curtailed;[31] and

(d) it is a ground upon which entry clearance or leave to enter the United Kingdom is to be refused or should normally be refused (on further application).[32]

3. New Restrictions on Studies Conditions

7.19 BCIA 2009, s 50, came into force on 21 July 2009.[33] It amends Immigration Act 1971, s 3(1)(c), by adding a new condition:[34]

(ia) a condition restricting his studies in the United Kingdom; . . .

7.20 BCIA 2009, s 3(1)(c)(ia), permits *any* restriction on a person's studies in the United Kingdom to be attached to a grant of limited leave to enter or remain under *any* provision of the Immigration Rules or *any* grant of leave to enter or remain outside the rules (LOTR).

7.21 By BCIA 2009, s 50(2), such a condition may be added on limited leave granted *before*, on, and after the passing of the BCIA 2009.[35] The effects of a failure to observe a condition attached to limited leave to enter and remain are those outlined above (see para **7.18**).

4. The Application of the Condition Restricting Studies in the United Kingdom

7.22 During the passage of the Borders, Citizenship and Immigration Bill through Parliament, the breadth of the power to impose *any* restrictions on studies on *anyone* with limited leave to enter or remain in the United Kingdom, was a recurrent concern mentioned in debate. It was observed that this could result, for example, in the imposition of study restrictions on migrant workers, family members, or refugees who are pursuing English classes; or prevent students from changing courses either internally at the same institution or to alternative institutions.[36]

7.23 In response to these concerns, Lord West of Spithead, Parliamentary Under-Secretary of State, Home Office, set out how he envisaged the powers would

[30] Immigration Act 1971, s 24(1)(b)(ii); see also generally the Immigration Act 1971, Part III.

[31] HC 395 of 1993–94 as amended, paras 322(3), 323 (i).

[32] HC 395 of 1993–94 as amended paras 320(7B)(b), (11).

[33] BCIA, s 58(3)(a).

[34] Immigration Act 1971, s 3(1)(c)(ia), inserted by BCIA 2009, s 50(1).

[35] Royal Assent was given on 21 July 2009.

[36] HL Comm 4 March 2009 vol 708 c772, per Baroness Hanham (Conservative).

be employed, by reference to Tier 4 (Students) of the PBS and the specified institutions:

> It is the Government's intention that the restriction on studies would be placed on those migrants granted leave to enter or remain as tier 4 migrants; that is, students. Furthermore, such a restriction will restrict a migrant to studying at a specified institution, rather than restricting their chosen course of study. I say to the noble Baroness, Lady Hanham, that I can provide an absolutely clear and unequivocal reassurance to the Committee that the Government do not intend to use this provision to prevent students from moving courses within the same sponsoring institution. By imposing a restriction on a migrant, so that he can study only at a specified institution, he would have to apply to the UK Border Agency to vary the conditions of his leave should he wish to change institution. This will allow the UK Border Agency to check that the institution to which the migrant wishes to move is a bona fide education provider, with a sponsor licence. Having the ability to link a student to a particular licensed institution is integral to the successful operation of tier 4, the student tier of the points-based system.[37]

Lord West of Spithead noted that it would apply to those under Tier 4 (Students) of the PBS in much the same way as a condition restricting employment applied to those with leave under Tier 2 (Skilled Workers) of the PBS.[38] 7.24

In respect of the commencement of the provision on Royal Assent and the transitional provision made, Lord West of Spithead noted that: 7.25

> . . . As soon as we have secured Royal Assent, it is our intention to amend the Immigration Rules, specifying that in addition to the conditions restricting a student's employment, we will also add a further condition restricting the student to studying at the educational institution that is acting as the student's sponsor under tier 4. As is usual practice, the Immigration Rules will be laid before Parliament for 21 days before coming into force, and we will look to publish revised guidance for tier 4 students around what this change will mean for them when we lay the rules.[39]

The shadow immigration minster, Damien Green MP (Conservative), remained unconvinced that such broad powers would ultimately be confined to their stated purpose in the light of the 'Government's tendency to legislate for powers whose nature and extent is realised only much later'.[40] He argued that the provisions ought to be confined to those whose leave is granted for the purpose of study in the UK.[41] In his view, changes in the requirements for eligibility for classification as an educational institution[42] were necessary to address the issue of bogus colleges.[43] 7.26

---

37 Ibid, c777.

38 Ibid, cc777–778.

39 Ibid, c779.

40 PBC Deb 6th Sitting 16 June 2009 c170.

41 Ibid, cc170–1.

42 With a view to bringing into line with the Company and Business Names Regulations 1981, SI 1981/1685.

43 PBC Deb 6th Sitting 16 June 2009 cc171–2.

7.27 Further, there were additional concerns about the power to impose restrictions on studies as a condition of leave, on the basis that it failed to adequately reflect the needs of students. The resulting bureaucracy, cost, potential hardship, and inconvenience generated by the application of these measures was said to risk deterring international students from studying in the UK. In particular, it was noted that there are a number of occasions when students legitimately seek to change institutions, for example where their PhD supervisor moves to an alternative institution, or where they discover that they have embarked upon an unsuitable course of study. Baroness Warwick of Undercliffe (Labour), Chief Executive of Universities UK, noted that the requirements would be applied in such a way as (i) to require students to submit a further application together with a relevant fee, and (ii) to prevent them from pursuing their course of studies until a positive determination in respect of their applications had been made. She stated that this would generate hardship.[44] In response to such concerns, Lord West of Spithead, Parliamentary Under-Secretary of State, Home Office, stated:

> . . . the revised guidance . . . that will be published when we make changes to the Immigration Rules in order to impose this condition on tier 4 students, will specify exactly what a student will need to do if he or she wishes to change institution, in terms of the requirement for him to submit a new application to the UK Border Agency. The revised guidance will also make clear the likely timeframes for consideration of an application, so that a student is able to submit his application to allow him to take up his studies at the new institution in good time.[45]

7.28 Other non-governmental organizations expressed concerns about the arbitrary application of the provision which could result in violations of both Article 8 (right to respect for private and family life)[46] and Article 2 of the First Protocol (right to education)[47] of the Convention for the Protection of Human Rights and Fundamental Freedoms (the Human Rights Convention).[48]

5. Retrospectivity

7.29 A key concern raised during the passage of the Borders, Citizenship and Immigration Bill through Parliament, was the retrospective quality of the provision. BCIA 2009, s 50(2), provides for a condition restricting studies to be added to limited leave to enter or remain granted *before* the passing of the Act (21 July 2009).

---

[44] HL Deb 11 February 2009 vol 7087 c1155.

[45] HL Comm 4 March 2009 vol 708 c778.

[46] See Parliamentary briefing for second reading in the House of Lords, JCWI <http://www.jcwi.org.uk>; Parliamentary briefing of JUSTICE, second reading briefing <http://www.justice.org.uk>.

[47] The right to education has some applicability to higher education, see *Leyla Sahin v Turkey* App No 4474/98 10 November 2005 (Grand Chamber).

[48] Rome, 4 November 1950; TS 71 (1953); Cmd 8969.

Baroness Hanham (Conservative) supported the proposition that the provisions should not apply to a grant of leave predating the date the passage of the Act.[49] One matter of particular concern centres on the need to notify existing students of the imposition of the new restrictions, especially where these students have changed address. Will the UKBA rely on deemed notification? Or must there be actual notification? Lord West of Spithead, Parliamentary Under-Secretary of State, Home Office, explained how BCIA 2009, s 50(2), is intended to operate in respect of students already in the UK, but made no mention of possible serious pitfalls over notification of new restrictions to existing students: 7.30

> . . . While we wish to be able to add the condition to all those who have been granted leave as a tier 4 student, if such a student changed institution between the launch of tier 4 and Royal Assent, without notifying the UK Border Agency of this change, he would not be subject to prosecution under Section 3(1)(c) of the Immigration Act 1971, nor would he be subject to removal under Section 10(1)(a) of the Immigration and Asylum Act 1999 for breaching his conditions of stay.[50]
>
> Furthermore, there is no intention to impose this condition on any of the students already in the United Kingdom under the terms of the current student rules that will be deleted on the introduction of tier 4. Only those students that UK Border Agency-licensed education providers bring to the UK under tier 4 from the end of March, or those existing students who will need to apply to extend their leave to remain under tier 4 after its launch in March, will be subject to this condition.[51]
>
> Once the rules are in force, the UK Border Agency will write to all migrants who had been granted leave to enter or remain under tier 4, informing them that they will, from the date of the letter, be subject to this condition. Hence, the condition will apply only from when the student is notified. At the same time, we will also inform these students of the potential consequences of any subsequent breach. Once subject to this condition, a tier 4 student would need to apply to the UK Border Agency to vary the conditions on their stay before moving to a new institution.[52]

C. THE FINGERPRINTING OF FOREIGN CRIMINALS SUBJECT TO AUTOMATIC DEPORTATION

1. Introduction

BCIA 2009, s 51, extends the existing powers of authorized persons to take fingerprints, so that fingerprints may be taken from 'foreign criminals' subject to automatic deportation. Whilst the fingerprints of those who commit crimes may 7.31

---

[49] HL Comm 4 March 2009 vol 708 c772.

[50] Ibid, cc778–9.

[51] Ibid, c779.

[52] Ibid. In respect of the constitutional principle that there must be notice of a decision for it to have legal effect, see *R v Secretary of State for the Home Department and another, ex parte Anufrijeva* [2003] UKHL 36; [2004] 1 AC 604, HL.

already be taken in a criminal context, the function of these measures is, as Lord West of Spithead, Parliamentary Under-Secretary of State, Home Office explained, to:

> . . . fix the identity of the individual whom we have put in prison for crimes in the UK and whom we wish to remove from the UK. Then we have a record when he tries to come back into the country . . .[53]

7.32 Like various other provisions in the BCIA 2009 and earlier Immigration Acts, section 51 of the BCIA 2009 exemplifies the tendency in immigration legislation to meld immigration control and criminal justice functions.

7.33 In order to understand the amendment brought about by BCIA 2009, s 51, it is necessary to outline the pre-existing power to take fingerprints under Immigration and Asylum Act 1999 (IAA), s 141, together with the scheme for the automatic deportation of foreign criminals under UK Borders Act 2007, ss 32–39.

2. Fingerprinting under the Immigration and Asylum Act 1999, s 141

7.34 IAA 1999, s 141, permits the taking of fingerprints by an authorized person from a person to whom the section applies.[54]

7.35 Authorized person means a constable, an immigration officer, a prison officer, an officer of the Secretary of State authorized for the purpose, or a person employed by a contractor in connection with the discharge of the contractor's[55] duties under a removal centre contract.[56]

7.36 Fingerprints may only be taken from a person falling within the list of persons specified under IAA 1999, s 141(7). There are six specified classes of person: A–F.[57] For these purposes only classes C and F are relevant. They cover persons in respect of whom a relevant immigration decision has been made and dependants of such persons.

7.37 Under IAA 1999, s 141(7)(c), one of the specified classes of person, 'C', refers to any person in respect of whom a relevant immigration decision has been made.

7.38 Prior to amendment by the BCIA 2009, IAA 1999, s 141(16), defines a 'relevant immigration decision' as meaning a decision of a kind mentioned in Nationality, Immigration and Asylum Act 2002, s 82(2)(g), (h), (i), (j), or (k). These decisions are:

1. a decision to remove a person unlawfully in the United Kingdom;
2. a decision to remove an illegal entrant;
3. a decision to remove the family member of an illegal entrant;
4. a decision to make a deportation order; and
5. a refusal to revoke a deportation order.

---

[53] Ibid, c786.
[54] IAA 1999, s 141(1).
[55] Ibid, ss 141(6) and 147.
[56] Ibid, s 141(5); see also para **3.48** in respect of fingerprints and designated customs officials.
[57] Ibid, s 141(7)(a)–(f).

Prior to amendment by the BCIA 2009, another one of the specified classes of persons, 'F', includes any person who is a dependant of any of those other persons in classes A–E.[58] It therefore includes dependants who fall within class 'C' (see paras 7.37–7.38 above). 7.39

A person is a dependant of another person for the purposes of class 'F' if he or she is that person's spouse or child under the age of 18, and does not have the right of abode in the United Kingdom or indefinite leave to enter or remain in the United Kingdom.[59] 7.40

Fingerprints may only be taken in the relevant period, which for persons falling within class 'C' begins on the service of notice on him of the relevant immigration decision and for those falling within class 'F' begins at the same time as the person whose dependant he or she is.[60] 7.41

For a person falling within class 'C', the relevant period ends on the earliest of the following: (i) the grant of leave to enter or remain in the United Kingdom, (ii) his leaving a control zone[61] or a supplementary control zone[62] (a juxtaposed controls provision in respect of the Channel Tunnel), or (iii) the time when the relevant immigration decision ceases to have effect, whether as a result of an appeal or otherwise; or if a deportation order has been made against him or her, its revocation or its otherwise ceasing to have effect.[63] For those falling within class 'F' the relevant period ends at the same time as it ends for the person whose dependant he or she is.[64] 7.42

Special provisions apply where fingerprints are to be taken from children under the age of 16.[65] 7.43

Written notice may be served upon those to whom the provisions apply requiring them to attend for fingerprinting.[66] Failure to comply with such a requirement may result in the arrest without warrant of the person concerned by a constable or an immigration officer,[67] the use of reasonable force to secure fingerprints,[68] the refusal to issue an Application Registration Card (ARC) or a Standard Acknowledgement Letter (SAL), the refusal of an asylum claim on non- compliance grounds,[69] or the making of adverse credibility findings.[70] 7.44

---

[58] Ibid, s 141(7)(f).
[59] Ibid, s 141(14).
[60] Ibid, s 141(2), (8).
[61] See the Channel Tunnel (International Arrangements) Order 1993, SI 1993/1813, art 2(1), Sch 1.
[62] Ibid.
[63] IAA 1999, s 141(9).
[64] Ibid.
[65] Ibid, s 141(3), (4), (12), (13).
[66] Ibid, s 142(1).
[67] Ibid, s 142(3).
[68] Ibid, ss 142, 146(2).
[69] Asylum Policy Instruction 'Non-Compliance'.
[70] Asylum and Immigration (Treatment of Claimants, etc.) Act 2004, s 8(1); see also Asylum Policy Instruction 'Fingerprinting', para 3 and Enforcement Instructions and Guidance 'Fingerprinting/taking fingerprints/powers'.

7.45 Fingerprints taken pursuant to IAA 1999, 141, could, potentially, be kept indefinitely. Provision has been made so that if fingerprints have not already been destroyed, they must be destroyed before the end of the specified period beginning with the day on which they were taken. The specified period is such period as the Secretary of State may specify by order, or if no period is specified, 10 years.[71] For dependants falling within class 'F' (see para **7.40** above), fingerprints must be destroyed when fingerprints taken from the person whose dependant he is have to be destroyed.[72] Where a person proves that he is a British citizen or a Commonwealth citizen with the right of abode in the United Kingdom, fingerprints must be destroyed as soon as reasonably practicable.[73]

7.46 By IAA 1999, s 145, authorized persons taking fingerprints must have regard to codes of practice specified in a direction given by the Secretary of State, a code of practice being one for the time being in force under the Police and Criminal Evidence Act 1984 (PACE).[74] PACE Code of Practice D makes further provision in respect of fingerprints.[75] In addition the Immigration (PACE Codes of Practice No 2 and Amendment) Directions 2000 provide for the destruction of fingerprints, if taken with consent, within 10 years. In practice 10 years appears to be the working time limit for the retention of fingerprints, although this could be easily altered by order of the Secretary of State.

7.47 The provisions for the retention of fingerprints must now be read subject to the judgment of the European Court of Human Rights (Grand Chamber) in *S and Marper v United Kingdom*[76] where the Court found, inter alia in respect of the retention of fingerprints, that the blanket and indiscriminate nature of the power of retention in respect of persons suspected but not convicted of criminal offences failed to strike a fair balance between the competing public and private interests, and that the state had overstepped any acceptable margin of appreciation in that regard. Accordingly, the retention of such information constituted a disproportionate interference with the applicant's right to respect for private life under the Human Rights Convention, Article 8 (right to respect for private life) and could not be regarded as necessary in a democratic society.

3. The Automatic Deportation of 'Foreign Criminals' under the UK Borders Act 2007, ss 32–38

7.48 UK Borders Act 2007 (UKBA 2007), ss 32–39, established an automatic deportation scheme for 'foreign criminals'.

---

71 IAA 1999, s 143(1), (15)(b).

72 Ibid, s 143 (9).

73 Ibid, s 143(2).

74 Ibid, s 145; see also para **3.48** in respect of fingerprints and designated customs officials.

75 Paras 4.10–4.15, Annex F; however, see also para **3.34**.

76 Application Nos 30562/04 and 30566/04 (4 December 2008).

A 'foreign criminal' is defined in UKBA 2007, s 32, as meaning a person:[77] 7.49

(a) who is not a British citizen;
(b) who is convicted in the United Kingdom of an offence; and
(c) to whom Condition 1 or 2 applies.

Condition 1 is that the person is sentenced to a period of imprisonment of at least 12 months and Condition 2 is that the offence is specified in an order made by the Secretary of State under the NIAA 2002, s 72(4)(a), and the person is sentenced to a period of imprisonment.[78] At present the provision is only in force in respect of Condition 1.[79] 7.50

Thereafter, further provision is made so that:[80] 7.51

(a) for the purpose of Immigration Act 1971, s 3(5)(a), the deportation of a foreign criminal is conducive to the public good;
(b) subject to specified exceptions, the Secretary of State must make a deportation order in respect of a foreign criminal; and
(c) revocation of an automatic deportation order may only be made where (i) a specified exception applies; (ii) the application is made while the foreign criminal is outside the UK; or (iii) the Secretary of State withdraws the decision that the automatic deportation order provisions apply or revokes a deportation order, *for the purpose of* general regulation and control and the subsequent making of a new decision that the automatic deportation order provisions apply and the making of such an order.

The specified exceptions, qualifying the statutory direction that deportation is conducive to the public good and, separately, that an automatic deportation order must be made, are found in UKBA 2007, s 33. They include exceptions where there is an exemption from immigration control; where rights under the Human Rights Convention or the Convention Relating to the Status of Refugees (Refugee Convention)[81] would be breached by removal; where the foreign criminal was under the age of 10 on the date of conviction; where rights under the Community Treaties would be breached by removal;[82] where extradition law applies; where mental health law applies; and where removal would contravene obligations under the Council of Europe Convention on Action against Trafficking in Human Beings.[83] 7.52

[77] UKBA 2007, s 32(1).

[78] Ibid, s 32(2)–(3); see also the Nationality, Immigration and Asylum Act 2002 (Specification of Particularly Serious Crimes) Order 2004, SI 2004/1910.

[79] UK Borders Act 2007 (Commencement No 3 and Transitional Provisions) Order 2008, SI 2008/1818.

[80] UKBA 2007, s 32(4)–(6).

[81] Geneva, 28 July 1951; UNTS 2545 (1954) and Protocol Relating to the Status of Refugees of 31 January 1967; UNTS 8791 (1967).

[82] The Community Treaties are defined in the European Communities Act 1972, s 1.

[83] Warsaw, 16 May 2005; CETS 197 (2008).

7.53 Further provision is made in respect of the timing of an automatic deportation order, appeal rights, and detention.[84]

7.54 A deportation order may not be made against a person belonging to the family of a foreign criminal after the end of the relevant period of eight weeks. Where the foreign criminal has not appealed in respect of an automatic deportation order, the relevant period begins when an appeal can no longer be brought, ignoring any possibility of an appeal out of time with permission; and where a foreign criminal has appealed in respect of an automatic deportation order, the relevant period begins when the appeal is no longer pending within the meaning of NIAA 2002, s 104.[85]

4. The New Provision for Fingerprinting Foreign Criminals Subject to Automatic Deportation

7.55 BCIA 2009, s 51, extends the power to take fingerprints from persons to include those persons in respect of whom a decision has been made that they are subject to automatic deportation.

7.56 BCIA 2009, s 51(3)(c), inserts a provision into IAA 1999, s 141(16)(b), so that a 'relevant immigration decision' is extended to include a decision that UKBA 2007, s 32(5), applies (ie a decision that the automatic deportation order provisions apply and that an automatic deportation order must be made), whether that decision was made *before, or on or after*, the day appointed for the commencement of BCIA 2009, s 51.

7.57 This has the effect of bringing a person in respect of whom a decision is made, in respect of the application of UKBA 2007, s 32(5), within class 'C' for fingerprinting purposes and engages the machinery set out above for the taking of fingerprints.

7.58 In the case of a 'foreign criminal' in respect of whom a decision under UKBA 2007, s 32(5), is made, the relevant period will begin on the date on which he or she is served with notice of the decision that the provision applies. The relevant period will end on the earliest of the following: (i) the grant of leave to enter or remain in the United Kingdom, (ii) his leaving a control zone[86] or a supplementary control zone[87] (a juxtaposed controls provision in respect of the Channel Tunnel), or (iii) the time when the relevant immigration decision ceases to have effect, whether as a result of an appeal or otherwise; or if a deportation order has been made against him, its revocation or its otherwise ceasing to have effect.[88]

7.59 BCIA 2009, s 51(2), makes a further amendment to IAA 1999, s 141, to reflect the non-availability of a power to deport certain persons belonging to the family of a foreign criminal (by virtue of so belonging) (see para 7.54 above). It does so by

---

[84] UKBA 2007, ss 34–36.

[85] Ibid, s 37; see also Immigration Act 1971, s 5(4), for the definition of belonging to another person's family.

[86] See the Channel Tunnel (International Arrangements) Order 1993, SI 1993/1813, art 2(1), Sch 1.

[87] Ibid.

[88] IAA 1999, s 141(9).

amending IAA 1999, s 141(7)(f), to insert a provision that excludes from its ambit those particular family members specified, from being dependants falling within class 'F'. Thus family members of a foreign criminal who are not liable to deportation by virtue of belonging to the family of a foreign criminal are exempted from the requirements imposed on foreign criminals in respect of fingerprinting under IAA 1999, s 141. For those who nonetheless fall within class 'F', fingerprints may only be taken in the relevant period beginning at the same time as the person whose dependants they are.[89] For persons falling within class 'F' as dependants, the relevant period ends at the same time as the person whose dependants they are.[90]

D. DETENTION AT PORTS IN SCOTLAND

1. The UK Borders Act 2007, ss 1–4

UKBA 2007, ss 1–4, provide for powers of detention at ports in England, Wales, and Northern Ireland.[91] To facilitate the use of the power, the Secretary of State has a power to designate immigration officers who he thinks are fit and proper for the purpose and suitably trained.[92] Such designation may be for a specified or permanent period and is subject to a power of revocation.[93] 7.60

Thereafter, a port is interpreted as including an airport or a hoverport. Further, a place is treated as a port in relation to an individual if a designated immigration officer believes an individual has gone there for the purpose of embarking on a ship or aircraft or has arrived there on disembarking from a ship or aircraft.[94] 7.61

A designated immigration officer at a port in England, Wales, or Northern Ireland may detain an individual if he or she thinks that the individual may be liable to arrest without warrant by a constable under Police and Criminal Evidence Act 1984 (PACE 1984), s 24(1), (2), or (3); or the Police and Criminal Evidence (Northern Ireland) Order 1989, SI 1989/1341, art 26(1), (2), or (3); or the constable thinks that an individual is subject to a warrant for arrest.[95] An individual may not be detained under this provision for longer than three hours.[96] 7.62

Where a designated immigration officer detains an individual, he or she must arrange for a constable to attend as soon as reasonably practicable; may search the individual and retain anything that might be used to assist escape or cause physical injury to the individual or another person; must retain anything found on a search which he thinks may be evidence of the commission of an offence; and must when 7.63

[89] Ibid, s 141(2), (8).
[90] Ibid.
[91] UKBA 2007, s 60(1).
[92] Ibid, s 1(1)–(2).
[93] Ibid, s 1(3).
[94] Ibid, s 4.
[95] Ibid, s 2(1).
[96] Ibid, s 2(3).

the constable arrives deliver the individual and anything found on the search to the constable.[97]

7.64 A designated immigration officer may use reasonable force for the purpose of exercising a power to detain under this provision.[98] Where an individual whom a designated immigration officer has detained or attempted to detain leaves the port, the immigration officer may pursue the individual and return the individual to the port.[99]

7.65 The exercise of the power of detention is supported by the provision of criminal offences for absconding from detention, assaulting an immigration officer exercising a power arising in relation to detention, and obstructing an immigration officer in the exercise of a power in relation to detention.[100]

2. Detention at Ports in Scotland Following Amendment to the UK Borders Act 2007 by the BCIA 2009

7.66 Under the BCIA 2009, provision is made to extend powers of detention to ports in Scotland. This is achieved by BCIA 2009, s 52, which amends UKBA 2007, ss 2, 3, and 60(1).

7.67 By BCIA 2009, s 52(1), a new s 2(1A) is inserted into UKBA 2007 providing a limited power to detain in Scotland that does *not* extend to situations where a designated immigration officer thinks a person may be liable to arrest without warrant:

> (1A) A designated immigration officer at a port in Scotland may detain an individual if the immigration officer thinks that the individual is subject to a warrant for arrest.

7.68 Thereafter, BCIA 2009, s 52(2), amends UKBA 2007, s 3, by providing that references to terms of imprisonment not exceeding *51 weeks*, to which a person in England and Wales is liable on conviction for an offence falling within that section, shall be treated as references to *12 months*.

7.69 BCIA 2009, s 52(3), amends UKBA 2009, s 60(1), so that the territorial scope of the powers of detention and enforcement by designated immigration officers under UKBA 2007, ss 1–4, extends to Scotland.

3. The Justification for the Extension of the Powers to Detain at Ports in Scotland

7.70 During the passage of the UK Borders Bill in 2007, the Government had been unsuccessful in convincing Scottish authorities of the merits of the extension to Scotland of the powers of immigration officers to detain an individual, with the

[97] Ibid, s 2(2); see also paras **3.33–3.34** in respect of the Police and Criminal Evidence Act 1984 (PACE).

[98] Ibid, s 2(4).

[99] Ibid, s 2(5).

[100] Ibid, s 3.

effect that immigration officers in ports in Scotland remained outside the scope of UKBA 2007, ss 1–4.[101] At the time the introduction of powers to detain were considered unnecessary as there were normally police at all Scottish ports and airports who could detain individuals where necessary.[102] However a loophole has been identified where a person cannot be held at immigration control by an immigration officer where the latter is aware of an outstanding warrant for arrest. The Scottish Government considered that this loophole should be closed.[103] BCIA 2009, s 52, amends the UKBA 2007 to extend to Scotland the power of designated immigration officers to detain persons at Scottish ports. At the Committee Stage of the Bill in the House of Commons, Phil Woolas MP, Minister of State, Home Office, stated:

> The extension of the powers to Scotland will mean that this important measure will cover the whole United Kingdom. In other words, our strategy is to bring police-like powers into the agency for a more effective partnership with the police.[104]

---

[101] PBC Deb 6th Sitting 16 June 2009 c178; see also HL Deb 4 March 2009 vol 708 c790, per Lord West of Spithead, Parliamentary Under-Secretary of State, Home Office.

[102] Legislative Consent Memorandum LCM (S3) 15.1 Session 3, 2009, para 5.

[103] Ibid, para 6.

[104] PBC Deb 6th Sitting 16 June 2009 c179.

8

THE TRANSFER OF CERTAIN IMMIGRATION JUDICIAL REVIEW APPLICATIONS TO THE UPPER TRIBUNAL

A. INTRODUCTION

8.01 Prior to the amendments made by the Borders, Citizenship and Immigration Act 2009 (BCIA 2009), s 53, applications for judicial review in immigration and nationality matters were dealt with exclusively in the High Court in England and Wales, the High Court in Northern Ireland, and the Court of Session in Scotland.[1] BCIA 2009, s 53, alters this position by providing for a certain class of immigration-based applications for judicial review to be heard in the Upper Tribunal.

8.02 In future, the High Court in England and Wales, the High Court in Northern Ireland, and the Court of Session in Scotland, on satisfaction of certain conditions, will be required to transfer to the Upper Tribunal, established under the Tribunals Courts and Enforcement Act 2007 (TCEA 2007),[2] any applications for judicial review calling into question a decision of the Secretary of State not to treat further submissions as an asylum claim or a human rights claim within the meaning of

[1] For England and Wales, see the Senior Courts Act 1981, ss 31 and 31A; see also CPR Pt 54, PD 54a, and PD 54d; for Northern Ireland see Judicature (Northern Ireland) Act 1978, ss 18 and 25A; and for Scotland see the Court of Session Rules, Chapter 58.

[2] TCEA 2007, ss 3, 7.

Nationality, Immigration and Asylum Act, 2002, Part 5. In practice such further submissions, making asylum or human rights claims, are so-called 'fresh claims', brought by an applicant after an initial claim and any onward appeal has failed to result in a grant of leave to enter or remain in the United Kingdom or has failed to arrest removal or deportation.

BCIA 2009, s 53, is not yet in force. It comes into force on such day as the Lord Chancellor may by order appoint.[3] No order may be made unless the functions of the Asylum and Immigration Tribunal under Nationality, Immigration and Asylum Act 2002, Part 5, have been transferred to the First-tier and/or the Upper Tribunal.[4] 8.03

B. OVERVIEW OF THE TWO-TIER TRIBUNAL STRUCTURE UNDER THE TRIBUNALS, COURTS AND ENFORCEMENT ACT 2007

1. Introduction

The Tribunals Service was established in April 2006, as an Executive Agency of the Ministry of Justice, with a view to bringing the various tribunals together in a single system, with a unified administration, separate from their relevant sponsoring Government departments. The TCEA 2007 further integrated the tribunals through the establishment of a two-tier tribunal system: the First-tier Tribunal and the Upper Tribunal, which began work on 3 November 2008. Various tribunals have now been subsumed into this system. These innovations were made as part of a process that began with the Report of the Review of Tribunals, *Tribunals for Users, One System, One Service*, by Sir Andrew Leggatt[5] and continued with the White Paper *Transforming Public Services: Complaints, Redress and Tribunals*.[6] 8.04

2. The Structure of the Two-tier Tribunal System

The new tribunal system is overseen by the Senior President of Tribunals, currently Lord Justice Carnwath. The Senior President's role, amongst other things, is to provide judicial leadership and guidance to the tribunals. In carrying out the functions of that office, he must have regard to:[7] 8.05

(a) the need for tribunals to be accessible;
(b) the need for proceedings before tribunals to be fair and to be handled quickly and efficiently;

[3] BCIA 2009, s 58(4)(a).
[4] Ibid, s 58(16); see also HC Written Ministerial Statements 8 May 2009 vol 492 c30 WS for the statement of Phil Woolas MP, Minister of State, Home Office, announcing the intention to transfer the functions of the Asylum and Immigration Tribunal to the First-tier Tribunal and the Upper Tribunal.
[5] HMSO 2001.
[6] 2004, Cm 6243.
[7] TCEA 2007, s 2.

(c) the need for members of tribunals to be experts in the subject matter of, or the law to be applied in, cases in which they decide matters; and
(d) the need to develop innovative methods of resolving disputes that are of a type that may be brought before tribunals.

8.06 In addition, the Administrative Justice and Tribunals Council[8] has the function of keeping the administrative justice system under review; considering ways to make the system accessible, fair, and efficient; advising specified persons on the development of the system and referring proposals for change to them; and making proposals for research into the system.[9]

8.07 In respect of the new tribunals, the TCEA 2007 makes provision for the appointment and transfer in of judges and members, as the case may be, and the designation of those serving in pre-existing tribunals as judges and members, as the case may be.[10] Specified categories of court judges including Court of Appeal, High Court, and Court of Session judges; circuit judges; county court judges in Northern Ireland; sheriffs in Scotland; and district judges in England and Wales, are *ex officio* judges of the tribunals[11] and are able to serve by request of the Senior President.[12]

8.08 There are two tribunals in the new tribunal system: the First-tier Tribunal and the Upper Tribunal. Each tribunal is divided up into separate chambers each with their own president or two presidents.[13] The First-tier Tribunal is presently divided into five chambers[14] and the Upper Tribunal is presently divided into three chambers.[15]

8.09 The rules of practice are governed by the various Tribunal Procedure Rules[16] made by the Tribunal Procedure Committee, together with Practice Directions made by the Senior President of Tribunals and by individual chamber presidents.[17] As far as immigration law is concerned, there are three major changes envisaged. The first is the wholesale transfer of the current immigration appellate process into the two-tier Tribunal. We deal with this in the next section. The second concerns the power of the Upper Tribunal to deal with judicial review applications, which previously would have gone exclusively to the High Courts or the Court of Session. Although both changes are equally important, the judicial review changes are something of a novelty, were hotly debated in the course of the Bill's passage through Parliament, and take up a very large part of this chapter. The third change is to how immigration decisions will eventually reach the Court of Appeal.

---

[8] Ibid, s 44.
[9] Ibid, Sch 7, Part 2, para 13(1).
[10] Ibid, ss 4 and 5.
[11] Ibid, s 6.
[12] Ibid, Sch 2 para 6; Sch 3 para 6.
[13] Ibid, ss 3–7.
[14] Social Entitlement; General Regulatory, War Pensions, and Armed Forces Compensation; Health Education and Social Care; and Tax.
[15] Administrative Appeals, Lands, and Tax and Chancery.
[16] eg The Tribunal Procedure (Upper Tribunal) Rules 2008, SI 2698/2008.
[17] TCEA 2007, ss 22–23.

3. Statutory Appeals under the Two-tier Tribunal System

Appeals to the Upper Tribunal, where permitted, are on a point of law and subject to a permission application, initially to the First-tier Tribunal and, if refused, the Upper Tribunal itself.[18] The Upper Tribunal is a superior court of record.[19] 8.10

Appeals against the decisions of the Upper Tribunal, where permitted, are on a point of law, to the Court of Appeal in England and Wales, to the Court of Appeal in Northern Ireland, and to the Inner House of the Court of Session in Scotland, subject to a permission application, initially to the Upper Tribunal or, if refused, the relevant appellate court.[20] 8.11

In England and Wales and Northern Ireland if an appeal from a decision by the Upper Tribunal has travelled through the First-tier Tribunal, in respect of permission (or leave in Northern Ireland) to appeal to the Court of Appeal, permission to appeal will not be granted unless the Upper Tribunal or the relevant appellate court, considers that:[21] 8.12

(a) the proposed appeal would raise some important point of principle or practice; or
(b) there is some other compelling reason for the relevant appellate court to hear the appeal.

The test for permission to appeal is substantially the same as the test for a second appeal (the second appeal test) to the Court of Appeal in England and Wales from a decision of a county court or the High Court, which was itself made on appeal.[22] 8.13

The Government proposes to integrate the Asylum and Immigration Tribunal into the two-tier structure described above. It is proposed that the First-tier Tribunal and the Upper Tribunal will simply replace the Asylum and Immigration Tribunal. There will be no change to initial appeal rights, save that these will be heard, at first instance, by a separate immigration and asylum chamber in the First-tier Tribunal, and thereafter on appeal, with permission of the First-tier Tribunal or, where refused by the Upper Tribunal, by a separate immigration and asylum chamber of the Upper Tribunal.[23] 8.14

The key change lies in the onward appeals process, with the scheme outlined above replacing the current reconsideration and appeal process in the single-tier 8.15

[18] Ibid, s 11, see legal opinion by Michael Fordham QC and Charlotte Kilroy, 10 October 2008 on behalf of the Public Law project for an analysis of the effects of this in an asylum and immigration context.

[19] TCEA 2007, s 3(5).

[20] Ibid, s 13.

[21] Ibid, s 13(6); Appeals from the Upper Tribunal to the Court of Appeal Order 2008, SI 2008/2834.

[22] CPR, r 52.13.

[23] *Immigration Appeals: Fairer Decisions; Faster Justice*: *Government Response to Consultation* (UK Border Agency, Tribunals Service) (May 2009); Undated correspondence from Chief Executive, Tribunals Service to stakeholders.

Asylum and Immigration Tribunal.[24] The latter was created as a single-tier tribunal by the Asylum and Immigration (Treatment of Claimants, etc.) Act 2004[25] and only started to function in 2005. Prior to that a two-tier system operated with immigration adjudicators hearing immigration appeals at first instance with the possibility of an onward appeal to the Immigration Appeal Tribunal.

8.16 For the First-tier Tribunal, the rules of procedure will be a modified version of the existing Asylum and Immigration Tribunal procedure rules. For the Upper Tribunal, the Tribunals Service held a consultation (ending 29 September 2009) over the modification of the existing Upper Tribunal procedure rules,[26] in order to reflect the particular needs of asylum and immigration appeals.[27]

4. An Overview of the Judicial Review Functions of the Upper Tribunal

(a) *England and Wales and Northern Ireland*

8.17 Under the TCEA 2007, ss 15(1)–(2) and 16(6), power is conferred upon the Upper Tribunal to grant forms of relief available in judicial review proceedings in England and Wales and Northern Ireland (a mandatory order, a prohibiting order, a quashing order, a declaration, or an injunction; or where so included as a claim arising from a matter to which the application relates: damages, restitution, or the recovery of a sum due, if the Tribunal is satisfied that such an award would have been made, had the claim been made in an action begun in the High Court by the applicant at the time of making the application).[28] Specific further provision is made in respect of quashing orders.[29] The powers to grant relief may only be exercised subject to satisfaction of conditions.[30] Those conditions require either that on an application to the Tribunal certain specified conditions are met,[31] or that the Tribunal is authorized to proceed even though not all of the conditions are met. In the latter case, this will occur where a case has either been transferred to the Upper Tribunal from the High Court[32] pursuant to Senior Courts Act 1981, s 31A,[33] or Judicature (Northern Ireland) Act 1978, s 25A,[34] as the case may be.

[24] See the Nationality, Immigration and Asylum Act 2002, ss 103A–103E and Asylum and Immigration (Treatment of Claimants, etc.) Act 2004, s 26, Sch 2.

[25] Section 26.

[26] The Tribunal Procedure (Upper Tribunal) Rules 2008, SI 2008/2698.

[27] The Tribunal Procedure (Upper Tribunal) Rules 2008 consultation on the rule amendments for Asylum and Immigration Upper Tribunal Chamber, Tribunal Service at <http://www.tribunals.gov.uk>.

[28] See Senior Courts Act 1981, s 30, for the powers of the High Court in England and Wales and the Judicature (Northern Ireland) Act 1978, ss 18 and 20, in respect of Northern Ireland.

[29] TCEA 2007, s 17.

[30] Ibid, s 15(2).

[31] Ibid, ss 15(2)(a), 18.

[32] Ibid, ss 15(2)(b), 19(3),(4).

[33] As amended by TCEA 2007, s 19(1).

[34] As amended by TCEA 2007, s 19(2).

The Lord Chief Justice of England and Wales made a Direction on 29 October 2008 with effect in relation to an application for judicial review made on or after 3 November 2008, specifying two classes of judicial review which, subject to satisfaction of other conditions, must be transferred from the High Court to the Upper Tribunal (see paras **8.28–8.31** below), or which may be begun by a claim in the latter (see paras **8.20–8.21** below): 8.18

(a) any decision of the First-tier Tribunal on an appeal against a review decision of the Criminal Injuries Compensation Authority; and

(b) any decision of the First-tier Tribunal made under the new Tribunal Procedure Rules or the TCEA 2007, s 9, where there is no right of appeal to the Upper Tribunal against the decision; and the decision *is not an excluded decision* within the TCEA 2007, s 11(5) (b), (c), or (f) (data protection and freedom of information appeals against a national security certificate and appeals of a description specified by the Lord Chancellor).

The Direction specified that it does not have effect where an application seeks, whether or not alone, a declaration of incompatibility under Human Rights Act 1998, s 4. 8.19

An application for judicial review of a matter falling within the jurisdiction of the Upper Tribunal *may* subject to certain conditions, or *must* subject to certain conditions, be transferred from the High Court (see paras **8.28–8.31** below). In addition, an application that would have to be transferred where begun in the High Court *may also be made instead to the Upper Tribunal.* Where an application is made to the Upper Tribunal seeking relief or for permission to apply for relief, if Conditions 1 to 4 are met (see para **8.21** below), the Upper Tribunal has the function of deciding the application; otherwise it must by order transfer the application to the High Court.[35] 8.20

The four Conditions are:[36] 8.21

(a) Condition 1: that the application does not seek any relief other than a mandatory, prohibiting, or quashing order; or a declaration or injunction; permission (or leave) to apply for any such relief; an award of damages, restitution, or the recovery of a sum due; interests and costs;

(b) Condition 2: that the application does not call into question anything done by the Crown Court;

(c) Condition 3: that the application falls within a class specified in a Direction by the Lord Chief Justice (or nominee) with the agreement of the Lord Chancellor (see para **8.18** above); and

(d) Condition 4: that the judge presiding at the hearing of the application is either a judge of the High Court or the Court of Appeal in England and Wales or

[35] TCEA 2007, s 18(1)–(3).

[36] Ibid, s 18(4)–(8); Constitutional Reform Act 2005, Sch 2, Part 1.

Northern Ireland, or a judge of the Court of Session; or such other persons as may be agreed from time to time between the Lord Chief Justice, the Lord President, or the Lord Chief Justice of Northern Ireland, as the case may be, and the Senior President of Tribunals.

8.22 An application for relief by way of judicial review may only be made if permission from the Upper Tribunal has been obtained.[37] In cases arising under the law of England and Wales and Northern Ireland the Upper Tribunal is required to apply the same principles of law that the High Court applies in dealing with applications for relief.[38] In particular, the Upper Tribunal may not grant permission to make the application unless it considers that an applicant has sufficient interest in the matter to which the application relates.[39] Further, it may refuse to grant permission or withhold relief where there has been undue delay in making the application and granting the relief sought on the application would be likely to cause substantial hardship to, or substantially prejudice the rights of, any person or would be detrimental to good administration.[40]

8.23 Relief awarded by the Upper Tribunal has the same effect as corresponding relief granted by the High Court and is enforceable in the same way.[41] For this purpose, in cases arising under the law of Northern Ireland a mandatory order corresponds to an order of mandamus, a prohibiting order to an order of prohibition, and a quashing order to an order of certiorari.[42]

8.24 Where the Upper Tribunal refuses to grant permission to apply for relief an applicant may appeal against that refusal to the Court of Appeal with permission. The more restrictive second appeal test for permission to appeal to the Court of Appeal,[43] (see paras **8.12** and **8.75**), is inapplicable to a decision from the Upper Tribunal in this circumstance. If the Upper Tribunal refuses permission (or leave) to apply for judicial review, the appellant appeals, and the Court of Appeal grants permission (or leave in Northern Ireland) to apply for judicial review, the Court may go on to decide the application for relief.[44]

8.25 Judges presiding over judicial review cases transferred from the High Court may be drawn from the High Court or the Court of Appeal in England and Wales and the same in Northern Ireland, may be a judge from the Court of Session, or may be such other persons as may be agreed from time to time between the Lord Chief Justice of England and Wales, the Lord Chief Justice of Northern Ireland, or the

---

[37] TCEA 2007, s 16(2); The Tribunal Procedure (Upper Tribunal) Rules 2008, SI 2698/2008, r 28(1).

[38] TCEA 2007, s 15(4), (5).

[39] Ibid, s 16(3).

[40] Ibid, s 16(4)–(5); see also Senior Courts Act 1981, s 31, in respect of the equivalent provision for the High Court in England and Wales and the Judicature (Northern Ireland) Act 1978, s 18 in respect of Northern Ireland.

[41] TCEA 2007, 15(3), 16(7).

[42] Ibid, s 15(6).

[43] Ibid, s 13 (7).

[44] Ibid, s 16(8).

Lord President (in Scotland, see para **8.26**), as the case may be, and the Senior President of Tribunals.[45] Thus, a Tribunal judge other than a High Court judge or an appellate court judge many hear an application for judicial review, where so agreed.

(b) *Scotland*

8.26 In Scotland, the Upper Tribunal has the function of deciding applications transferred to it from the Court of Session.[46] Its powers of review are the same as those of the Court of Session in an application to the supervisory jurisdiction of that court.[47] In dealing with an application before it, the Tribunal is required to apply the same principles as the Court of Session would apply in deciding an application.[48] Any order of the Tribunal made in respect of the above has the same effect as a corresponding order granted by the Court of Session and is enforceable as though it were granted by that court.

C. BACKGROUND AND LEGISLATIVE PROCESS

1. The Framework for the Transfer of Judicial Review Applications Prior to the BCIA 2009

8.27 The High Court in England and Wales and the High Court in Northern Ireland have power to transfer applications for judicial review and applications for permission (or leave in Northern Ireland) to apply for judicial review to the Upper Tribunal.[49] The Court of Session also has power to transfer an application made to the supervisory jurisdiction of the Court of Session to the Upper Tribunal.[50] Under the existing framework an order for transfer is mandatory in certain circumstances[51] and discretionary in others.[52] In both circumstances, a series of conditions must first be fulfilled before a transfer can take place.

(a) *England and Wales*

8.28 In England and Wales, if Conditions 1–4 are met, the High Court *must* by order transfer the application to the Upper Tribunal. In addition if Conditions 1, 2, and 4 are met, but Condition 3 is not, the High Court *may* by order transfer the application to the Upper Tribunal *if it appears to the High Court to be just and convenient to*

[45] Ibid, s 18(8).

[46] Ibid, ss 20(1) and 21(1).

[47] Ibid, s 21(2).

[48] Ibid, s 21(3).

[49] Senior Courts Act 1981, s 31A as inserted by TCEA 2007, s 19(1); Judicature (Northern Ireland) Act 1978, s 25A, as inserted by TCEA 2007, s 19(2).

[50] TCEA 2007, s 20.

[51] Senior Courts Act 1981, s 31A(2) as inserted by TCEA 2007, s 19(1); Judicature (Northern Ireland) Act 1978, s 25A(2) as inserted by TCEA 2007, s 19(2) and TCEA, s 20(1)(a).

[52] Senior Courts Act 1981, s 31A (3) as inserted by TCEA 2007, s 19(1); Judicature (Northern Ireland) Act 1978, s 25A(3) as inserted by TCEA 2007, s 19(2) and TCEA 2007, s 20(1)(b).

do so.[53] In this latter scenario, applications for judicial review on matters *other* than those specified in Condition 3 may be transferred. Thus a wide range of applications could potentially be transferred.

8.29 The Conditions are:[54]

(a) Condition 1: that the application does not seek anything other than relief under Senior Courts Act 1981, s 31(1)(a) and (b) (a mandatory, prohibiting, or quashing order, or a declaration or injunction under Senior Courts Act 1981, s 31(2)); permission to apply for any such relief; an award of damages, restitution or the recovery of a sum due under Senior Courts Act 1981, s 31(4); interests and costs;

(b) Condition 2: that the application does not call into question anything done by the Crown Court;

(c) Condition 3: that the application falls within a class specified in a Direction by the Lord Chief Justice (or nominee) with the agreement of the Lord Chancellor under Tribunals, Courts and Enforcement Act 2007, s 18(6), (see para **8.18** above); and

(d) Condition 4: that the application does not call into question any decision made under the Immigration Acts;[55] the British Nationality Act 1981; any instrument having effect under any of the aforementioned enactments; or any other provision of law for the time being in force which determines British citizenship, British overseas territories citizenship, the status of a British National (Overseas), or British Overseas citizenship.

8.30 The effect of Condition 4 is to place a statutory bar on the transfer of immigration and nationality applications for judicial review and applications for permission to apply for judicial review to the Upper Tribunal.

(b) *Northern Ireland*

8.31 In Northern Ireland, if Conditions 1–4 are met, the High Court *must* by order transfer the application to the Upper Tribunal. In addition if Conditions 1, 2, and 4 are met, but Condition 3 is not, the High Court *may* by order transfer the application to the Upper Tribunal *if it appears to the High Court to be just and convenient to do so.*[56] The four Conditions are, broadly speaking, the same as in England and Wales, although the prerogative orders are mandamus, certiorari, and prohibition and Condition 1 varies slightly, having regard to the forms of relief available by way of an injunction and damages.[57]

[53] Senior Courts Act, s 31A(2),(3), as inserted by TCEA 2007, s 19(1).
[54] Ibid, s 31A(4)–(7), as inserted by TCEA 2007, s 19(1).
[55] See UK Borders Act 2007, s 61(2).
[56] Judicature (Northern Ireland) Act 1978, s 25A (2)–(4), as inserted by TCEA 2007, s 19(2).
[57] Ibid.

(c) *Scotland*

In Scotland, where an application is made to the supervisory jurisdiction of the Court of Session, the Court *must*, if Conditions 1, 2, and 4 are met, and *may*, if Conditions 1, 3, and 4 are met, but Condition 2 is not; by order transfer the application to the Upper Tribunal.[58] 8.32

The Conditions are:[59] 8.33

(a) Condition 1: that the application does not seek anything other than an exercise of the supervisory jurisdiction of the Court of Session (including the making of any order in connection with or in consequence of the exercise of that jurisdiction);
(b) Condition 2: that the application falls within a class specified for this purpose by act of sederunt made with the consent of the Lord Chancellor, (however no class of application may be specified that includes an application the subject matter of which is a devolved Scottish matter; that is, it concerns the exercise of functions in or as regards Scotland and does not relate to a reserved matter within the meaning of the Scotland Act 1998). By the Act of Sederunt (Transfer of Judicial Review Applications from the Court of Session) 2008,[60] an application which challenges a procedural decision or a procedural ruling of the First-tier Tribunal is specified as a class of application;
(c) Condition 3: that the subject matter of the application is not a devolved Scottish matter; and
(d) Condition 4: is the same as Condition 4 for England and Wales and for Northern Ireland (see para **8.29**).

2. The Original Clause in the Borders, Citizenship and Immigration Bill for the Transfer of Judicial Review to the Upper Tribunal

During the passage through Parliament of the Tribunals, Courts and Enforcement Bill (which became the TCEA 2007) in 2006–2007, the Government had accepted that applications for judicial review in immigration cases were particularly sensitive and that there should be a statutory bar on their transfer, at least until there had been a proper opportunity to review how the transfer of applications for judicial review (in other areas of law) to the Upper Tribunal had worked.[61] However, a clause for the transfer of immigration and nationality law applications for judicial review to the Upper Tribunal was nonetheless contained in the Borders, Citizenship and 8.34

[58] TCEA 2007, s 20(1).

[59] Ibid, s 20(2)–(5).

[60] SI 2008/357, in force 10 November 2008.

[61] HL Comm 13 December 2006 vol 687 c68–70, per Baroness Ashton of Upholland, Parliamentary Under-Secretary of State, Department for Constitutional Affairs; See also HL Deb 1 Apr 2009 vol 709 c1125, per Lord Kingsland (Conservative), Opposition Spokesperson for Constitutional and Legal Affairs/Justice.

Immigration Bill as introduced into the House of Lords[62] before any opportunity for such a review. The clause reflected proposals outlined by the UK Border Agency in its consultation paper *Consultation: Immigration Appeals Fair Decisions; Faster Justice*.[63] Those proposals sought the straightforward removal of Condition 4 (see para **8.29** above). Were this provision to have been enacted its effect would have been to allow for the transfer of *any* immigration or nationality judicial review to the Upper Tribunal, subject to satisfaction of specified requirements.[64]

3. The Rationale for the Transfer of Judicial Review Provisions

8.35 There are three key factors accounting for the Government's aim of removing the statutory bar on the transfer of immigration and nationality judicial review applications from the High Court in England and Wales, the High Court in Northern Ireland, and the Court of Session in Scotland, to the Upper Tribunal:

(a) pressure from the judiciary;
(b) the desire to enforce immigration control; and
(c) centripetal forces working to create a single tribunal service.

(a) *Pressure from the Judiciary*

8.36 It is clear that members of the higher judiciary in the Court of Appeal and the High Court were key in calling for a lessening of the burden on the higher courts and in calling for the introduction of powers for the transfer of certain immigration related judicial review into the Upper Tribunal to assist in that task. Indeed, the proposals first outlined in *Immigration Appeals Fair Decisions; Faster Justice*,[65] for the removal of the statutory bar on such transfer, and the integration more generally of statutory immigration appeals into the new tribunal structure, were considered in a working group[66] under the joint chairmanship of a Court of Appeal judge, Lord Justice Richards and Lin Homer, Chief Executive of the UK Border Agency. Further, they appear to have been broadly endorsed by the President of the Queen's Bench Division, and the Master of the Rolls.[67]

8.37 The March 2008 Review by the Lord Chief Justice of England and Wales (as he then was), Lord Phillips of Worth Matravers, provides an account of the concerns of the higher judiciary in the superior courts about their large caseload, emanating from the particularly large level of immigration and asylum casework. Delay in the

[62] HL Bill 15 of 2008–09, clause 50.

[63] *Consultation: Immigration Appeals Fair Decisions; Faster Justice*, UK Border Agency, 21 August 2008, p 10.

[64] Ibid.

[65] Ibid.

[66] *Consultation: Immigration Appeals Fair Decisions; Faster Justice*, UK Border Agency, 21 August 2008, p 1.

[67] See responses to *Immigration Appeals Fair Decisions; Faster Justice* by the Master of the Rolls and the President of the Queen's Bench Division <http://www.ukba.homeoffice.gov.uk>.

overall dispensing of justice and poor distribution of court resources on account of the deployment of High Court and Court of Appeal judges in non-complex issues were key matters Lord Phillips identified as arising from a high caseload and the structure of the immigration appellate system.[68]

(b) *The Desire to Enforce Immigration Control*

It would be wrong however to view the measures exclusively in terms of judicial concerns. A constant theme of Government policy from 1997 onwards has been the desire to speed up the determination of asylum and immigration cases, given their link, in the opinion of the Government, with efficient enforcement of immigration control.[69] To this extent these proposals simply represent continuity with previous policy. As Phil Woolas MP, Minister of State, Home Office, explained during the Committee Stage of the Bill in the House of Commons: 8.38

> What we are trying to achieve is a more efficient system that can speed up decisions, because it is the speed of decision in the immigration system that has caused such difficulty.[70]

More cynical observers might, as part of this, also be inclined to view the measures as an attempt to inhibit the constitutional role of the higher judiciary given their tendency at least in some of the more contentious areas such as asylum, to facilitate the 'creative expansion of 'pegs' at common law upon which cases may be hung'.[71] 8.39

(c) *Centripetal Forces Working to Create a Single Tribunal Service*

Lord Justice Carnwath, Senior President of Tribunals, described tribunals, in distinction to courts, as possessing the main distinguishing features of the specialized expertise of their members (such as doctors or accountants) and the flexibility of their procedures to resolve the needs of the particular client group.[72] The establishment of an independent tribunal service, together with the creation of a two-tier tribunal structure, with the Upper Tribunal exercising powers of judicial review in relation to the other areas now covered by the tribunal service, signals a development in the role of tribunals, an increase in their status, and an extension of their functional competence. Under the TCEA 2007, tribunal judges have been endowed with a standing to match that of their court-based brethren.[73] In complement to this, the Upper Tribunal is now a superior court of record[74] (although such status alone does 8.40

---

[68] The Lord Chief Justice's Review of the Administration of Justice in the Courts, HC 448, March 2008, paras 5.69–5.72, 5.75 and paras 5.101–5.103.

[69] Fairer, Faster and Firmer—A Modern Approach to Immigration and Asylum (Cm 4018, 1998) para 7.14, Secure Borders, Safe Haven Integration and Diversity in Modern Britain (Cm 5387, 2002) para 4.66, Fair, effective, transparent and trusted, Rebuilding confidence in our immigration system, Home Office, July 2006, p 12, Controlling our borders: making migration work for Britain (Cm 6472, 2005) para 26, p17.

[70] PBC 16 June 2009 c183.

[71] R Rawlings, 'Review, Revenge and Retreat' (2005) 68(3) MLR 380 at 390–1.

[72] Sir Robert Carnwath, 'Tribunal Justice—a New Start' Public Law [2009] PL 48–69 at 48.

[73] TCEA 2007, s 1.

[74] Ibid, s 3(5).

not foreclose the possibility of it being subject to judicial review in the High Court). To this extent, the lifting of the statutory bar on the transfer of certain immigration judicial review applications represents not only a response to the difficulties discussed above but is also a reflection of the growth in the role of tribunals in the legal system.

4. Criticisms during the Passage of the Bill and the Consultation Process

8.41 There were several key criticisms of the original clause providing for the transfer of immigration and nationality applications for judicial review to the Upper Tribunal, made both during the initial consultation process,[75] and during the passage of the Bill. A principal objection of the Administrative Law Bar Association (ALBA) was that the constitutional role of the High Court was being neutered.[76] There was no general view that the proposals amounted to an ouster clause, to exclude (as opposed to empowering the judiciary to transfer proceedings to the Upper Tribunal) the role of the higher courts, as had been attempted in the Asylum and Immigration (Treatment of Claimants, etc.) Bill.[77] However, there was criticism that the practical effect would be to block or oust access *to a High Court judge* independent of the process, where the UK Border Agency *or the tribunal itself* had acted unlawfully.[78]

8.42 The Joint Committee on Human Rights was concerned to ensure that complex judicial review cases and those concerning human rights were decided in the Upper Tribunal by judges of the standing of a High Court Judge:

> 1.28 We accept that there may be good reason why many immigration judicial reviews that are currently heard by the High Court, and which do not raise issues of any great difficulty or complexity, should be transferred to the Upper Tribunal. We remain concerned, however, that immigration and asylum cases which raise complex issues of fact and law, or in which human rights such as life, liberty or freedom from torture are at stake, should continue to be decided by judges of the standing of a High Court Judge. The Bill's transfer of immigration and nationality cases to the Upper Tribunal does not guarantee this: a High Court judge *may* sit on the Upper Tribunal, but this is not guaranteed.[79]

8.43 Their recommendation was for a sifting mechanism, ensuring that more significant and complex cases either remain in the High Court or are heard by a High Court judge in the Upper Tribunal.[80] The Home Affairs Committee took a similar view.[81]

---

[75] *Consultation: Immigration Appeals Fair Decisions; Faster Justice*, UK Border Agency, 21 August 2008.

[76] *Response to Immigration Appeals Fair Decisions; Faster Justice*, Administrative Law Bar Association.

[77] 2003–04.

[78] *Response to Immigration Appeals Fair Decisions; Faster Justice*, ILPA and JCWI.

[79] JCHR Legislative Scrutiny: Borders, Citizenship and Immigration Bill, 9th Report (2008–09) HL Paper 62 HC 375.

[80] Ibid, at para 1.29.

[81] Home Affairs Committee: Borders, Citizenship and Immigration Bill, 5th Report (2008–09), HC 425 p 23 para 78.

In respect of the role of High Court judges in the Upper Tribunal on applications for judicial review, the Designated Judges of the Asylum and Immigration Tribunal noted the continuing role of judicial review as a reality of public administration for the Home Office: 8.44

> 8.1 . . . It perhaps does not matter whether judicial review applications are heard by the High Court or by High Court judges sitting in the Upper Tribunal; but the Home Office has simply to accept that judicial review is a reality of public administration which, however inconvenient, it cannot remove. Any judicial system inevitably produces decisions which are amenable to legitimate challenge, and the Upper Tribunal will not be immune from this simply because its judges include High Court judges, whose decisions, when they sit in the High Court, are automatically accepted as potentially subject to appeal.[82]

By according judges of the calibre of High Court judges and Court of Appeal judges a role within it, an immigration and asylum chamber of the Upper Tribunal may develop an improved facility in the application of general principles of public and administrative law to its day-to-day decision-making and judgments. However, notwithstanding the actual and prospective use of limited numbers of judges of the High Court and the Court of Appeal in the Upper Tribunal and the transferral of certain immigration applications for judicial review of executive action or omission to the Upper Tribunal, the independent, constitutional role of the High Court itself is diminished, as ALBA noted. 8.45

Lord Kingsland (Conservative), Opposition Spokesperson for Constitutional and Legal Affairs/Justice, at the Report Stage of the Bill in the House of Lords, argued that the removal of the statutory bar against the transfer of judicial review cases to the Upper Tribunal was premature, and breached the Government's own undertaking made during the passage of the TCEA 2007 (see para **8.34**). There had been no scope to assess how the system was working before enacting further legislation.[83] Lord Thomas of Gresford (Liberal Democrat), at the Committee Stage of the Bill in the House of Lords, argued that there was a risk that this would result in injustice to the litigant, a risk of inadequate handling of judicial reviews leading to an increase in the workload of the Court of Appeal, and reduced supervision of the Home Office.[84] He also argued that the breadth of the clause was too wide given that it extended to nationality issues, which only accounted for some two to three judicial review applications each year, some of which could in any event be brought by private law proceedings for an application for a declaration.[85] 8.46

Others argued that the pressure on the higher courts could not be resolved by these proposals. The Home Affairs Committee cited poor initial decision-making by the Home Office and the significant backlog of decisions in asylum cases as a 8.47

[82] *Response to Immigration Appeals Fair Decisions; Faster Justice*, Designated Judges of the Asylum and Immigration Tribunal.

[83] HL Deb 1 April 2009 vol 709 c1125.

[84] HL Comm 4 March 2009 vol 708 c792.

[85] HL Comm 4 March 2009 vol 708 cc792–3.

key problem.[86] In March 2000, the Bowman Report on judicial review had noted the high level of settlement in immigration cases after permission was granted and had recommended, not that cases be transferred out of the judicial review process of the High Court, but that the Home Office should be encouraged to examine the strength of their case at the earliest opportunity with a view to settlement where appropriate.[87]

8.48 Lord Kingsland (Conservative), Opposition Spokesperson for Constitutional and Legal Affairs/Justice, at the Committee Stage of the Bill in the House of Lords, stated that there was a need to assess properly the factors underlying the expansion of judicial review and that these measures would simply redistribute existing problems to the Upper Tribunal.[88]

8.49 During the consultation on the removal of the statutory bar to transfer of immigration applications for judicial review,[89] further factors were identified by respondents as causes of delay and of the volume of cases. Poor quality initial decisions, the faults of the current appeals structure, the withdrawal of appeal rights leading to the growth of judicial review, the emphasis on speed as opposed to quality, the Home Office failure to comply with case management directions, and the lack of adequate provision for legal representation,[90] were all identified as key factors which would need to be addressed before an appropriate solution could be found.[91]

8.50 Separate concerns were raised in relation to Scotland, where there was real concern at the lack of consultation with Scottish bodies and the failure to await the review by Lord Gill, Lord Justice Clerk, of the civil courts in Scotland. It was argued that removal of the jurisdiction of the Court of Session, a national supreme court, to a non-national body would infringe the Concordat between the DCA (the former Department for Constitutional Affairs) and the Scottish Government.[92]

---

[86] Home Affairs Committee: Borders, Citizenship and Immigration Bill 5th Report (2008–09) HC 425 para 77, p 23.

[87] Sir Jeffrey Bowman, Review of the Crown Office list: a report to the Lord Chancellor, March 2000, Dep 00/681 cited in House of Commons Library Research Paper 09/47, Borders Immigration and Citizenship Bill, Bill 86 of 2008–09, p 78.

[88] HL Comm 4 March 2009 vol 708 c794.

[89] *Consultation: Immigration Appeals Fair Decisions; Faster Justice*, UK Border Agency (21 August 2008).

[90] House of Commons Library Research Paper 09/47, Borders Immigration and Citizenship Bill, Bill 86 of 2008–09, p 77.

[91] See generally responses to *Immigration Appeals, Fair Decisions; Faster Justice* available at <http://www.bia.homeoffice.gov.uk>.

[92] *Response to Immigration Appeals Fair Decisions; Faster Justice*, Jonathan Mitchell QC, para 7–10. See also Scottish Refugee Council, *Briefing on the Borders, Citizenship and Immigration Bill*, February 2009, para 2.

D. THE TRANSFER OF CERTAIN APPLICATIONS FOR JUDICIAL REVIEW

1. Introduction

BCIA 2009, s 53, represents the Government's compromise in relation to concerns articulated by both Houses of Parliament during the passage of the Bill. It is similar, though less generous to applicants, to an earlier amendment made to the Bill during its passage in the House of Lords.[93] It operates by leaving intact the general statutory bar found in Condition 4 (see para **8.29** above), on the transfer of immigration and nationality judicial review applications, or applications for permission (or leave) to apply for judicial review as the case may be, to the Upper Tribunal in England and Wales, Northern Ireland, and Scotland. Instead, it provides for a more limited power of transfer, only in relation to those judicial review applications calling into question decisions on whether or not to treat *further* submissions as an asylum claim or a human rights claim. 8.51

2. The Transfer of Certain Immigration Applications for Judicial Review in England and Wales

The provision made for the transfer of certain judicial review applications to the Upper Tribunal is found in BCIA 2009, s 53(1). This provision amends Senior Courts Act 1981, 31A, by inserting new provisions. It is to be commenced by order (see **para 8.03** above), after the functions of the Asylum and Immigration Tribunal have been transferred to the two-tier tribunal system. In practice a direction identifying the specified class of immigration applications for judicial review that are to be transferred will need to be made by the Lord Chief Justice (see Condition 3 at paras **8.18** and **8.29** above), to render the operation of the provisions effective.[94] 8.52

As set out above (see para **8.28**), Senior Courts Act 1981, s 31A,[95] sets out the circumstances where the High Court must transfer, and where it may transfer, to the Upper Tribunal an application for permission to apply for judicial review, or an application for judicial review, by reference to four conditions (see para **8.29** above).[96] BCIA 2009, s 53(1), inserts two new paragraphs into Senior Courts Act 1981, s 31A. The first paragraph inserted, Senior Courts Act 1981, s 31A(2A), provides that: 8.53

> If Conditions 1, 2, 3 and 5 are met, but Condition 4 is not, the High Court *must* by order transfer the application to the Upper Tribunal.[97]

[93] HL Bill 86, clause 55(2).
[94] Senior Courts Act 1981, s 31A(6), as inserted by TCEA 2007, s 19(1); TCEA 2007, s 18(6).
[95] As inserted by TCEA, s 19(1).
[96] Senior Courts Act 1981, s 31A(1)–(7), as inserted by TCEA 2007, s 19(1).
[97] Ibid, s 31A(2A), as inserted by BCIA 2009, s 53(1)(a).

8.54 The second paragraph inserted, Senior Courts Act 1981, s 31A(8), provides that (see para **8.64** below):

> Condition 5 is that the application calls into question a decision of the Secretary of State not to treat submissions as an asylum claim or a human rights claim within the meaning of Part 5 of the Nationality, Immigration and Asylum Act 2002 wholly or partly on the basis that they are not significantly different from material that has previously been considered (whether or not it calls into question any other decision).[98]

8.55 Senior Courts Act 1981, s 31A(8), adds a new Condition 5 to the existing list of four conditions (see para **8.29** above) and Senior Courts Act 1981, s 31(2A), sets out the necessary combination of conditions that will need to be fulfilled. Upon satisfaction of those conditions, the transfer from the High Court to the Upper Tribunal of an application for judicial review or for permission to apply for judicial review is mandatory.

8.56 The effect of the above will be that whilst the general statutory bar on the transfer of immigration and nationality cases found in Condition 4 (see para **8.29** above) will remain in place, the High Court will in future be *required* to transfer any application for judicial review if Conditions 1, 2, 3 (see para **8.29** above), and Condition 5 (see para **8.54** above) are met although Condition 4 is not. Although transfer to the Tribunal will be mandatory as far as the High Court is concerned, this will be subject to satisfaction of Condition 3, through the designation of the class of certain claims (falling within Condition 5) in a Direction by the Lord Chief Justice (see paras **8.18** and **8.29** above. Thus there is a necessary role for a member of the judiciary in deciding to allocate claims to the Upper Tribunal.

3. The Transfer of Certain Immigration Applications for Judicial Review in Northern Ireland

8.57 The provision made for the transfer of certain judicial review applications to the Upper Tribunal is found in BCIA 2009, s 53(2). This provision amends Judicature (Northern Ireland) Act 1978, s 25A, by inserting new provisions. The provisions apply to the High Court in Northern Ireland and have an identical effect to the provisions outlined above in respect of England and Wales (see paras **8.53–8.56**).

8.58 BCIA 2009, s 53(2), is to be commenced by order (see para **8.03** above), after the functions of the Asylum and Immigration Tribunal have been transferred to the two-tier tribunal system. In practice a direction identifying the specified class of immigration applications for judicial review (see paras **8.18** and **8.29** above) that are to be transferred will need to be made by the Lord Chief Justice—see Condition 3 at para **8.29** above—to render the operation of the provisions effective.[99]

---

98 Ibid, s 31A(8), as inserted by BCIA 2009, s 53(1)(b).

99 Judicature (Northern Ireland) Act 1978, s 25A(6) as inserted by TCEA 2007, s 19(2); TCEA 2007, s 18(6).

As noted above (see para **8.31**), Judicature (Northern Ireland) Act 1978, s 25A,[100] sets out the circumstances where the High Court must transfer, and where it may transfer, to the Upper Tribunal an application for leave to apply for judicial review, or an application for judicial review, by reference to four conditions (see para **8.29** above).[101] The amendments made by BCIA 2009, s 53(2), add a Condition 5 in the same terms as that added for England and Wales (see para **8.54** above), and an additional requirement for a mandatory transfer to the Upper Tribunal upon satisfaction of a new combination of conditions, the latter being the same as that added for England and Wales (see para **8.53** above).[102] The effect will be the same as that for England and Wales (see paras **8.55–8.56** above). 8.59

4. The Transfer of Certain Immigration Applications for Judicial Review in Scotland

The provision made for the transfer of certain judicial review applications to the Upper Tribunal is found in BCIA 2009, s 53(3). This provision amends TCEA 2007, s 20, by inserting new provisions.[103] The provisions apply to the Court of Session and have an essentially similar effect to the provisions outlined above in respect of England and Wales (see paras **8.53–8.56**). 8.60

BCIA 2009, s 53(3), is to be commenced by order (see para **8.03** above), after the functions of the Asylum and Immigration Tribunal have been transferred to the two-tier tribunal system. In practice an act of sederunt, made with the consent of the Lord Chancellor, identifying the specified class of immigration applications for judicial review that are to be transferred, will need to be made (see Condition 2 at para **8.33** above) to render the operation of the provisions effective.[104] 8.61

As noted above (see para **8.32**), TCEA 2007, s 20, sets out the circumstances where the Court of Session must transfer, and where it may transfer, to the Upper Tribunal an application to the supervisory jurisdiction of the Court of Session, by reference to four conditions (see para **8.33** above).[105] The amendments made by BCIA 2009, s 53(3), add a Condition 5[106] in the same terms as that added for England and Wales (see para **8.54** above). In addition, there is a further requirement for a mandatory transfer to the Upper Tribunal upon satisfaction of a new combination of conditions so that, if Conditions 1, 2 and 5 are met but Condition 4 is not, the Court of Session must by order transfer the application to the Upper Tribunal.[107] 8.62

[100] As inserted by the TCEA 2007, s 19(2).
[101] Judicature (Northern Ireland) Act 1978, s 25A, as inserted by TCEA 2007, s 19(2).
[102] Ibid, s 25A(2A) and (8), as inserted by BCIA 2009, s 53(2).
[103] TCEA 2007, ss 20(1)(aa) and 20(5A), as inserted by BCIA 2009, s 53(3).
[104] Senior Courts Act 1981, s 31A(6) as inserted by TCEA 2007, s 19(1); TCEA 2007, s 18(6).
[105] TCEA 2007, s 20.
[106] Ibid, s 20(5A), as inserted by BCIA 2009, s 53(3).
[107] Ibid, s 20(1)(aa), as inserted by BCIA 2009, s 53(3).

8.63 The effect of the above will be that whilst the general statutory bar on the transfer of immigration and nationality cases found in Condition 4 (see para **8.29** above) will remain in place, the Court of Session will in future be *required* to transfer any application for judicial review if Conditions 1 and 2 (see para **8.33** above) and Condition 5 (see para **8.54**) are met although Condition 4 is not. Although transfer to the Tribunal will be mandatory as far as the Court of Session is concerned, this will be subject to satisfaction of Condition 2 through the designation of the class of claims falling within Condition 5 in an act of sederunt, made with the consent of the Lord Chancellor (see paras **8.33** and **8.61** above). Thus there is a necessary role for members of the judiciary in deciding to allocate claims to the Upper Tribunal.

5. Condition 5

8.64 For England and Wales, Northern Ireland, and Scotland, Condition 5 is fulfilled where:[108]

(a) the application calls into question a decision of the Secretary of State not to treat submissions as *an asylum claim* or *a human rights claim* within the meaning of Nationality, Immigration and Asylum Act 2002 (NIAA 2002), Part 5;

(b) wholly or partly on the basis that they are not significantly different from material that has previously been considered (whether or not it calls into question any other decision).

8.65 For the purposes of NIAA 2002, Part 5, an asylum claim means:[109]

> . . . a claim made by a person to the Secretary of State at a place designated by the Secretary of State that to remove the person from or require him to leave the United Kingdom would breach the United Kingdom's obligations under the Refugee Convention,[110]

8.66 For the purposes of NIAA 2002, Part 5, a human rights claim means:[111]

> . . . a claim made by a person to the Secretary of State at a place designated by the Secretary of State that to remove the person from or require him to leave the United Kingdom would be unlawful under section 6 of the Human Rights Act 1998 (c 42) (public authority not to act contrary to Convention) as being incompatible with his Convention rights.[112]

---

[108] Senior Courts Act 1981, s 31A(8), as inserted by BCIA 2007, s 53(1)(b); Judicature (Northern Ireland) Act 2007, s 25A(8), as inserted by BCIA 2009, s 53(2)(b); and TCEA 2007, s 20(5A), as inserted by BCIA 2009, s 53(3)(b).

[109] NIAA 2002, s 113(1), as in force (a substituted definition under s 12 of the Immigration, Asylum and Nationality Act 2006 being not yet in force); see further *SS and others (Ankara Agreement—no in-country right of appeal) Turkey* [2006] UKAIT 00074.

[110] Geneva, 28 July 1951; UNTS 2545 (1954) and Protocol Relating to the Status of Refugees of 31 January 1967; UNTS 8791 (1967).

[111] NIAA 2002, s 113(1), as in force (a substituted definition being not yet in force).

[112] Convention for the Protection of Human Rights and Fundamental Freedoms (the Human Rights Convention) Rome, 4 November 1950; TS 71 (1953); Cmd 8969.

For Condition 5 to apply the application must call into question a decision of the Secretary of State not to treat submissions as *an asylum claim* or *a human rights claim*. Commonly, the Secretary of State makes such a decision when *further submissions* are made by an applicant, seeking leave to enter or remain in, or to resist removal or deportation from, the United Kingdom by reference to the Refugee Convention or the Human Rights Convention, *following* exhaustion of an initial claim for asylum and/or human and any onward appeal rights. 8.67

In considering such fresh or further submissions the Secretary of State applies paragraph 353 of the Immigration Rules:[113] This provides that: 8.68

Fresh Claims

353. When a human rights or asylum claim has been refused or withdrawn or treated as withdrawn under paragraph 333C of these Rules and any appeal relating to that claim is no longer pending, the decision maker will consider any further submissions and, if rejected, will then determine whether they amount to a fresh claim. The submissions will amount to a fresh claim if they are significantly different from the material that has previously been considered. The submissions will only be significantly different if the content:

(i) had not already been considered; and
(ii) taken together with the previously considered material, created a realistic prospect of success, notwithstanding its rejection.

This paragraph does not apply to claims made overseas.

Where further submissions are made, the Secretary State first considers them for their merit. It is only *if* they are rejected that he proceeds to consider whether they amount to a fresh claim by applying the test set out in paragraph 353 of the Immigration Rules.[114] 8.69

Where further submissions, albeit rejected on their merits, are determined by the Secretary of State as amounting to a fresh claim, then a further substantive appeal may proceed to the Asylum and Immigration Tribunal (the First-tier Tribunal when the functions of the Asylum and Immigration Tribunal are transferred) under the NIAA 2002, Part 5. 8.70

Where the further submissions are determined by the Secretary of State not to amount to a fresh claim, no further appeal may follow. The only remedy available in such a circumstance, where merited, is an application for judicial review. Indeed it is against such determinations that many applications for judicial review are made.[115] These are the so-called fresh claim applications for judicial review that are the subject of concern in Condition 5. 8.71

[113] HC 395 of 1993–94 as amended.

[114] See Asylum Policy Instructions 'Further Submissions'.

[115] See *ZT (Kosovo) v Secretary of State* [2009] UKHL 6 and *WM (Democratic Republic of Congo) v Secretary of State* [2006] EWCA Civ 1495; [2007] Imm AR 337.

E. APPLICATIONS FOR PERMISSION TO APPEAL TO THE COURT OF APPEAL

1. Introduction

8.72 In respect of applications for judicial review generally, the transfer of applications into the Upper Tribunal or the commencement of such applications there, does not presage an alteration thereafter to the test for securing permission to appeal to the Court of Appeal against decisions of the Upper Tribunal on applications for judicial review. In England and Wales, the test will remain that found in the Civil Procedure Rules (CPR), r 52.3(6), that permission to appeal may be given only where the court considers that the appeal would have a real prospect of success or there is some other compelling reason why the appeal should be heard. The test remains unaltered as an application for judicial review decided by the Upper Tribunal does not fall within the class of cases in respect of which the higher appeal threshold permitted under TCEA 2007, s 13(6), for giving permission to appeal (the second appeal test) may be applied (see para **8.12** above and para **8.75** below). This is so because applications for judicial review do not fall within TCEA 2007, s 13(7).[116]

8.73 However, the transfer of asylum and immigration functions to the two-tier tribunal structure heralds changes in England and Wales and in Northern Ireland to the test for giving permission to appeal to the Court of Appeal in immigration and asylum cases, where there have been two appeals, one to the Lower Tribunal and a second thereafter to the Upper Tribunal.

2. Requirements for Permission to Appeal to the Court of Appeal from the Asylum and Immigration Tribunal

8.74 In England and Wales on an application under the current law for permission to appeal to the Court of Appeal, on a point of law from a determination of the Asylum and Immigration Tribunal,[117] permission will be given only where the court considers that the appeal would have a real prospect of success or there is some other compelling reason why the appeal should be heard.[118]

3. Requirements for Permission to Appeal to the Court of Appeal from the Upper Tribunal

8.75 Upon the transfer of the functions of the Asylum and Immigration Tribunal into the two-tier tribunal structure, established under the TCEA 2007, a higher, second

[116] See Further Opinion of Sir Richard Buxton, 8 June 2009, and HC Deb 14 July 2009 vol 496 c 217, per Phil Woolas MP, Minister of State, Home Office.

[117] NIAA 2002, ss 103B, 103E.

[118] See CPR, r 52.3(6).

appeal test (see paras **8.12** and **8.72** above) will apply for the purpose of securing permission to appeal to the Court of Appeal from decisions of the Upper Tribunal in England and Wales and Northern Ireland in immigration and asylum appeals. The second appeal test applies to decisions made by the Upper Tribunal provided that they have first travelled through the First-tier Tribunal.[119] Permission to appeal to the Court of Appeal in England and Wales or leave to appeal to the Court of Appeal in Northern Ireland will not be granted unless the Upper Tribunal or, where the Upper Tribunal refuses permission, the relevant appellate court, considers that the proposed appeal would raise some important point of principle or practice or there is some other compelling reason for the relevant appellate court to hear the appeal.[120]

(a) *The 'Important Point of Principle or Practice' Requirement*

The 'important point of principle or practice' test adopts the language of Access to Justice Act 1999, s 55(1), and CPR r 52.13, which limits second appeals from decisions of county court or High Court judges that were themselves made on appeal. The test was explained by the then Vice-President of the Court of Appeal, Brooke LJ, in *Tanfern Ltd v Cameron-MacDonald*: 8.76

> This reform introduces a major change to our appeal procedures. It will no longer be possible to pursue a second appeal to the Court of Appeal merely because the appeal is 'properly arguable' or 'because it has a real prospect of success' . . . The new statutory provision is even tougher—the relevant point of principle or practice must be an important one—and it has effect even if the would-be appellant won in the lower court before losing in the appeal court. The decision of the first appeal court is now to be given primacy unless the Court of Appeal itself considers that the appeal would raise an important point of principle or practice, or that there is some other compelling reason for it to hear this second appeal.[121]

In *Uphill v BRB(Residuary) Ltd*[122] Dyson LJ stated that if the principle is clear in law, but the lower court has applied it wrongly, no appeal will lie, even though the principle that has not been applied correctly was an important one, as an important point of principle or practice arises only in relation to a point that is not yet established. However, there was perhaps a glimmer of light in *Cramp v Hastings Borough Council*[123] where Brooke LJ, Vice-President of the Court of Appeal, Civil Division, recalled that the guidance of Dyson LJ in *Uphill* was not meant to be exhaustive, although it contained helpful guidance in the majority of cases and that the Court of Appeal has a degree of flexibility in relation to second appeals. In that case he concluded that it would: 8.77

---

119 TCEA 2007, ss 11(1), 13(6), (7).

120 Ibid, s 13(6) and the Appeals from the Upper Tribunal to the Court of Appeal Order 2008, SI 2008/2834.

121 [2000] EWCA Civ 3023; [2001] 1 WLR 1311 [42].

122 [2005] EWCA Civ 60; [2005] 3 All ER 264 [18].

123 [2005] EWCA Civ 1005; [2005] 4 All ER 1014; [2005] HLR 48 [65]–[66].

. . . be quite wrong for the court to feel that the judgment in *Uphill* represented a fetter on its power to put things right if it has occasion to believe that things are going wrong in an important way in the practical operation of the statutory scheme in Part VII of the [Housing Act 1996]. . .

8.78 The effect of the application of the second appeal test was considered by a former Lord Justice of Appeal, Sir Richard Buxton, in his legal opinion of 8 June 2009 for the Joint Council for the Welfare of Immigrants (JCWI). In his opinion he noted that (under the second appeal test) in an immigration appeal on points of law, where the United Kingdom's international obligations are engaged (eg under the Refugee Convention, the Human Rights Convention, or the Treaty on European Union), where *there is a real prospect of success*—that is that there is a real prospect of showing that the decision of the Upper Tribunal, if implemented, will place the UK in breach of its international obligations—an individual will be denied any relief from the Court of Appeal *unless the second appeal test is also satisfied*. He stated that it must be obvious that this cannot be right. Further, a liberal interpretation by the Court of Appeal of the alternative 'some other compelling reason' limb of the second appeal test (to alleviate the problem) would, he argued, seem unlikely, as this would appear at odds with Parliament's intentions behind the provision of a second appeal test.

8.79 The Joint Committee on Human Rights expressed its concerns about the potential implications arising from the application of the second appeal test and sought to inhibit the application of it, stating:

1.32 We agree with the opinion of Sir Richard Buxton that in a case where there is a real prospect that the decision of the Upper Tribunal is in breach of the UK's international human rights obligations, that issue demands the attention of a court of the stature of the Court of Appeal. We recommend a simple amendment to the Bill to ensure that the Lord Chancellor's power to impose the restrictive 'second appeal' test on appeals to the Court of Appeal is not available in immigration and nationality cases . . .[124]

8.80 Those concerns were reflected during the passage of the Bill in the House of Lords through an amendment to the Bill being made, preventing the more restrictive second appeal test from applying.[125] That protective amendment was reversed during proceedings in the House of Commons[126] and does not appear in the BCIA 2009. During the Report Stage of the Bill in the House of Lords, Lord West of Spithead, Parliamentary Under-Secretary of State, Home Office, argued that such protection was both unnecessary and unhelpful from the point of view of allocation of higher court resources but confirmed:

. . . I accept that there may be some cases which raise the real prospect the decision of the Upper Tribunal is in breach of the UK's human rights obligations, but these are precisely the sort of cases that would meet the test . . .[127]

---

[124] JCHR Legislative Scrutiny: Borders, Citizenship and Immigration Bill, 9th Report (2008–09) HL Paper 62 HC 375 para 1.32.

[125] Borders, Citizenship and Immigration Bill [HL] Bill 86, clause 55(4).

[126] PBC 16 June 2009 c190.

[127] HL Deb 1 April 2009 vol 709 c1130.

This was repeated by Phil Woolas MP, Minister of State, Home Office, during the Committee Stage and the Report Stage of the Bill in the House of Commons,[128] although there was no further elaboration as to how, precisely, the Government anticipates the second appeal test being met in light of the issues identified by Sir Richard Buxton. In a letter of 31 July 2009 to Paul Rowen MP (Liberal Democrat), Phil Woolas MP indicated the Government's view that cases involving international obligations would be very likely to raise important points of principle or practice or provide a sufficient compelling reason for granting permission to appeal. Further, he did not consider that an application for permission to appeal, where the appellant had won at first instance but lost in the Upper Tribunal, would be refused permission to appeal to the Court of Appeal where there was a real prospect of success and the issues concerned the appellant's human rights. 8.81

The interpretation of the new requirements imposed by the second appeal test, and in particular the extent to which breaches of international obligations arising under the Refugee Convention, the Human Rights Convention, or the EC Treaty found 'some other compelling reason' for the purpose of securing permission to appeal under the second limb of the second appeal test, will be a matter for the courts to resolve. 8.82

In the context of immigration and asylum appeals from the Upper Tribunal, if the approach to tribunals advanced in cases like *Cooke v Secretary of State for Social Security*[129] (per Hale LJ as she then was) and *Secretary of State for the Home Department v AH (Sudan)*[130] (per Baroness Hale) is followed, where (even without the second appeal test to contend with) Baroness Hale in considering the issues surrounding whether to grant permission to appeal displayed a degree of caution on account of the great expertise of tribunals in relation to specialized areas of law and their independent two-tier appellate structure, the Court of Appeal will be adopting a distinctly non-interventionist approach to decisions of the Upper Tribunal. 8.83

Indeed, in respect of appeals to the Court of Appeal, the Senior President of Tribunals set out his expectation of how the scheme might operate noting: 8.84

> . . . If the Upper Tribunal is doing its job properly, its decisions should come to be regarded as sufficiently expert and authoritative for onward appeals to be rare, particularly given the hands-off approach advocated in recent House of Lords decisions . . .
>
> . . . There is scope for rethinking the traditional allocation, as between courts and tribunals, of responsibilities for definitive interpretation of substantive law, including human rights law, in specialist fields.[131]

[128] PBC 16 June 2009 c182, HC Deb 14 July 2009 vol 496 c210.

[129] [2001] EWCA Civ 734, [15]–[18] per Hale LJ (as she then was). This was cited with approval in Hooper [2007] EWCA Civ at 495; see also *Hooper v Secretary of State for Work and Pensions* [2007] EWCA Civ 495 at [40]–[41].

[130] *AH (Sudan) v Secretary of State for the Home Department* [2007] UKHL 49; [2008] 1 AC 678 at [30], per Baroness Hale.

[131] R Carnwath, 'Tribunal Justice—a New Start' *Public Law* [2009] PL 48–69, at 68–69.

9

CHILDREN AND TRAFFICKING

A. INTRODUCTION

9.01 The Borders, Citizenship and Immigration Act 2009 (BCIA 2009), s 54, modifies and expands the definition of exploitation in the offences of trafficking people for exploitation in Asylum and Immigration (Treatment of Claimants, etc.) Act 2004 (AITCA 2004), s 4. The effect is to plug a lacuna in the provision made, with a view to ensuring that trafficking, involving victims who play an entirely passive role in situations where they are used, or attempts are made to use them, for the purpose of obtaining services or benefits of any kind, are protected.

9.02 In addition, BCIA 2009, s 55, imposes statutory duties on the Secretary of State and the Director of Border Revenue, to make arrangements ensuring that specified functions are discharged with regard to the need to safeguard and promote the welfare of children who are in the UK. A further duty is imposed upon a person exercising one of those specified functions, in so exercising the function, to have regard to guidance given by the Secretary of State for the purpose of the performance of the duty.

B. TRAFFICKING

1. Introduction

9.03 Trafficking is viewed as a source of concern internationally, regionally within Europe, and in the United Kingdom. The UK is considered a receiving and transit state for trafficking purposes[1] and was ranked internationally as having a 'high' incidence of trafficking.[2]

[1] HL Deb 11 February 2009 vol 707, c1175, per Baroness Butler-Sloss.

[2] Trafficking in Persons: Global Patterns, United Nations Office on Drugs and Crime, April 2006, p 20.

Recently, there have been a series of measures adopted at international, regional, and national levels with a view to combating trafficking. The UK has sought to address the issue through victim-centred approaches as exemplified by its ratification of the Council of Europe Convention Against Trafficking in Human Beings[3] on 17 December 2008 (and the measures taken to give effect to it), the Government's Action Plan on Tackling Human Trafficking, the UK Human Trafficking Centre, and through criminalization of conduct. A source of difficulty with approaches at all levels has lain with the definition of the term 'trafficking'. 9.04

2. Existing Framework for the Offences of Trafficking People for Exploitation

The AITCA 2004, s 4, provides for the criminalization of trafficking through the creation of three United Kingdom-wide criminal offences of trafficking people for exploitation. 9.05

Firstly, by AITCA 2004, s 4(1), it is an offence for a person to arrange or facilitate the arrival in, or the entry into, the United Kingdom of an individual ('the passenger') where he intends to exploit the passenger in the United Kingdom or elsewhere, or he believes that another person is likely to do so. 9.06

Secondly, by AITCA 2004, s 4(2), it is an offence if a person arranges or facilitates travel within the UK by an individual ('the passenger') in respect of whom he believes an offence under s 4(1) (see para **9.06**) may have been committed where he intends to exploit the passenger in the UK or elsewhere, or he believes that another person is likely to do so. 9.07

Thirdly, by AITCA 2004, s 4(3), it is an offence for a person to arrange or facilitate the departure from the United Kingdom of an individual ('the passenger') where he intends to exploit the individual outside the UK, or believes that another person is likely to do so. 9.08

AITCA 2009, s 4(4)(a)–(d), sets out the circumstances in which an individual is exploited for the purpose of these offences. Prior to amendment, a person is exploited if and only if: 9.09

(a) he is the victim of behaviour that contravenes Article 4 (slavery and forced labour) of the Convention for the Protection of Human Rights and Fundamental Freedoms (the Human Rights Convention);[4]
(b) he is encouraged, required or expected to do anything as a result of which he or another person would commit an offence under the Human Organ Transplants Act 1989 (repealed with savings), the Human Tissue (Scotland) Act 2006, Part 1 or the Human Tissue Act 2004, ss 32 or 33;
(c) he is subjected to force, threats or deception designed to induce him:
 (i) to provide services of any kind,
 (ii) to provide another person with benefits of any kind, or
 (iii) to enable another person to acquire benefits of any kind; or

[3] Warsaw, 16 May 2005; CETA 197 (2008).
[4] Rome, 4 November 1950; TS 71 (1953); Cmd 8969.

(d) he is requested or induced to undertake any activity, having been chosen as the subject of the request or inducement on the grounds that:
   (i) he is mentally or physically ill or disabled, he is young or he has a family relationship with a person, and
   (ii) a person without the illness, disability, youth or family relationship would be likely to refuse the request or resist the inducement.

9.10 By AITCA 2004, s 4(5), a person guilty of an offence under s 4 is liable on conviction on indictment, to imprisonment for a term not exceeding 14 years, to a fine, or to both; or on summary conviction, to imprisonment for a term not exceeding 12 months, to a fine not exceeding the statutory maximum, or to both.

3. The Substituted Definition of Exploitation in AITCA 2009, s 4(4)(d)

9.11 BCIA 2009, s 54, is not yet in force. It comes into force on such day as the Secretary of State may by order appoint.[5] By BCIA 2009, s 57(4)(b), it extends to England and Wales and Northern Ireland only. It is inapplicable in Scotland where the existing definition will continue to apply, unless and until amended.

9.12 The amendment made by BCIA 2009, s 54, to AITCA 2009, s 4(4)(d), seeks to plug a lacuna in the offence of trafficking people for exploitation generated by the above definition of 'exploitation' (see para **9.09**). Specifically the requirement in s 4(4)(d) for an individual to have been *requested or induced* to *undertake an activity* has, as a recent criminal case exemplifies,[6] proved inadequate in capturing the position of victims of trafficking who are entirely passive, for example, very young children and babies who cannot, as such, be requested or induced to do anything.[7]

9.13 BCIA 2009, s 54, amends the definition in AITCA 2004, s 4(4)(d), to rectify this difficulty. It achieves this by substituting a new provision that omits altogether the requirement for a request or inducement to undertake an activity.

9.14 Following substitution, a person is exploited under AITCA 2004, s 4(4)(d), in circumstances where a person uses or attempts to use him for any purpose listed in s 4(4)(c)(i)–(iii) (see para **9.09**), having chosen him for that purpose on the ground that:

(i) he is mentally or physically ill or disabled, he is young or he has a family relationship with a person; and
(ii) a person without the illness, disability, youth or family relationship would be likely to refuse to be used for that purpose.

---

[5] BCIA 2009, s 58(4)(b).

[6] See 'Woman Smuggled Baby into the UK to qualify for housing priority', *Guardian*, 12 April 2008 for the case of Peace Sandberg.

[7] HL Deb 1 April 2009 vol 709 c1138, per Lord West of Spithead, Parliamentary Under-Secretary of State, Home Office. See also Protocol to Prevent, Suppress and Punish Trafficking in Persons, Especially Women and Children, supplementing the United Nations Convention against Transnational Organised Crime (Palermo Protocol) (New York, 15 November 2000, (25 December 2003, No 39574)), art 3.

C. DUTY REGARDING THE WELFARE OF CHILDREN

1. Introduction

BCIA 2009, s 55, represents the response of the Government to widespread criticism of the omission of immigration and nationality functions from the duty, introduced by Children Act 2004, s 11, on public authorities to make arrangements for ensuring that their functions are discharged having regard to the need to safeguard and promote the welfare of children. 9.15

However, BCIA 2009, s 55, should also be viewed as part of the wider move on the part of the Government towards bringing child welfare concerns into the mainstream of social policy,[8] a move which has hitherto only been extended to immigration law and policy to a limited degree (see para **9.17** below).[9] As part of this, after some considerable criticism from various human rights organizations, the United Kingdom has removed its immigration and nationality reservation[10] (September 2008) in relation to the Convention on the Rights of the Child.[11] 9.16

2. The Existing Framework

UK Borders Act 2007, s 21(1), introduced an obligation on the Secretary of State to issue a code of practice designed to ensure that in exercising its functions, the Border and Immigration Agency (now the UK Border Agency) took appropriate steps to ensure that while children are in the UK they are *safe from harm*. The *Code of Practice for Keeping Children in the Immigration System Safe from Harm* was issued pursuant to this obligation.[12] By UK Borders Act 2007, s 21(2), as enacted, the Border and Immigration Agency (which was absorbed into the UK Border Agency in April 2008, see para **1.16**) was obliged to: 9.17

(a) have regard to the code in the exercise of its functions; and
(b) take appropriate steps to ensure that persons with whom it makes arrangements for the provision of services have regard to the code.

The provisions of UK Borders Act 2007, s 21, have been modified by BCIA 2009, s 34 (see paras **4.24–4.26**), so the obligation no longer falls on the UK Border Agency but rather now falls on designated customs officials and officials of the 9.18

[8] See for example the whole of the Children Act 2004; see also *Every Child Matters*, Cm 5860 (2003).

[9] See UK Borders Act 2007, s 21, and the UK Border Agency, *Code of Practice for Keeping Children Safe From Harm*, December 2008, issued under UK Borders Act 2007, s 21.

[10] Convention on the Rights of the Child (New York, 20 November 1989; 1577 UNTS 3 (1989)); United Kingdom of Great Britain and Northern Ireland: Partial Withdrawal of Reservations, 4 December 2008.

[11] New York, 20 November 1989; 1577 UNTS 3 (1989).

[12] UK Borders Act 2007 (Code of Practice on Children) Order 2008, SI 2008/3158.

Secretary of State exercising customs functions; immigration officers and officials of the Secretary of State exercising functions relating to immigration, asylum, or nationality; the Secretary of State in so far as the Secretary of State has general customs functions and functions relating to immigration, nationality, or asylum; and the Director of Border Revenue and any person exercising functions of the Director.

3. An Overview of the Proposed Framework

9.19 BCIA 2009, s 55, is not in force. It comes into force on such day as the Secretary of State may by order appoint.[13] A reference in another enactment to the Immigration Acts includes a reference to BCIA 2009, s 55.[14]

9.20 BCIA 2009, s 55, extends to England and Wales, Scotland, and Northern Ireland.[15]

9.21 Once BCIA 2009, s 55, is in force, the UK Borders Act 2007, s 21, (and the code issued pursuant to it) ceases to have effect.[16]

9.22 Whilst BCIA 2009, s 55, does not introduce any new functions that replace existing functions,[17] it does introduce a new and more demanding obligation on the Secretary of State, in place of that found in UK Borders Act 2007, s 21, (to keep children safe from harm), namely an obligation to make arrangements to ensure that specified functions are discharged having regard to *the need to safeguard and promote the welfare of children* who are in the United Kingdom. In so doing it aligns the duty imposed with that imposed on public authorities under Children Act 2004, s 11(2).

9.23 During the passage of the Children Bill (which became the Children Act 2004), Earl Howe had endeavoured to amend what is now s 11 (duty to safeguard and promote the welfare of children) of that Act to include immigration officials among the agencies listed in s 11. He pressed his amendment to a vote that was lost by only nine votes.[18] During the subsequent passage of the Children and Young Persons Bill (which became the Children and Young Persons Act 2008) the Government indicated that it would introduce a duty on the UK Border Agency, which was equivalent to that in Children Act 2004, s 11.[19] BCIA 2009 gives effect to that undertaking.

---

[13] BCIA 2009, s 58(4)(b).

[14] Ibid, s 55(7); see also the definition of 'the Immigration Acts' in the UK Borders Act 2007, s 61(2).

[15] Ibid, s 57(1).

[16] Ibid, s 55(8).

[17] See *Arrangements to Safeguard and Promote the Welfare of Children for those Exercising UK Border Agency Functions and Director of Border Revenue Functions*, 11 June 2009, p 2.

[18] HL Deb 15 July 2004 vol 663 cc1460–5.

[19] *Home Office and DCSF Signal Duty on the UK Border Agency to Protect Children*, Home Office and Department for Children, Schools and Families press release 24 June 2008; see also House of Commons Library Research Paper 09/47 Borders Citizenship and Immigration Bill [HL], pp 82–8.

The provisions were welcomed by the Joint Committee of Human Rights: 9.24

1.14 During the Bill's Committee stage, the Minister said 'we have no intention of treating children in the immigration system any differently from other children in the UK. Quite the opposite . . . every child matters as much if they are subject to immigration control as if they are British citizens.' This is a most welcome change in policy. Both we and our predecessor Committee have highlighted serious human rights concerns about the treatment of children in the UK subject to immigration control, including, for example, the inappro priate use of detention, the effect on them of heavy handed enforcement methodssuch as dawn raids and forced removals, and the use of inappropriate methods for testing their age. We have consistently identified as one of the root problems the fact that children subject to immigration control are treated less favourably than UK national children because they have been excluded from the protection of the UN Convention on the Rights of the Child by the UK's immigration reservation. The provisions concerning child welfare in this Bill provide the opportunity to begin to address some of those deep-rooted human rights problems experienced by children who are subject to immigration control.[20]

4. The Duty Imposed upon the Secretary of State

By BCIA 2009, s 55(1), the Secretary of State must make arrangements for ensuring that: 9.25

(a) specified *functions* (see para **9.28** below) are discharged having regard to the need to safeguard and promote the welfare of children who are in the United Kingdom; and
(b) any services provided by another person, pursuant to arrangements made by the Secretary of State, which relate to the discharge of the specified *functions* (see para **9.28** below), are provided with regard to the need to safeguard and promote the welfare of children in the United Kingdom.

Although self-evident on the face of the provision, it is worth noting that BCIA 2009, s 55, only extends to those *children* (see para **9.27** below) who are *present* in the UK (see paras **9.34–9.39** below). 9.26

By BCIA 2009, s 55(6), children are defined as persons who are under the age of 18. Those persons lawfully assessed as 18 years old or older will fall outside the scope of the obligation. 9.27

The specified functions of which mention is made in BCIA 2009, s 55(1)(a) and (b) are:[21] 9.28

(a) any function of the Secretary of State in relation to immigration, asylum or nationality;

[20] JCHR 9th Report (2008–09) Legislative Scrutiny: Borders, Citizenship and Immigration Bill, HL Paper 62 HC 375, pp 7–8.
[21] BCIA 2009, s 55(2).

(b) any function conferred by or by virtue of the Immigration Acts[22] on an immigration officer;
(c) any general customs function of the Secretary of State; and
(d) any customs function conferred on a designated customs official.

9.29 By BCIA 2009, s 55(6), 'customs function', 'designated customs official', and 'general customs function' have the meanings given by BCIA 2009, Part 1.

5. The Duty Imposed upon Persons Exercising the Specified Functions

9.30 By BCIA 2009, s 55(3), a person exercising any of the specified functions must, in so exercising them, have regard to any *guidance* given to the person by the Secretary of State for the purpose specified in BCIA 2009, s 55(1).

9.31 In June 2009 the UK Border Agency issued a draft working document[23] on the guidance to accompany this duty. It is apparently modelled on the statutory guidance accompanying Children Act 2004, s 11, together with the existing code of practice on children. However, concerns have already been voiced[24] that that draft guidance does not meet the fulsome assurances given during the passage of the BCIA 2009 (see para **9.40**) that this would be modelled on guidance under s 11 of the Children Act 2004.

6. Issues Arising

(a) *The Functions and Services to which the Duties Imposed Apply*

9.32 The obligation upon the Secretary of State under BCIA 2009, s 55(1), only applies in respect of the specified functions set out in BCIA 2009, ss 55(2). During the Committee Stage of the Bill in the House of Lords, Lord West of Spithead, Parliamentary Under-Secretary of State, Home Office, clarified the nature of the specified functions, stating:

> . . . I remind the Committee that the duty will apply to any function carried out in relation to immigration, asylum nationality and any general customs or border revenue function carried out on behalf of the Secretary of State. This will include the handling of children whose contact with the border force is as passengers who are in transit through the UK and who seek a short stay of 48 hours to accomplish that.
>
> Passengers who are in direct transit and transferring straightaway to a connecting flight do not need to seek entry to the UK and no immigration function is carried out. The duty would not therefore apply in those circumstances, although staff will of course involve the

[22] See UK Borders Act 2007, s 61(2).

[23] Communication from the UK Border Agency to the Immigration Law Practitioners' Association (ILPA), Arrangements to safeguard and promote the welfare of children for those exercising UK Border Agency Functions and Director of Border Revenue Functions, 11 June 2009, version 1.6

[24] See ILPA response to the draft working document (August 2009), available at <http://www.ilpa.org.uk/submissions>.

police if there are reasonable grounds for believing a child in these circumstances may be at risk of harm.[25]

9.33 The Secretary of State is also obliged to make arrangements to ensure that services provided by another person, pursuant to arrangements made by the Secretary of State that relate to the discharge of a specified function, are provided having regard to the need to safeguard and promote the welfare of children who are in the United Kingdom. In this way, independent contractors, detention and escorting services are brought within the scope of the duty.

(b) *The Limitation Requiring the Children to be in the United Kingdom*

9.34 At the Committee Stage of the Bill in the House of Lords, Lord West of Spithead, Parliamentary Under-Secretary of State, Home Office, explained the restriction on the ambit of the duties imposed in relation to children, that is to those children *in* the United Kingdom in the following terms:

> Whether the duty applies is absolutely determined by whether the child is in the UK or overseas . . . it is a matter of where the child is.[26]

9.35 The rationale for this was explained by Lord West of Spithead, Parliamentary Under-Secretary of State, Home Office, in a letter to Baroness Hanham (Conservative):

> . . . UK officials overseas are not in a position where they can require a certain response from the agencies of another country. Nor can they seek to impose the standards needed to fulfil a duty in the UK on another country's agencies. Moreover, in some countries international 'minimum standards' agreements already exist and it would be wrong for UK officials to seek to over-ride or disagree with these in individual cases simply because of the way this duty was perceived in the UK.[27]

9.36 Further, it was noted by Lord West of Spithead, in the debate at the Report Stage of the Bill in the House of Lords that rights under the Convention on the Rights of the Child only inhere to those within a state's jurisdiction,[28] that an extension of the duty would interfere with the territorial sovereignty of other states, that it would give rise to a risk of the creation of a route of entry in cases where conditions in which children are brought up fall below standards customary in the United Kingdom,[29] and that it would be at variance with international agreements in the case of juxtaposed controls given the UK's limited jurisdiction at those locations.[30]

9.37 The effect of the limitation to children in the United Kingdom is that UKBA staff who are exercising immigration functions outside of the UK, for example at sites of

25 HL Deb 4 March 2009 vol 708 c820.

26 HL Deb 4 March 2009 vol 708 c822.

27 Lord West of Spithead, Parliamentary Under-Secretary of State, Home Office, Letter to Baroness Hanham and others, *Borders, Citizenship and Immigration Bill—Committee Day 3 and 4*, DEP 2009-1047.

28 HL Deb 1 April 2009 vol 709 c1146.

29 HL Deb 1 April 2009 vol 709 c1147.

30 HL Deb 1 April 2009 vol 709 c1148.

juxtaposed controls, during escorted removals, at entry clearance offices, or airports or vessels outside of the UK during transfers to other European Union Member States, will not be within the scope of the statutory obligations. However, those exercising functions in relation to children who are physically present in the UK, including those with temporary admission, will be within the scope. In addition, the draft working document, *Arrangements to Safeguard and Promote the Welfare of Children for those Exercising UK Border Agency Functions and Director of Border Revenue Functions*, 11 June 2009, at p 11 confirms that asylum seeking children are also within the scope of the duties.

9.38 At the Report Stage of the Bill in the House of Lords, Lord Avebury (Liberal Democrat) sought, without success, to introduce a clause removing the requirement for children to be in the United Kingdom:

> As the Minister will be aware from our earlier debates, we would like this clause to apply to all UKBA staff whenever or wherever they come into contact with any child. Staff based abroad, who are exercising immigration functions at juxtaposed controls, at entry clearance points and during escorted removals from the UK, should carry out their duties in relation to children with whom they come into contact whether that child is in the UK or not.[31]

9.39 In seeking to assuage the concerns of Opposition peers, Lord West of Spithead, Parliamentary Under-Secretary of State, Home Office, in a letter to Baroness Hanham (Conservative), gave a modest assurance, stating that:

> . . . In the case of UKBA staff dealing with entry clearance applications overseas, I can provide an assurance that they will seek to apply the duty in the country in which they are based but they will do this as a matter of policy not as a statutory requirement.[32]

(c) *The Meaning of 'Welfare of Children' and 'Safeguarding and Promoting the Welfare of Children' in BCIA 2009, s 55(1)*

9.40 During the Report Stage of the Bill in the House of Lords, Lord West of Spithead, Parliamentary Under-Secretary of State, Home Office, clarified the intended meaning of 'welfare of children', stating:

> As noble Lords know, the intention of Clause 53 is to mirror as closely as possible the effect of Section 11 of the Children Act 2004 . . . For that to happen, all agencies involved need to share the same understanding of what we mean by welfare. In fact, DCSF's statutory guidance on Section 11, the guidance on which we intend to draw heavily for Clause 53, already defines the word 'welfare'. It may help if I quote from paragraph 2.7 of that guidance which states:
>
>> In this guidance, welfare is defined . . . in terms of children's health and development, where health means "physical or mental health" and development means "physical, intellectual, emotional, social or behavioural development".

---

[31] HL Deb 1 April 2009 vol 709 c1144.

[32] Lord West of Spithead, Parliamentary Under-Secretary of State, Home Office, Letter to Baroness Hanham and others, *Borders, Citizenship and Immigration Bill—Committee Day 3 and 4*, DEP 2009-1047.

The following paragraph states:

> Safeguarding and promoting the welfare of children,

is defined as,

> protecting children from maltreatment; preventing impairment of children's health or development; ensuring that children are growing up in circumstances consistent with the provision of safe and effective care; and undertaking that role so as to enable those children to have optimum life chances and to enter adulthood successfully.

The existing definition of welfare focuses on those elements which are most crucial to children's well-being . . .[33]

(d) *The Standard of Performance of the Obligation*

The obligation imposed by BCIA 2009, s 55(1) and (2), is merely to make arrangements for ensuring that *the specified functions are discharged*, having regard to the need to safeguard and promote the welfare of children in the United Kingdom. During the Committee Stage of the Bill in the House of Lords, Lord West of Spithead, Parliamentary Under-Secretary of State, Home Office, noted that this was a distinct and separate requirement from the more demanding one, found in Children (Scotland) Act 1995, s 17, made in respect of children *looked after* by local authorities; requiring that the duty to safeguard and promote the welfare of children shall be a paramount concern. The duty imposed on the Secretary of State, in contrast, is to have regard to the need to safeguard and promote the welfare of children when exercising specific functions.[34] 9.41

The Refugee Children's Consortium[35] welcomed the new duty but expressed concern about its confinement to children *within* the United Kingdom and the absence of any statutory requirement to issue guidance on the face of the Act. It also emphasized the need for the guidance to be drawn up jointly between the UK Border Agency and the Department for Schools Children and Families. The Immigration Law Practitioners Association (ILPA) argued that the provisions would be of limited use in the absence of the reform of existing age assessment practices in relation to children whose age is disputed.[36] 9.42

Whilst BCIA 2009, s 55, imposes a more demanding and onerous obligation in relation to the interests of children than that found in UK Borders Act 2007, s 21 and, further, whilst it imposes an equivalent duty on the UK Border Agency for the protection of children subject to immigration control to that which applies to public authorities in respect of children as contained in the analogous provision in Children Act 2004, s 11, it is not clear to what extent s 55 will be successful in effecting 9.43

---

[33] HL Deb 1 April 2009 vol 709 c1143.

[34] HL Deb 4 March 2009 vol 708 c833.

[35] Borders, Citizenship and Immigration Bill House of Lords' Second Reading Briefing, 11 February 2009, Refugee Children's Consortium.

[36] Borders Citizenship and Immigration Bill, House of Lords Committee Part 3, Clause 51 Duty regarding the welfare of children, Immigration Law Practitioners Association.

a cultural change within the UK Border Agency in respect of the treatment of children. The new duty under the BCIA 2009 will, after all, coexist with what some might consider to be other, child unfriendly, policies.

9.44 The impact of the duty under BCIA 2009, s 55, on individual children will depend on the contents of the guidance. A failure to have regard to the guidance or to misapply it in particular circumstances may render the UK Border Agency susceptible to legal challenge.

9.45 The role that the duties under BCIA 2009, s 55, will play in cases concerning the removal of children is also difficult to ascertain given that the United Kingdom's obligations under the Human Rights Convention are already coloured by the more exacting requirement in the CRC, which requires the 'best interests' of the child to be 'a primary consideration' in actions concerning children. However, it is clear that the obligations under BCIA 2009, s 55, will have some role to play in these cases.

7. The Duty Imposed upon the Director of Border Revenue

9.46 By BCIA 2009, s 55(4), a duty, analagous to that found in BCIA 2009, s 55(1), in respect of the Secretary of State, is imposed on the Director of Border Revenue.

9.47 The Director or Border Revenue *must make arrangements* for ensuring that:[37]

(a) the Director's functions[38] are discharged having regard to the need to safeguard and promote the welfare of children who are in the United Kingdom; and

(b) any services provided by another person pursuant to arrangements made by the Director in the discharge of such a function are provided having regard to safeguard and promote the welfare of children who are in the United Kingdom.

8. The Duty Imposed upon Persons Exercising a Function of the Director of Border Revenue

9.48 A person exercising a function of the Director of Border Revenue must, in exercising the function, have regard to any guidance given to the person by the Secretary of State for the purpose of the obligation imposed on the Director of Border Revenue by BCIA 2009, s 55(4); see Chapter 2 for the functions of the Director of Border Revenue

[37] BCIA 2009, s 55(4).

[38] Ibid, ss 6, 7, and, 9.

APPENDIX 1

Borders, Citizenship and Immigration Act 2009

CHAPTER 11

CONTENTS

PART 1
BORDER FUNCTIONS

BORDERS, CITIZENSHIP AND IMMIGRATION ACT 2009

2009 Chapter 11

An Act to provide for customs functions to be exercisable by the Secretary of State, the Director of Border Revenue and officials designated by them; to make provision about the use and disclosure of customs information; to make provision for and in connection with the exercise of customs functions and functions relating to immigration, asylum or nationality; to make provision about citizenship and other nationality matters; to make further provision about immigration and asylum; and for connected purposes.

[21st July 2009]

BE IT ENACTED by the Queen's most Excellent Majesty, by and with the advice and consent of the Lords Spiritual and Temporal, and Commons, in this present Parliament assembled, and by the authority of the same, as follows:—

PART 1
BORDER FUNCTIONS

General customs functions of the Secretary of State

1 General customs functions of the Secretary of State

(1) The functions of the Commissioners for Her Majesty's Revenue and Customs that are exercisable in relation to general customs matters are exercisable by the Secretary of State concurrently with the Commissioners.

(2) For the purposes of this Part, a "general customs matter" is a matter in relation to which the Commissioners, or officers of Revenue and Customs, have functions, other than—

(a) a matter listed in Schedule 1 to the Commissioners for Revenue and Customs Act 2005 (c. 11),

(b) any tax, duty or levy not mentioned in that Schedule,

(c) a matter in respect of which functions were transferred to the Commissioners from the Paymaster General under the Transfer of Functions (Office of Her Majesty's Paymaster General) Order 2006 (S.I. 2006/607),

(d) the subject matter of Directive 2005/60/EC on the prevention of the use of the financial system for the purpose of money laundering and terrorist financing (as amended from time to time), and

(e) the subject matter of Regulation (EC) No 1781/2006 on information on the payer accompanying transfers of funds (as amended from time to time).

(3) If a function is exercisable by the Commissioners—

(a) in relation to a general customs matter, and

(b) in relation to any other matter,

the function is exercisable by the Secretary of State in relation to the general customs matter only.

(4) So far as is appropriate for the purposes of or in connection with this section, references to the Commissioners for Her Majesty's Revenue and Customs, or to Her Majesty's Revenue and Customs, in an enactment, instrument or document to which this section applies are to be construed as including a reference to the Secretary of State.

(5) References in this section (other than in subsection (8))—
 (a) to functions of the Commissioners are to functions conferred by an enactment to which this section applies;
 (b) to functions of officers of Revenue and Customs are to functions conferred by an enactment to which section 3 (designation of general customs officials) applies.

(6) This section applies to—
 (a) an enactment passed or made before the end of the session in which this Act is passed, and
 (b) an instrument or document issued before the passing of this Act.

(7) This includes—
 (a) section 5(2)(b) of the Commissioners for Revenue and Customs Act 2005 (c. 11) (Commissioners' initial functions),
 (b) section 9 of that Act (ancillary powers),
 (c) section 25A(2) of that Act (certificates of debt),
 (d) section 31 of that Act (obstruction), and
 (e) section 33 of that Act (power of arrest) other than in its application to an offence under section 30 of that Act (impersonation),

but does not include any other enactment contained in that Act.

(8) In this Part "general customs function" means—
 (a) a function that is exercisable—
  (i) by the Secretary of State by virtue of this section, or
  (ii) by general customs officials by virtue of section 3,
 (b) a function that is conferred on general customs officials or the Secretary of State by or by virtue of any of sections 22 to 24 (investigations and detention), or
 (c) a function under Community law that is exercisable by the Secretary of State or general customs officials in relation to a matter—
  (i) in relation to which functions under Community law are exercisable by the Commissioners or officers of Revenue and Customs, and
  (ii) that is not listed in paragraphs (a) to (e) of subsection (2).

2 Power of Secretary of State to modify functions

(1) The Secretary of State may by order—
 (a) amend section 1(2) (matters that are general customs matters) so as to add, modify or remove a matter;
 (b) amend that section so as to exclude its application in relation to a function of the Commissioners for Her Majesty's Revenue and Customs or to modify or remove a reference to a function previously so excluded;
 (c) make provision for that section to apply in relation to a function conferred on the Commissioners by an enactment passed or made after the end of the session in which this Act is passed;
 (d) modify any enactment (including an enactment passed or made after the passing of this Act) in consequence of provision made under any of paragraphs (a) to (c);
 (e) make provision for a function of the Secretary of State or general customs officials to be treated, or not to be treated, as a general customs function.

(2) The power under subsection (1)(a) may not be exercised to add any of the following to section 1(2)—
 (a) a matter listed in Schedule 1 to the Commissioners for Revenue and Customs Act 2005 (c. 11),

(b) value added tax,
(c) a customs revenue matter (as to which, see section 7), or
(d) a matter listed at section 7(2)(e).

(3) The Secretary of State must consult the Treasury before exercising the power under this section.

General customs officials

3 Designation of general customs officials

(1) The Secretary of State by whom general customs functions are exercisable may designate—
(a) an immigration officer, or
(b) any other official in that Secretary of State's department,
as a general customs official.

(2) A general customs official—
(a) has, in relation to a general customs matter, the same functions as an officer of Revenue and Customs would have, and
(b) may exercise the functions conferred on the Secretary of State by section 1 (general customs functions of the Secretary of State).

(3) This does not prevent the exercise of the Secretary of State's functions by any other official of the Secretary of State.

(4) If a function within subsection (2) is exercisable—
(a) in relation to a general customs matter, and
(b) in relation to any other matter,
the function is exercisable by a general customs official in relation to the general customs matter only.

(5) So far as is appropriate for the purposes of or in connection with this section, references to an officer of Revenue and Customs, or to Her Majesty's Revenue and Customs, in an enactment, instrument or document to which this section applies are to be construed as including a reference to a general customs official.

(6) References in this section to functions of an officer of Revenue and Customs are to functions conferred by an enactment to which this section applies.

(7) This section applies to—
(a) an enactment passed or made, or an instrument or document issued, before this Act is passed, and
(b) subject to express provision to the contrary, an enactment passed or made, or an instrument or document issued, after this Act is passed.

(8) This includes—
(a) section 2(4) of the Commissioners for Revenue and Customs Act 2005 (c. 11) (continuation of anything begun by one officer by another),
(b) section 6 of that Act (officers' initial functions),
(c) section 25(1) and (5) of that Act (conduct of civil proceedings in a magistrates' court or in the sheriff court),
(d) section 25A(1) of that Act (certificates of debt),
(e) section 31 of that Act (obstruction),
(f) section 32 of that Act (assault), and
(g) section 33 of that Act (power of arrest) other than in its application to an offence under section 30 of that Act (impersonation), but does not otherwise include any enactment contained in that Act.

(9) This section has effect subject to—
(a) any limitation specified in the official's designation under section 4 (supplementary provisions about designation), and
(b) any designation of the official under section 11 (designation of customs revenue officials).

4 Designation: supplementary

(1) A designation under section 3 is subject to such limitations as may be specified in the designation.
(2) A limitation specified under subsection (1) may, in particular, relate to—
(a) the functions that are exercisable by virtue of the designation, or
(b) the purposes for which those functions are exercisable.
(3) A designation under section 3—
(a) may be permanent or for a specified period,
(b) may (in either case) be withdrawn, and
(c) may be varied.
(4) The power to designate, or to withdraw or vary a designation, is exercised by the Secretary of State giving notice to the official in question.
(5) The Secretary of State may designate an official under section 3 only if the Secretary of State is satisfied that the official—
(a) is capable of effectively carrying out the functions that are exercisable by virtue of the designation,
(b) has received adequate training in respect of the exercise of those functions, and
(c) is otherwise a suitable person to exercise those functions.

5 Directions by the Secretary of State

A general customs official must comply with the directions of the Secretary of State in the exercise of general customs functions.

The Director of Border Revenue

6 The Director of Border Revenue

(1) The Secretary of State must designate an official in the department of the Secretary of State by whom general customs functions are exercisable as the Director of Border Revenue.
(2) Before making a designation under this section, the Secretary of State must obtain the consent of the Treasury to the designation.

7 Customs revenue functions of the Director

(1) The functions of the Commissioners for Her Majesty's Revenue and Customs that are exercisable in relation to customs revenue matters are exercisable by the Director of Border Revenue concurrently with the Commissioners.
(2) For the purposes of this Part, each of the following is a "customs revenue matter"—
(a) agricultural levies (within the meaning given by section 6(8) of the European Communities Act 1972 (c. 68));
(b) anti-dumping duty (within the meaning of Council Regulation (EC) No. 384/96, as amended from time to time);

(c) countervailing duty (within the meaning of Council Regulation (EC) No. 2026/97, as amended from time to time);
(d) customs duties;
(e) duties of excise other than—
(i) amusement machine licence duty,
(ii) bingo duty,
(iii) gaming duty,
(iv) general betting duty,
(v) lottery duty,
(vi) pool betting duty, and
(vii) remote gaming duty;
(f) value added tax so far as relating to the export of goods from, or th import of goods into, the United Kingdom.

(3) Subsection (1) does not apply to—
(a) any function of making, by statutory instrument, any regulations, rules or an order;
(b) any function of issuing notices, directions or conditions that relate to value added tax and that apply generally to any person falling within their terms.

(4) If a function is exercisable by the Commissioners—
(a) in relation to a customs revenue matter, and
(b) in relation to any other matter, the function is exercisable by the Director in relation to the customs revenue matter only.

(5) So far as is appropriate for the purposes of or in connection with this section, references to the Commissioners for Her Majesty's Revenue and Customs, or to Her Majesty's Revenue and Customs, in an enactment, instrument or document to which this section applies are to be construed as including a reference to the Director.

(6) References in this section to functions of the Commissioners are to functions conferred by an enactment to which this section applies.

(7) This section applies to—
(a) an enactment passed or made before the end of the session in which this Act is passed, and
(b) an instrument or document issued before the passing of this Act.

(8) This includes—
(a) section 5(1)(b) and (2)(b) of the Commissioners for Revenue and Customs Act 2005 (c. 11) (Commissioners' initial functions),
(b) section 9 of that Act (ancillary powers),
(c) section 24(1), (2), (3)(e) and (4) to (7) of that Act (evidence),
(d) section 25(1), (1A), (5) and (6) of that Act (conduct of civil proceedings),
(e) section 25A(2) of that Act (certificates of debt),
(f) section 26 of that Act (rewards),
(g) section 31 of that Act (obstruction), and
(h) section 33 of that Act (power of arrest) other than in its application to an offence under section 30 of that Act (impersonation),

but does not include any other enactment contained in that Act.

(9) In this Part "customs revenue function" means—
(a) a function that is exercisable—
(i) by the Director by virtue of this section, or
(ii) by customs revenue officials by virtue of section 11,

(b) a function that is conferred on customs revenue officials or the Director by or by virtue of any of sections 22 to 24 (investigations and detention), or

(c) a function under Community law that is exercisable by the Director or customs revenue officials in relation to a customs revenue matter.

8 Power of Treasury to modify Director's functions

The Treasury may by order—

(a) amend section 7(2) (matters that are customs revenue matters) so as to add, modify or remove a matter;

(b) amend section 7(3) (functions to which that section does not apply) so as to add, modify or remove a function;

(c) make provision for that section to apply in relation to a function conferred on the Commissioners for Her Majesty's Revenue and Customs by an enactment passed or made after the end of the session in which this Act is passed;

(d) modify any enactment (including an enactment passed or made after the passing of this Act) in consequence of provision made under any of paragraphs (a) to (c).

9 Delegation of Director's functions

(1) The Director of Border Revenue may make arrangements to delegate a function of the Director.

(2) The delegation of a function under this section—

(a) does not prevent the exercise of the function by the Director, and

(b) does not prevent the exercise of the function by a customs revenue official (see section 11).

(3) Where the Director delegates a function under this section—

(a) the Director must monitor the exercise of the function by the person to whom it is delegated, and

(b) the person must comply with the directions of the Director in exercising that function.

10 Compliance with directions etc.

(1) This section applies to—

(a) the Director of Border Revenue in the exercise of the Director's customs revenue functions, and

(b) a person to whom such functions are delegated under section 9.

(2) A person to whom this section applies must comply with any directions of a general nature given by the Treasury.

(3) A person to whom this section applies must apply—

(a) any concession published by the Commissioners for Her Majesty's Revenue and Customs and available generally to any person falling within its terms, and

(b) any interpretation of the law issued by the Commissioners (whether or not published).

(4) A person to whom this section applies must also—

(a) comply with any other guidance issued by the Commissioners (whether or not published), and

(b) take account of any other material published by the Commissioners.

Customs revenue officials

11 Designation of customs revenue officials

(1) The Director of Border Revenue may designate—
(a) an immigration officer, or
(b) any other official in the department of the Secretary of State by whom general customs functions are exercisable,
as a customs revenue official.
(2) A customs revenue official—
(a) has, in relation to a customs revenue matter, the same functions as an officer of Revenue and Customs would have, and
(b) may exercise the functions conferred on the Director by section 7 (customs revenue functions).
(3) If a function within subsection (2) is exercisable—
(a) in relation to a customs revenue matter, and
(b) in relation to any other matter,
the function is exercisable by a customs revenue official in relation to the customs revenue matter only.
(4) So far as is appropriate for the purposes of or in connection with this section, references to an officer of Revenue and Customs, or to Her Majesty's Revenue and Customs, in an enactment, instrument or document to which this section applies are to be construed as including a reference to a customs revenue official.
(5) References in this section to functions of an officer of Revenue and Customs are to functions conferred by an enactment to which this section applies.
(6) This section applies to—
(a) an enactment passed or made, or an instrument or document issued, before this Act is passed, and
(b) subject to express provision to the contrary, an enactment passed or made, or an instrument or document issued, after this Act is passed.
(7) This includes—
(a) section 2(4) of the Commissioners for Revenue and Customs Act 2005 (c. 11) (continuation of anything begun by one officer by another),
(b) section 6 of that Act (officers' initial functions),
(c) section 25(1), (1A) and (5) of that Act (conduct of civil proceedings),
(d) section 25A(1) of that Act (certificates of debt),
(e) section 26 of that Act (rewards),
(f) section 31 of that Act (obstruction),
(g) section 32 of that Act (assault), and
(h) section 33 of that Act (power of arrest) other than in its application to an offence under section 30 of that Act (impersonation),
but does not otherwise include any enactment contained in that Act.
(8) This section has effect subject to—
(a) any limitation specified in the official's designation under section 12 (supplementary provisions about designation), and
(b) any designation of the official under section 3 (designation of general customs officials).

12 Designation: supplementary

(1) A designation under section 11 is subject to such limitations as may be specified in the designation.
(2) A limitation specified under subsection (1) may, in particular, relate to—
  (a) the functions that are exercisable by virtue of the designation, or
  (b) the purposes for which those functions are exercisable.
(3) A designation under section 11—
  (a) may be permanent or for a specified period,
  (b) may (in either case) be withdrawn, and
  (c) may be varied.
(4) The power to designate, or to withdraw or vary a designation, is exercised by the Director of Border Revenue giving notice to the official in question.
(5) The Director may designate an official under section 11 only if the Director is satisfied that the official—
  (a) is capable of effectively carrying out the functions that are exercisable by virtue of the designation,
  (b) has received adequate training in respect of the exercise of those functions, and
  (c) is otherwise a suitable person to exercise those functions.

13 Directions by the Director

A customs revenue official must comply with the directions of the Director of Border Revenue in the exercise of customs revenue functions.

Use and disclosure of information

14 Use and disclosure of customs information

(1) A person to whom this section applies may—
  (a) use customs information acquired by that person in connection with a function exercisable by that person for the purpose of any other function exercisable by that person, and
  (b) disclose customs information to any other person to whom this section applies for the purpose of a function exercisable by that person.
(2) The persons to whom this section applies are—
  (a) a designated customs official,
  (b) an immigration officer,
  (c) the Secretary of State by whom general customs functions are exercisable,
  (d) any other Minister of the Crown in the department of that Secretary of State,
  (e) the Director of Border Revenue, and
  (f) a person acting on behalf of a person mentioned in paragraphs (a) to (e).
(3) This section is subject to any provision that restricts or prohibits the use or disclosure of information and that is contained in—
  (a) this Part,
  (b) any other enactment, or
  (c) an international or other agreement to which the United Kingdom or Her Majesty's Government is party.

(4) In subsection (3) the reference to an enactment does not include an enactment contained in, or in an instrument made under—
(a) an Act of the Scottish Parliament,
(b) a Measure or Act of the National Assembly for Wales, or
(c) Northern Ireland legislation.

(5) This section is without prejudice to—
(a) the use by a person to whom it applies of information other than customs information;
(b) the disclosure by or to a person to whom it applies of information other than customs information.

(6) In this Part—
"customs function" means a general customs function or a customs revenue function;
"customs information" means information acquired or capable of being acquired as a result of the exercise of a customs function;
"customs revenue information" means information acquired or capable of being acquired as a result of the exercise of a customs revenue function;
"designated customs official" means a general customs official or a customs revenue official.

(7) It is immaterial for the purposes of subsection (6)—
(a) whether the information was acquired or is capable of being acquired by the person by whom it is held or another person;
(b) whether the information was also acquired or is also capable of being acquired in the exercise of any other function.

15 Prohibition on disclosure of personal customs information

(1) A person who is or was a relevant official, the Secretary of State by whom general customs functions are exercisable or another Minister of the Crown in that Secretary of State's department may not disclose personal customs information to a person who is not—
(a) a relevant official, or
(b) a Minister of the Crown in that department.

(2) A person who is or was a relevant official may not disclose personal customs revenue information to a Minister of the Crown.

(3) In this Part "relevant official" means—
(a) a designated customs official,
(b) an immigration officer,
(c) the Director of Border Revenue, or
(d) a person acting on behalf of—
(i) the Secretary of State by whom general customs functions are exercisable, or
(ii) a person mentioned in paragraphs (a) to (c).

(4) In this Part—
"personal customs information" means customs information relating to a person that—
(a) identifies that person, or
(b) enables that person to be identified (either by itself or in combination with other information);
"personal customs revenue information" means customs revenue information relating to a person that—
(a) identifies that person, or

(b) enables that person to be identified (either by itself or in combination with other information).

(5) A person—

(a) does not breach subsection (1) by disclosing information the person knows was acquired otherwise than as the result of the exercise of a customs function;

(b) does not breach subsection (2) by disclosing information the person knows was acquired otherwise than as the result of the exercise of a customs revenue function.

(6) Subsections (1) and (2) are also subject to—

(a) section 16 (exceptions to the prohibition in this section), and

(b) any enactment (other than an enactment contained in this Part) permitting disclosure, where the disclosure in question does not contravene any restriction imposed by the Commissioners for Her Majesty's Revenue and Customs on the disclosure of customs revenue information.

(7) This section does not apply to information supplied by or on behalf of Her Majesty's Revenue and Customs or the Revenue and Customs Prosecutions Office. This is without prejudice to any other restriction on the disclosure of such information.

(8) In subsection (6) the reference to an enactment does not include an enactment contained in, or in an instrument made under—

(a) an Act of the Scottish Parliament,

(b) a Measure or Act of the National Assembly for Wales, or

(c) Northern Ireland legislation.

16 Exceptions to section 15 prohibition

(1) A person does not breach section 15(1) or (2) by making a disclosure—

(a) to which any of subsections (3) to (8) applies, and

(b) which, in the case of a disclosure of customs revenue information, does not contravene any restriction imposed by the Commissioners for Her Majesty's Revenue and Customs.

(2) Subsection (1)(b) does not apply if the person making the disclosure knows that the information was acquired otherwise than as the result of the exercise of a customs revenue function.

(3) This subsection applies to a disclosure which is made for the purposes of—

(a) a customs function,

(b) a function relating to immigration, asylum or nationality,

(c) a function relating to national security, or

(d) a function relating to the prevention or detection of crime.

(4) This subsection applies to a disclosure which is made to a person exercising public functions (whether or not within the United Kingdom) for the purposes of any of those functions.

(5) This subsection applies to a disclosure which—

(a) is made for the purposes of civil proceedings (whether or not within the United Kingdom) relating to a function within subsection (3),

(b) is made for the purposes of a criminal investigation or criminal proceedings (whether or not within the United Kingdom), or

(c) is made in pursuance of an order of a court.

(6) This subsection applies to a disclosure which is made with the consent of each person to whom the information relates.

(7) This subsection applies to a disclosure which is made in order to comply with an obligation of the United Kingdom, or Her Majesty's Government, under an international or other agreement.

(8) This subsection applies to a disclosure—

(a) to a person specified in regulations made jointly by the Treasury and the Secretary of State, or

(b) of a kind specified in such regulations.

17 Prohibition on further disclosure

(1) A person to whom information is disclosed in reliance on section 16 or this section may not disclose that information without the consent of a relevant official (which may be general or specific).

(2) A person does not breach subsection (1) by making a disclosure—

(a) to which any of subsections (3) to (8) of section 16 applies, and

(b) which, in the case of a disclosure of customs revenue information, does not contravene any restriction imposed by the Commissioners for Her Majesty's Revenue and Customs.

(3) Subsection (2)(b) does not apply if the person making the disclosure knows that the information was acquired otherwise than as the result of the exercise of a customs revenue function.

(4) This section is also subject to any other enactment permitting disclosure.

(5) In subsection (4) the reference to an enactment does not include an enactment contained in, or in an instrument made under—

(a) an Act of the Scottish Parliament,

(b) a Measure or Act of the National Assembly for Wales, or

(c) Northern Ireland legislation.

18 Offence of wrongful disclosure

(1) A person commits an offence if the person breaches section 15(1) or (2) or 17(1).

(2) It is a defence for a person charged with an offence under this section to prove that the person reasonably believed—

(a) that the disclosure was lawful, or

(b) that the information had already and lawfully been made available to the public.

(3) A prosecution for an offence under this section—

(a) may be brought in England and Wales only with the consent of the Director of Public Prosecutions or the Director of Revenue and Customs Prosecutions;

(b) may be brought in Northern Ireland only with the consent of the Director of Public Prosecutions for Northern Ireland.

(4) This section is without prejudice to the pursuit of any remedy or the taking of any action in relation to a breach of section 15(1) or (2) or 17(1) (whether or not this section applies to the breach).

(5) A person guilty of an offence under this section is liable—

(a) on conviction on indictment to imprisonment for a term not exceeding 2 years, or to a fine, or to both;

(b) on summary conviction—

(i) in England and Wales, to imprisonment for a term not exceeding 12 months, or to a fine not exceeding the statutory maximum, or to both;

(ii) in Scotland, to imprisonment for a term not exceeding 12 months, or to a fine not exceeding the statutory maximum, or to both;

(iii) in Northern Ireland, to imprisonment for a term not exceeding 6 months, or to a fine not exceeding the statutory maximum, or to both.

(6) In relation to an offence under this section committed before the commencement of section 282 of the Criminal Justice Act 2003 (c. 44) (increase in maximum sentence on summary conviction of offence triable either way), the reference in subsection (5)(b)(i) to 12 months has effect as if it were a reference to 6 months.

19 Application of statutory provisions

(1) Nothing in sections 14 to 17 authorises the making of a disclosure which—

(a) contravenes the Data Protection Act 1998 (c. 29), or

(b) is prohibited by Part 1 of the Regulation of Investigatory Powers Act 2000 (c. 23).

(2) Information whose disclosure is prohibited by section 15(1) or (2) or 17(1) is exempt information by virtue of section 44(1)(a) of the Freedom of Information Act 2000 (c. 36).

(3) Sections 15(6), 16 and 17(2) and (4) are to be disregarded in determining for the purposes of subsection (2) whether the disclosure of personal customs information is prohibited by section 15(1) or (2) or 17(1).

(4) In section 23 of the Commissioners for Revenue and Customs Act 2005 (c. 11) (freedom of information), after subsection (1) insert—

"(1A) Subsections (2) and (3) of section 18 are to be disregarded in determining for the purposes of subsection (1) of this section whether the disclosure of revenue and customs information relating to a person is prohibited by subsection (1) of that section."

20 Supply of Revenue and Customs information

(1) After section 41 of the UK Borders Act 2007 (c. 30) insert—

"41A Supply of information to UK Border Agency

(1) HMRC and the RCPO may each supply a person to whom this section applies with information for use for the purpose of the customs functions exercisable by that person.

(2) This section applies to—

(a) a designated customs official,

(b) the Secretary of State by whom general customs functions are exercisable,

(c) the Director of Border Revenue, and

(d) a person acting on behalf of a person mentioned in paragraphs (a) to (c).

(3) This section applies to a document or article which comes into the possession of, or is discovered by, HMRC or the RCPO, or a person acting on behalf of HMRC or the RCPO, as it applies to information.

(4) A person to whom this section applies—

(a) may retain for a purpose within subsection (1) a document or article supplied by virtue of subsection (3);

(b) may dispose of a document or article supplied by virtue of subsection (3).

(5) A power conferred by this section on HMRC or the RCPO may be exercised on behalf of HMRC or the RCPO by a person who is authorised (generally or specifically) for the purpose.

(6) In this section and section 41B "customs function" and "general customs function" have the meanings given by Part 1 of the Borders, Citizenship and Immigration Act 2009.

41B UK Border Agency: onward disclosure

(1) A person to whom information is supplied under section 41A may not disclose that information.
(2) But subsection (1) does not apply to a disclosure—
(a) which is made for the purpose of a customs function, where the disclosure does not contravene any restriction imposed by the Commissioners for Her Majesty's Revenue and Customs;
(b) which is made for the purposes of civil proceedings (whether or not within the United Kingdom) relating to a customs function;
(c) which is made for the purpose of a criminal investigation or criminal proceedings (whether or not within the United Kingdom);
(d) which is made in pursuance of an order of a court;
(e) which is made with the consent (which may be general or specific) of HMRC or the RCPO, depending on by whom or on whose behalf the information was supplied;
(f) which is made with the consent of each person to whom the information relates.
(3) Subsection (1) is subject to any other enactment permitting disclosure.
(4) The reference in subsection (1) to information supplied under section 41A includes a reference to documents or articles supplied by virtue of subsection (3) of that section.
(5) The reference in that subsection to a person to whom information is supplied includes a reference to a person who is or was acting on behalf of that person.
(6) In subsection (3) "enactment" does not include—
(a) an Act of the Scottish Parliament,
(b) an Act of the Northern Ireland Assembly, or
(c) an instrument made under an Act within paragraph (a) or (b)."

(2) In section 42(1) of that Act (wrongful disclosure) after "section 41" insert "or 41B".

21 Duty to share information

(1) In section 36 of the Immigration, Asylum and Nationality Act 2006 (c. 13) (duty to share information), in subsection (1), for paragraph (a) substitute—
"(a) designated customs officials,
(aa) immigration officers,
(ab) the Secretary of State in so far as the Secretary of State has general customs functions,
(ac) the Secretary of State in so far as the Secretary of State has functions relating to immigration, asylum or nationality,
(ad) the Director of Border Revenue and any person exercising functions of the Director,".
(2) In subsection (6)(a) of that section, after "persons" insert "or descriptions of persons".
(3) In subsection (9) of that section, at the appropriate place insert—
""designated customs official" and "general customs function" have the meanings given by Part 1 of the Borders, Citizenship and Immigration Act 2009,".

Investigations and detention

22 Application of the PACE orders

(1) Subject as follows, the PACE orders—
 (a) apply to criminal investigations conducted by designated customs officials and relating to a general customs matter or customs revenue matter as they apply to relevant investigations conducted by officers of Revenue and Customs, and
 (b) apply to persons detained by designated customs officials as they apply to persons detained by officers of Revenue and Customs.

(2) Each of the following is a PACE order for the purposes of this section—
 (a) the Police and Criminal Evidence Act 1984 (Application to Revenue and Customs) Order 2007 (S.I. 2007/3175);
 (b) the Police and Criminal Evidence (Application to Revenue and Customs) Order (Northern Ireland) 2007 (S.R. 2007/464).

(3) In the application of the PACE orders by virtue of this section—
 (a) subject to the following provisions of this subsection, references in those orders to an officer of Revenue and Customs are to be read as references to a designated customs official;
 (b) references in those orders to the Commissioners are to be read as references to—
  (i) the Secretary of State in relation to general customs matters, or
  (ii) the Director of Border Revenue in relation to customs revenue matters;
 (c) references in those orders to Her Majesty's Revenue and Customs or to Revenue and Customs are to be read as references to—
  (i) the Secretary of State in so far as the Secretary of State has general customs functions,
  (ii) the Director of Border Revenue, and
  (iii) designated customs officials;
 (d) references in those orders to an office of Revenue and Customs are to be read as references to an office of the UK Border Agency;
 (e) references in those orders to a designated office of Revenue and Customs are to be read as references to a designated office of the UK Border Agency;
 (f) references in those orders to a relevant indictable offence are to be read as references to an indictable offence that relates to a general customs matter or a customs revenue matter;
 (g) references in those orders to a relevant investigation are to be read as references to a criminal investigation conducted by a designated customs official that relates to a general customs matter or a customs revenue matter;
 (h) references in those orders to a person being in Revenue and Customs detention are to be read as references to a person being in UK Border Agency detention;
 (i) references in those orders to an officer of Revenue and Customs of at least the grade of officer are to be read as references to a designated customs official of at least the grade of immigration officer or executive officer;
 (j) references in those orders to an officer of Revenue and Customs of at least the grade of higher officer are to be read as references to a designated customs official of at least the grade of chief immigration officer or higher executive officer;
 (k) references in those orders to an officer of Revenue and Customs of at least the grade of senior officer are to be read as references to a designated customs official of at least the grade of immigration inspector or senior executive officer;

(l) any other references in those orders to an officer of Revenue and Customs occupying a specified post or grade are to be read as references to the Secretary of State.

(4) For the purposes of this section—

(a) a person is in UK Border Agency detention if—

(i) the person has been taken to an office of the UK Border Agency after being arrested for an offence, or

(ii) the person is arrested at an office of the UK Border Agency after attending voluntarily at the office or accompanying a designated customs official to it,

and is detained there or is detained elsewhere in the charge of a designated customs official, and

(b) "office of the UK Border Agency" means premises wholly or partly occupied by designated customs officials.

(5) This section does not apply to the following provisions of the PACE orders—

(a) in article 2(1) of the Police and Criminal Evidence Act 1984 (Application to Revenue and Customs) Order 2007 (S.I. 2007/3175), the definitions of "the Commissioners", "office of Revenue and Customs", "relevant indictable offence" and "relevant investigation";

(b) article 2(2) of that order (Revenue and Customs detention);

(c) article 7 of that order (restriction on other powers to apply for production of documents);

(d) article 19 of that order (authorisation);

(e) in article 2(1) of the Police and Criminal Evidence (Application to Revenue and Customs) Order (Northern Ireland) 2007 (S.R. 2007/464), the definitions of "the Commissioners", "office of Revenue and Customs", "relevant indictable offence" and "relevant investigation";

(f) article 2(2) of that order (Revenue and Customs detention);

(g) article 7 of that order (restriction on other powers to apply for production of documents);

(h) article 15 of that order (authorisation).

(6) A person may be transferred—

(a) between UK Border Agency detention and Revenue and Customs detention;

(b) between Revenue and Customs detention and UK Border Agency detention;

(c) between UK Border Agency detention and police detention;

(d) between police detention and UK Border Agency detention.

(7) The references to police detention in subsection (6)—

(a) in relation to England and Wales, are to be construed in accordance with the Police and Criminal Evidence Act 1984 (c. 60);

(b) in relation to Northern Ireland, are to be construed in accordance with the Police and Criminal Evidence (Northern Ireland) Order 1989 (S.I. 1989/1341 (N.I. 12)).

(8) Expressions used in this section that are defined in a PACE order have the same meaning as in that PACE order.

(9) This section does not affect the generality of sections 1(4), 3(5), 7(5) and 11(4) (construction of statutory etc. references to the Commissioners for Her Majesty's Revenue and Customs, officers of Revenue and Customs and Her Majesty's Revenue and Customs).

23 Investigations and detention: England and Wales and Northern Ireland

(1) The Secretary of State may by order provide for any provision of an enactment listed in subsection (2) that relates to investigations of offences conducted by police officers or to persons detained by the police to apply, subject to such modifications as the order may specify, in relation to—
   (a) investigations conducted by designated customs officials,
   (b) persons detained by designated customs officials,
   (c) investigations conducted by immigration officers, or
   (d) persons detained by immigration officers.

(2) Those enactments are—
   (a) the Police and Criminal Evidence Act 1984 (c. 60), and
   (b) the Police and Criminal Evidence (Northern Ireland) Order 1989 (S.I. 1989/1341 (N.I. 12)).

(3) An order under this section may make, in relation to designated customs officials, immigration officers, the Secretary of State or the Director of Border Revenue, provision similar to that which may be made in relation to officers of Revenue and Customs or the Commissioners for Her Majesty's Revenue and Customs under—
   (a) section 114 of the Police and Criminal Evidence Act 1984, or
   (b) article 85 of the Police and Criminal Evidence (Northern Ireland) Order 1989.

(4) If an order under this section provides that a function may be exercised only by a person acting with the authority of the Secretary of State or the Director of Border Revenue, a certificate of the Secretary of State or (as the case may be) the Director that the person had authority to exercise the function is conclusive evidence of that fact.

(5) An order under this section may amend or repeal section 22 (application of the PACE orders).

24 Investigations and detention: Scotland

(1) After section 26B of the Criminal Law (Consolidation) (Scotland) Act 1995 (c. 39) insert—

"**26C Investigations by designated customs officials**

(1) In the application of this Part of this Act to investigations conducted by designated customs officials—
   (a) references to an officer are to a designated customs official;
   (b) references to an authorised officer are to a designated customs official acting with the authority (which may be general or specific) of—
      (i) the Secretary of State in relation to investigations relating to general customs matters, or
      (ii) the Director of Border Revenue in relation to investigations relating to customs revenue matters;
   (c) references to the Commissioners for Her Majesty's Revenue and Customs are to—
      (i) the Secretary of State in relation to investigations relating to general customs matters, or
      (ii) the Director of Border Revenue in relation to investigations relating to customs revenue matters;
   (d) references to an office of Revenue and Customs are to premises wholly or partly occupied by designated customs officials;

(e) references to a superior officer are to—
(i) an immigration officer not below the grade of Inspector,
(ii) a person of the grade of Senior Executive Officer, or
(iii) a person of a grade equivalent to that within subparagraph (i) or (ii).
(2) In this section "customs revenue matter", "designated customs official" and "general customs matter" have the meanings given by Part 1 of the Borders, Citizenship and Immigration Act 2009."

(2) The amendment made by this section does not affect the generality of sections 1(4), 3(5), 7(5) and 11(4) (construction of statutory etc. references to the Commissioners for Her Majesty's Revenue and Customs, officers of Revenue and Customs and Her Majesty's Revenue and Customs).

25 Short-term holding facilities

In section 147 of the Immigration and Asylum Act 1999 (c. 33) (removal centres and detained persons: interpretation), in the definition of "short-term holding facility"—
(a) after "used" insert "—(a)", and
(b) at the end insert ", or
(b) for the detention of—
(i) detained persons for a period of not more than seven days or for such other period as may be prescribed, and
(ii) persons other than detained persons for any period."

Transfer of property etc.

26 Transfer schemes

(1) The Commissioners for Her Majesty's Revenue and Customs may make one or more schemes for the transfer of specified property, rights or liabilities or property, rights or liabilities of a specified description between—
(a) the Commissioners or officers of Revenue and Customs, and
(b) the Secretary of State, the Director of Border Revenue or designated customs officials.

(2) A scheme under subsection (1) may, in particular—
(a) create interests or rights, or impose liabilities, in relation to property, rights or liabilities transferred by virtue of the scheme or retained by a transferor;
(b) apportion property, rights or liabilities between a transferor and a transferee.

(3) A scheme under subsection (1) may—
(a) provide for anything done by or in relation to a transferor in connection with anything transferred to have effect as if done by or in relation to a transferee;
(b) permit anything (including any legal proceedings) relating to anything transferred by the scheme which is in the process of being done by or in relation to a transferor when the transfer takes effect to be continued by or in relation to a transferee;
(c) provide for references to a transferor in an agreement (whether written or not), instrument or other document relating to anything transferred by the scheme to be treated as references to a transferee;
(d) include other incidental, supplementary, consequential, transitional or transitory provision or savings.

(4) A scheme under subsection (1) may provide for a transfer of property, rights or liabilities—
   (a) whether or not they would otherwise be capable of being transferred,
   (b) without any instrument or other formality being required, and
   (c) irrespective of any requirement for consent that would otherwise apply.
(5) The Commissioners may make one or more schemes providing for—
   (a) any specified thing or anything of a specified description done by or in relation to the Commissioners or an officer of Revenue and Customs in connection with a relevant function to have effect as if done by or in relation to the Secretary of State, the Director or a designated customs official;
   (b) any specified thing or anything of a specified description (including any legal proceedings) relating to a relevant function done by or in relation to the Commissioners or an officer of Revenue and Customs to be continued by or in relation to the Secretary of State, the Director or a designated customs official.
(6) A scheme under this section—
   (a) comes into force in accordance with its terms;
   (b) may be amended or revoked.
(7) In this section—
   "relevant function" means a function which before the passing of this Act was exercisable by the Commissioners or officers of Revenue and Customs (whether or not it remains so exercisable) and that—
      (a) is conferred by or by virtue of this Part on the Secretary of State, the Director or a designated customs official, or
      (b) is a function under Community law that is exercisable by the Secretary of State, the Director or a designated customs official; "specified" means specified in the scheme.

27 Facilities and services

(1) Her Majesty's Revenue and Customs may make facilities and services available to any person by whom functions relating to immigration, asylum or nationality, or customs functions, are exercisable for the purposes of the exercise of any of those functions.
(2) A person by whom functions relating to immigration, asylum or nationality, or customs functions, are exercisable may make facilities and services available to Her Majesty's Revenue and Customs for the purposes of the exercise of a function of Her Majesty's Revenue and Customs.

Inspection and oversight

28 Inspections by the Chief Inspector of the UK Border Agency

(1) In section 48 of the UK Borders Act 2007 (c. 30) (establishment of the Border and Immigration Inspectorate), in subsection (1) for "the Border and Immigration Agency" substitute "the UK Border Agency".
(2) After that subsection insert—
   "(1A) The Chief Inspector shall monitor and report on the efficiency and effectiveness of the performance of functions by the following—
      (a) designated customs officials, and officials of the Secretary of State exercising customs functions;

(b) immigration officers, and officials of the Secretary of State exercising functions relating to immigration, asylum or nationality;

(c) the Secretary of State in so far as the Secretary of State has general customs functions;

(d) the Secretary of State in so far as the Secretary of State has functions relating to immigration, asylum or nationality;

(e) the Director of Border Revenue and any person exercising functions of the Director.

(1B) The Chief Inspector shall monitor and report on the efficiency and effectiveness of the services provided by a person acting pursuant to arrangements relating to the discharge of a function within subsection (1A)."

(3) In subsection (2) of that section—

(a) omit the words from the beginning to "Agency;",

(b) in paragraph (a), for "within the Border and Immigration Agency" substitute "among the persons listed in subsections (1A) and (1B) (the "listed persons")",

(c) in paragraph (b), for "the Border and Immigration Agency" substitute "the listed persons", and

(d) after paragraph (g) insert—

"(ga) practice and procedure in relation to the prevention, detection and investigation of offences,

(gb) practice and procedure in relation to the conduct of criminal proceedings,

(gc) whether customs functions have been appropriately exercised by the Secretary of State and the Director of Border Revenue,".

(4) After that subsection insert—

"(2A) Unless directed to do so by the Secretary of State, the Chief Inspector shall not monitor and report on the exercise by the listed persons of—

(a) functions at removal centres and short term holding facilities, and under escort arrangements, in so far as Her Majesty's Chief Inspector of Prisons has functions under section 5A of the Prison Act 1952 in relation to such functions, and

(b) functions at detention facilities, in so far as Her Majesty's Inspectors of Constabulary, the Scottish inspectors or the Northern Ireland inspectors have functions by virtue of section 29 of the Borders, Citizenship and Immigration Act 2009 in relation to such functions."

(5) Omit subsection (3) of that section.

(6) After that subsection insert—

"(3A) In this section "customs function", "designated customs official" and "general customs function" have the meanings given by Part 1 of the Borders, Citizenship and Immigration Act 2009."

(7) In section 53 of that Act (relationship with other bodies), in subsection (1)—

(a) in paragraph (a), for "the Border and Immigration Agency" substitute "a person listed in section 48(1A) or (1B)", and

(b) in paragraph (b), for "the Agency" substitute "such a person".

(8) In subsection (3) of that section, for "the Agency" insert "a person listed in section 48(1A) or (1B)".

(9) In section 56(2)(a) of that Act (Senior President of Tribunals), for "the Border and Immigration Agency" substitute "the UK Border Agency".

(10) The person holding the office of the Chief Inspector of the Border and Immigration Agency immediately before the day on which this section comes into force is to be treated, on and after that day, as if appointed as the Chief Inspector of the UK Border Agency under section 48(1) of the UK Borders Act 2007 (c. 30).

29 Inspections by Her Majesty's Inspectors of Constabulary etc.

(1) The Secretary of State may make regulations conferring functions on Her Majesty's Inspectors of Constabulary, the Scottish inspectors or the Northern Ireland inspectors in relation to—
 (a) designated customs officials, and officials of the Secretary of State exercising customs functions;
 (b) immigration officers, and officials of the Secretary of State exercising functions relating to immigration, asylum or nationality;
 (c) the Secretary of State in so far as the Secretary of State has general customs functions;
 (d) the Secretary of State in so far as the Secretary of State has functions relating to immigration, asylum or nationality;
 (e) the Director of Border Revenue and any person exercising functions of the Director;
 (f) persons providing services pursuant to arrangements relating to the discharge of a function of a person mentioned in paragraphs (a) to (e).

(2) Regulations under subsection (1) may—
 (a) in relation to Her Majesty's Inspectors of Constabulary, apply (with or without modification) or make provision similar to any provision of sections 54 to 56 of the Police Act 1996 (c. 16) (inspection);
 (b) in relation to the Scottish inspectors, apply (with or without modification) or make provision similar to any provision of section 33 or 34 of the Police (Scotland) Act 1967 (c. 77) (inspection);
 (c) in relation to the Northern Ireland inspectors, apply (without or without modification) or make provision similar to any provision of section 41 or 42 of the Police (Northern Ireland) Act 1998 (c. 32) (inspection).

(3) Regulations under subsection (1)—
 (a) may enable a Minister of the Crown to require an inspection to be carried out;
 (b) must provide for a report of an inspection to be made and, subject to any exceptions required or permitted by the regulations, published;
 (c) must provide for an annual report by Her Majesty's Inspectors of Constabulary;
 (d) may make provision for payment to or in respect of Her Majesty's Inspectors of Constabulary, the Scottish inspectors or the Northern Ireland inspectors.

(4) An inspection carried out by virtue of this section may not address a matter of a kind which the Comptroller and Auditor General may examine under section 6 of the National Audit Act 1983 (c. 44).

(5) An inspection carried out by virtue of this section must be carried out jointly by Her Majesty's Inspectors of Constabulary and the Scottish inspectors—
 (a) if it is carried out wholly in Scotland, or
 (b) in a case where it is carried out partly in Scotland, to the extent that it is carried out there.

(6) In this section—
(a) "the Scottish inspectors" means the inspectors of constabulary appointed under section 33(1) of the Police (Scotland) Act 1967;
(b) "the Northern Ireland inspectors" means the inspectors of constabulary appointed under section 41(1) of the Police (Northern Ireland) Act 1998.

30 Complaints and misconduct

(1) In section 41 of the Police and Justice Act 2006 (c. 48) (power to confer functions on the Independent Police Complaints Commission in respect of the exercise of immigration functions)—
(a) after subsection (1)(b) insert—
"(c) the provision of services pursuant to arrangements relating to the discharge of a function within paragraph (a) or (b).", and
(b) after subsection (2) insert—
"(2A) The Secretary of State may make regulations conferring functions on the Independent Police Complaints Commission in relation to—
(a) the exercise by designated customs officials, and officials of the Secretary of State, of customs functions within the meaning of Part 1 of the Borders, Citizenship and Immigration Act 2009;
(b) the exercise by the Director of Border Revenue, and any person exercising functions of the Director, of customs revenue functions within the meaning of that Part of that Act;
(c) the provision of services pursuant to arrangements relating to the discharge of a function within paragraph (a) or (b)."
(2) In each of subsections (4) and (7) of that section, after "subsection (1)" insert "or (2A)".
(3) In the title to that section, after "functions" insert "and customs functions".

Other provisions

31 Prosecution of offences

(1) The Attorney General may by order assign to the Director of Revenue and Customs Prosecutions a function of—
(a) instituting criminal proceedings in England and Wales,
(b) assuming the conduct of criminal proceedings in England and Wales, or
(c) providing legal advice,
relating to a criminal investigation of a kind specified in the order by a person to whom this section applies.
(2) This section applies to—
(a) designated customs officials,
(b) immigration officers,
(c) officials of the Secretary of State,
(d) the Secretary of State,
(e) the Director of Border Revenue,
(f) a person acting on behalf of a person mentioned in paragraphs (a) to (e), and
(g) constables.

(3) For the purposes of the Commissioners for Revenue and Customs Act 2005 (c. 11)—
(a) functions assigned to the Director of Revenue and Customs Prosecutions by virtue of this section are to be treated as functions of the Director under or by virtue of that Act, and
(b) proceedings conducted by the Director by virtue of this section are to be treated as proceedings conducted by the Director under that Act.
(4) Sections 37 to 37B of the Police and Criminal Evidence Act 1984 (c. 60) (guidance etc.) have effect, in relation to a person arrested following a criminal investigation in relation to which functions are conferred by virtue of this section, as if references to the Director of Public Prosecutions were references to the Director of Revenue and Customs Prosecutions.
(5) An order under this section—
(a) may include incidental, supplementary and consequential provision;
(b) may make transitional or transitory provision or savings;
(c) may be amended or revoked.
(6) The reference in this section to instituting criminal proceedings is to be construed in accordance with section 15(2) of the Prosecution of Offences Act 1985 (c. 23).
(7) In this section "criminal investigation" means any process—
(a) for considering whether an offence has been committed,
(b) for discovering by whom an offence has been committed, or
(c) as a result of which an offence is alleged to have been committed.

32 Payment of revenue to the Commissioners

(1) The Director of Border Revenue must pay money received by way of revenue or security for revenue in the exercise of the Director's customs revenue functions to the Commissioners for Her Majesty's Revenue and Customs.
(2) The Secretary of State must pay money received by way of revenue in the exercise of the Secretary of State's general customs functions to the Commissioners.
(3) A payment under subsection (1) or (2) must be made—
(a) at such times and in such manner as the Treasury directs, and
(b) after deduction of payments in connection with drawback and repayments.
(4) If the Commissioners think that the funds available to the Director or the Secretary of State may be insufficient to make a payment in connection with drawback or a repayment, the Commissioners may—
(a) pay money to the Director or the Secretary of State (as the case may be) to enable the payment or repayment to be made, or
(b) make the payment or repayment on behalf of the Director or the Secretary of State (as the case may be).
(5) Subsection (4) applies whether or not the reason for a deficiency is or may be that an amount has been paid or retained on the basis of an estimate that has proved or may prove to be inaccurate.
(6) A payment by the Commissioners under that subsection is to be treated for the purposes of the Commissioners for Revenue and Customs Act 2005 (c. 11) as a disbursement of a kind specified in section 44(3) of that Act.
(7) In this section—
"repayments" includes—
(a) payments in respect of actual or deemed credits relating to any tax, duty or levy, and

(b) payments of interest (or repayment supplement) on—
(i) repayments, or
(ii) payments treated as repayments;

"revenue" means—
(a) taxes, duties and levies,
(b) the proceeds of forfeitures made and penalties imposed under the customs and excise Acts (within the meaning of section 1 of the Customs and Excise Management Act 1979 (c. 2)),
(c) a sum paid, or the proceeds of sale, under paragraph 16 of Schedule 3 to that Act, and
(d) the proceeds of penalties imposed in accordance with Regulation (EC) No 1889/2005 on controls of cash entering or leaving the Community (including penalties imposed under that Regulation as amended from time to time);

"security for revenue" means any sum paid as security for a tax or duty.

33 Power to require payment into the Consolidated Fund

(1) The Treasury may by order make provision for—
(a) requiring the payment of sums received by the Secretary of State or the Director in the exercise of their functions into the Consolidated Fund;
(b) permitting the deduction of disbursements before such payments are made;
(c) requiring the Secretary of State or the Director to provide accounts of the receipt and disposal of revenue;
(d) permitting the Treasury to make payments to the Secretary of State or the Director out of the Consolidated Fund to enable them to make disbursements.

(2) An order under this section may amend or repeal section 32 (payment of revenue to the Commissioners).

34 Children

(1) In section 21 of the UK Borders Act 2007 (c. 30) (code of practice relating to children), in subsection (1), for "the Border and Immigration Agency takes" substitute "the persons listed in subsection (4A) take".

(2) In subsection (2) of that section—
(a) for "The Agency" substitute "Those persons",
(b) in paragraph (a), for "its" substitute "their", and
(c) in paragraph (b), for "it makes" substitute "they make".

(3) After subsection (4) of that section insert—

"(4A) The persons are—
(a) designated customs officials, and officials of the Secretary of State exercising customs functions,
(b) immigration officers, and officials of the Secretary of State exercising functions relating to immigration, asylum or nationality,
(c) the Secretary of State in so far as the Secretary of State has general customs functions,
(d) the Secretary of State in so far as the Secretary of State has functions relating to immigration, asylum or nationality, and
(e) the Director of Border Revenue and any person exercising functions of the Director."

(4) In subsection (5) of that section omit paragraph (a).

(5) After that subsection insert—

"(5A) In this section "customs function", "designated customs official" and "general customs function" have the meanings given by Part 1 of the Borders, Citizenship and Immigration Act 2009."

(6) This section ceases to have effect on the coming into force of section 55 (duty regarding welfare of children).

Supplementary

35 Power to modify enactments

(1) The Secretary of State may by order provide for an enactment (or a description of enactments) to apply in relation to—

(a) relevant persons, or

(b) the exercise of functions by relevant persons,

with such modifications as the Secretary of State considers necessary or expedient.

(2) In this section—

(a) "relevant persons" means—

(i) the Secretary of State by whom general customs functions are exercisable,

(ii) the Director of Border Revenue, and

(iii) designated customs officials, immigration officers and officials in the department of that Secretary of State, and

(b) a reference to relevant persons includes a reference to any description of relevant persons.

(3) An order under this section may, in particular, include provision for or in connection with—

(a) extending to relevant persons an exemption or protection afforded by an enactment to any other description of persons;

(b) providing for the disclosure of information to, or the doing of other things in relation to, relevant persons.

(4) The Secretary of State must consult the Commissioners for Her Majesty's Revenue and Customs before making an order under this section that—

(a) makes provision in relation to a general customs matter or a customs revenue matter, or

(b) makes provision in relation to the exercise of a customs function.

36 Power to make supplementary etc. provision

(1) The Secretary of State may by order make—

(a) such incidental, supplementary or consequential provision, or

(b) such transitional or transitory provision or savings,

as the Secretary of State considers appropriate for the general purposes, or any particular purpose, of this Part, or in consequence of, or for giving full effect to, any provision made by or under this Part.

(2) An order under subsection (1) may amend, repeal, revoke or otherwise modify any enactment (including this Act).

(3) The power to make an order under subsection (1) includes power to repeal or revoke an enactment which is spent.

(4) Nothing in this Part affects the generality of the power conferred by this section.

37 Subordinate legislation

(1) Orders and regulations under this Part must be made by statutory instrument.
(2) An order or regulations under this Part may—
 (a) include incidental, supplementary and consequential provision;
 (b) make transitional or transitory provision or savings;
 (c) make different provision for different cases or circumstances.
(3) A statutory instrument containing an order or regulations to which subsection
(4) applies may not be made unless a draft of the instrument has been laid before, and approved by a resolution of, each House of Parliament.
(4) This subsection applies to—
 (a) an order under section 2 (power of Secretary of State to modify functions);
 (b) an order under section 8 (power of Treasury to modify Director's functions);
 (c) regulations under section 16(8) (power to permit disclosure);
 (d) an order under section 23 (application of provisions about investigations and detention: England and Wales and Northern Ireland);
 (e) an order under section 35 (power to modify enactments);
 (f) an order under section 36 (power to make supplementary etc. provision) that amends or repeals primary legislation.
(5) A statutory instrument containing only—
 (a) regulations under section 29 (inspections by Her Majesty's Inspectors of Constabulary etc.), or
 (b) an order under section 36 that does not amend or repeal primary legislation, is subject to annulment in pursuance of a resolution of either House of Parliament.
(6) A statutory instrument containing an order under section 33 (power to require payment into the Consolidated Fund) is subject to annulment in pursuance of a resolution of the House of Commons.
(7) In this section "primary legislation" means—
 (a) an Act of Parliament,
 (b) an Act of the Scottish Parliament,
 (c) a Measure or Act of the National Assembly for Wales, or
 (d) Northern Ireland legislation.
(8) This section does not apply to an order under section 31 (prosecution of offences).

38 Interpretation

In this Part—

"Community law" means—
 (a) all the rights, powers, liabilities, obligations and restrictions from time to time created or arising by or under the Community Treaties, and
 (b) all the remedies and procedures from time to time provided for by or under the Community Treaties,

as in accordance with the Community Treaties are without further enactment to be given legal effect or used in the United Kingdom;

"customs function" has the meaning given by section 14(6);

"customs information" has the meaning given by section 14(6);

"customs revenue function" has the meaning given by section 7(9);

"customs revenue information" has the meaning given by section 14(6);

"customs revenue matter" has the meaning given by section 7(2);

"customs revenue official" means a customs revenue official designated under section 11(1);
"designated customs official" has the meaning given by section 14(6);"enactment" includes—
(a) an enactment contained in subordinate legislation within the meaning of the Interpretation Act 1978 (c. 30);
(b) an enactment contained in, or in an instrument made under, an Act of the Scottish Parliament;
(c) an enactment contained in, or in instrument made under, Northern Ireland legislation;
(d) an enactment contained in, or in an instrument made under, a Measure or Act of the National Assembly for Wales;
"function" means any power or duty (including a power or duty that is ancillary to another power or duty);
"general customs function" has the meaning given by section 1(8);
"general customs matter" has the meaning given by section 1(2);
"general customs official" means a general customs official designated under section 3(1);
"personal customs information" has the meaning given by section 15(4);
"personal customs revenue information" has the meaning given by section 15(4);
"relevant official" has the meaning given by section 15(3).

PART 2
CITIZENSHIP

Acquisition of British citizenship by naturalisation

39 Application requirements: general

(1) In paragraph 1 of Schedule 1 to the British Nationality Act 1981 (c. 61) (requirements for naturalisation as a British citizen under section 6(1) of that Act), in sub-paragraph (1)(a), omit ", or the alternative requirement specified in sub-paragraph (3) of this paragraph".
(2) For sub-paragraph (2) of that paragraph substitute—
"(2) The requirements referred to in sub-paragraph (1)(a) of this paragraph are—
(a) that the applicant ("A") was in the United Kingdom at the beginning of the qualifying period;
(b) that the number of days on which A was absent from the United Kingdom in each year of the qualifying period does not exceed 90;
(c) that A had a qualifying immigration status for the whole of the qualifying period;
(d) that on the date of the application A has probationary citizenship leave, permanent residence leave, a qualifying CTA entitlement, a Commonwealth right of abode or a permanent EEA entitlement;
(e) that, where on the date of the application A has probationary citizenship leave granted for the purpose of taking employment in the United Kingdom, A has been in continuous employment since the date of the grant of that leave; and

(f) that A was not at any time in the qualifying period in the United Kingdom in breach of the immigration laws."

(3) Omit sub-paragraph (3) of that paragraph.

(4) In paragraph 2 of that Schedule (which becomes sub-paragraph (1) of that paragraph) (discretion of Secretary of State on applications for naturalisation under section 6(1)), for paragraph (a) substitute—

"(a) treat the applicant as fulfilling the requirement specified in paragraph 1(2)(b) although the number of days on which the applicant was absent from the United Kingdom in a year of the qualifying period exceeds 90;".

(5) After paragraph (b) of sub-paragraph (1) of that paragraph, insert—

"(ba) treat the applicant as fulfilling the requirement specified in paragraph 1(2)(c) where the applicant has had a qualifying immigration status for only part of the qualifying period;

(bb) treat the applicant as fulfilling the requirement specified in paragraph 1(2)(d) where the applicant has had probationary citizenship leave but it expired in the qualifying period;".

(6) Omit paragraph (c) of that sub-paragraph.

(7) Before paragraph (d) of that sub-paragraph, insert—

"(ca) treat the applicant as fulfilling the requirement specified in paragraph 1(2)(e) although the applicant has not been in continuous employment since the date of the grant mentioned there;".

(8) In paragraph (d) of that sub-paragraph—

(a) for "1(2)(d)" substitute "1(2)(f)", and

(b) for "period there mentioned" substitute "qualifying period".

(9) After that sub-paragraph insert—

"(2) If in the special circumstances of a particular case that is an armed forces case or an exceptional Crown service case the Secretary of State thinks fit, the Secretary of State may for the purposes of paragraph 1 waive the need to fulfil all or any of the requirements specified in paragraph 1(2).

(3) An armed forces case is a case where, on the date of the application, the applicant is or has been a member of the armed forces.

(4) An exceptional Crown service case is a case where—

(a) the applicant is, on the date of the application, serving outside the United Kingdom in Crown service under the government of the United Kingdom; and

(b) the Secretary of State considers the applicant's performance in the service to be exceptional."

(10) After sub-paragraph (4) (inserted by subsection (9) above) insert—

"(5) In paragraph 1(2)(e) and sub-paragraph (1)(ca) of this paragraph, "employment" includes self-employment."

(11) After paragraph 2 insert—

"2A (1) A person has a qualifying immigration status for the purposes of paragraph 1(2) if the person has—

(a) qualifying temporary residence leave;

(b) probationary citizenship leave;

(c) permanent residence leave;

(d) a qualifying CTA entitlement;

(e) a Commonwealth right of abode; or
(f) a temporary or permanent EEA entitlement.

(2) A person who is required for those purposes to have a qualifying immigration status for the whole of the qualifying period need not have the same qualifying immigration status for the whole of that period."

40 Application requirements: family members etc.

(1) In section 6 of the British Nationality Act 1981 (c. 61) (acquisition of British citizenship by naturalisation), in subsection (2), for "is married to a British citizen or is the civil partner of a British citizen" substitute "has a relevant family association".

(2) After that subsection insert—

"(3) For the purposes of this section and Schedule 1, a person ("A") has a relevant family association if A has a connection of a prescribed description to a person of a prescribed description.

(4) If in the special circumstances of any particular case the Secretary of State thinks fit, the Secretary of State may for the purposes of subsection (3) treat A as having a relevant family association on the date of the application although the relevant family association ceased to exist before that date."

(3) For paragraph 3 of Schedule 1 to that Act (requirements for naturalisation as a British citizen under section 6(2) of that Act) substitute—

"3 (1) Subject to paragraph 4, the requirements for naturalisation as a British citizen under section 6(2) are, in the case of any person ("A") who applies for it—

(a) the requirements specified in sub-paragraph (2) of this paragraph;
(b) the requirement specified in sub-paragraph (3) of this paragraph;
(c) that A is of good character;
(d) that A has a sufficient knowledge of the English, Welsh or Scottish Gaelic language; and
(e) that A has sufficient knowledge about life in the United Kingdom.

(2) The requirements referred to in sub-paragraph (1)(a) are—

(a) that A was in the United Kingdom at the beginning of the qualifying period;
(b) that the number of days on which A was absent from the United Kingdom in each year of the qualifying period does not exceed 90;
(c) that, subject to sub-paragraph (5)—
(i) A had a relevant family association for the whole of the qualifying period, and
(ii) A had a qualifying immigration status for the whole of that period;
(d) that on the date of the application—
(i) A has probationary citizenship leave, or permanent residence leave, based on A's having the relevant family association referred to in section 6(2), or
(ii) A has a qualifying CTA entitlement or a Commonwealth right of abode; and
(e) that A was not at any time in the qualifying period in the United Kingdom in breach of the immigration laws.

(3) The requirement referred to in sub-paragraph (1)(b) is—

(a) that A's intentions are such that, in the event of a certificate of naturalisation as a British citizen being granted to A, A's home or (if A has more than one) A's principal home will be in the United Kingdom;

(b) that A intends, in the event of such a certificate being granted to A, to enter into, or continue in, service of a description mentioned in sub paragraph (4); or

(c) that, in the event of such a certificate being granted to A—

(i) the person with whom A has the relevant family association referred to in section 6(2) ("B") intends to enter into, or continue in, service of a description mentioned in sub paragraph (4); and

(ii) A intends to reside with B for the period during which B is in the service in question.

(4) The descriptions of service referred to in sub-paragraph (3) are—

(a) Crown service under the government of the United Kingdom;

(b) service under an international organisation of which the United Kingdom, or Her Majesty's government in the United Kingdom, is a member; or

(c) service in the employment of a company or association established in the United Kingdom.

(5) Where the relevant family association referred to in section 6(2) is (in accordance with regulations under section 41(1)(a)) that A is the partner of a person who is a British citizen or who has permanent residence leave—

(a) the requirement specified in sub-paragraph (2)(c)(i) is fulfilled only if A was that person's partner for the whole of the qualifying period, and

(b) for the purposes of sub-paragraph (2)(c)(ii), A can rely upon having a qualifying immigration status falling within paragraph 4A(1)(a), (b) or (c) only if that partnership is the relevant family association upon which the leave to which the status relates is based.

(6) For the purposes of sub-paragraph (5), A is a person's partner if—

(a) that person is A's spouse or civil partner or is in a relationship with A that is of a description that the regulations referred to in that sub-paragraph specify, and

(b) the marriage, civil partnership or other relationship satisfies the conditions (if any) that those regulations specify.

(7) For the purposes of sub-paragraph (5), the relationship by reference to which A and the other person are partners need not be of the same description for the whole of the qualifying period."

(4) For paragraph 4 of that Schedule substitute—

"4 If in the special circumstances of any particular case the Secretary of State thinks fit, the Secretary of State may for the purposes of paragraph 3 do all or any of the following, namely—

(a) treat A as fulfilling the requirement specified in paragraph 3(2)(b), although the number of days on which A was absent from the United Kingdom in a year of the qualifying period exceeds 90;

(b) treat A as having been in the United Kingdom for the whole or any part of any period during which A would otherwise fall to be treated under paragraph 9(1) as having been absent;

(c) treat A as fulfilling the requirement specified in paragraph 3(2)(c)(i) (including where it can be fulfilled only as set out in paragraph 3(5)) where a relevant family association of A's has ceased to exist;

(d) treat A as fulfilling the requirement specified in paragraph 3(2)(c)(ii) (including where it can be fulfilled only as set out in paragraph 3(5)) where A has had a qualifying immigration status for only part of the qualifying period;

(e) treat A as fulfilling the requirement specified in paragraph 3(2)(d) where A has had probationary citizenship leave but it expired in the qualifying period;
(f) treat A as fulfilling the requirement specified in paragraph 3(2)(e) although A was in the United Kingdom in breach of the immigration laws in the qualifying period;
(g) waive the need to fulfil either or both of the requirements specified in paragraph 3(1)(d) and (e) if the Secretary of State considers that because of A's age or physical or mental condition it would be unreasonable to expect A to fulfil that requirement or those requirements;
(h) waive the need to fulfil all or any of the requirements specified in paragraph 3(2)(a), (b), (c) or (d) (including where paragraph 3(2)(c) can be fulfilled only as set out in paragraph 3(5)) if—
(i) on the date of the application, the person with whom A has the relevant family association referred to in section 6(2) is serving in service to which section 2(1)(b) applies, and
(ii) that person's recruitment for that service took place in the United Kingdom."

(5) After that paragraph insert—
"4A (1) Subject to paragraph 3(5), a person has a qualifying immigration status for the purposes of paragraph 3 if the person has—
(a) qualifying temporary residence leave based on a relevant family association;
(b) probationary citizenship leave based on a relevant family association;
(c) permanent residence leave based on a relevant family association;
(d) a qualifying CTA entitlement; or
(e) a Commonwealth right of abode.
(2) For the purposes of paragraph 3 and this paragraph, the leave mentioned in sub-paragraph (1)(a), (b) or (c) is based on a relevant family association if it was granted on the basis of the person having a relevant family association.
(3) A person who is required for the purposes of paragraph 3 to have, for the whole of the qualifying period, a qualifying immigration status and a relevant family association need not, for the whole of that period—
(a) have the same qualifying immigration status; or
(b) (subject to paragraph 3(5)) have the same relevant family association.
(4) Where, by virtue of sub-paragraph (3)(a), a person relies upon having more than one qualifying immigration status falling within sub-paragraph (1)(a), (b) or (c)—
(a) subject to paragraph 3(5), it is not necessary that the leave to which each status relates is based on the same relevant family association, and
(b) in a case where paragraph 3(5) applies, the relationship by reference to which the persons referred to in paragraph 3(5) are partners need not be of the same description in respect of each grant of leave."

41 The qualifying period

(1) After paragraph 4A of Schedule 1 to the British Nationality Act 1981 (c. 61) (inserted by section 40(5) above), insert—
"The qualifying period for naturalisation as a British citizen under section 6
4B (1) The qualifying period for the purposes of paragraph 1 or 3 is a period of years which ends with the date of the application in question.

(2) The length of the period is determined in accordance with the following provisions of this paragraph.
(3) In the case of an applicant who does not meet the activity condition, the number of years in the period is—
(a) 8, in a case within paragraph 1;
(b) 5, in a case within paragraph 3.
(4) In the case of an applicant who meets the activity condition, the number of years in the period is—
(a) 6, in a case within paragraph 1;
(b) 3, in a case within paragraph 3.
(5) The applicant meets the activity condition if the Secretary of State is satisfied that the applicant—
(a) has participated otherwise than for payment in prescribed activities; or
(b) is to be treated as having so participated."

(2) In section 41 of that Act (regulations etc.), in subsection (1), after paragraph (bb) insert—
"(bc) for amending paragraph 4B(3)(a) or (b) or (4)(a) or (b) of Schedule 1 to substitute a different number for the number for the time being specified there;
(bd) for determining whether a person has, for the purposes of an application for naturalisation under section 6, participated in activities prescribed for the purposes of paragraph 4B(5)(a) of Schedule 1;
(be) for determining whether a person is to be treated for the purposes of such an application as having so participated;".

(3) After subsection (1A) of that section insert—
"(1B) Regulations under subsection (1)(bc) may make provision so that—
(a) the number specified in sub-paragraph (3)(a) of paragraph 4B of Schedule 1 is the same as the number specified in subparagraph (4)(a) of that paragraph;
(b) the number specified in sub-paragraph (3)(b) of that paragraph is the same as the number specified in sub-paragraph (4)(b) of that paragraph.
(1C) Regulations under subsection (1)(bd) or (be)—
(a) may make provision that applies in relation to time before the commencement of section 41 of the Borders, Citizenship and Immigration Act 2009;
(b) may enable the Secretary of State to make arrangements for such persons as the Secretary of State thinks appropriate to determine whether, in accordance with those regulations, a person has, or (as the case may be) is to be treated as having, participated in an activity."

(4) In subsection (7) of that section, after "this section" insert "(other than regulations referred to in subsection (8))".

(5) After subsection (7) of that section insert—
"(8) Any regulations (whether alone or with other provision)—
(a) under subsection (1)(a) for prescribing activities for the purposes of paragraph 4B(5)(a) of Schedule 1; or
(b) under subsection (1)(bc), (bd) or (be), may not be made unless a draft has been laid before and approved by a resolution of each House of Parliament."

Acquisition of British citizenship by birth

42 Children born in UK etc. to members of the armed forces

(1) Section 1 of the British Nationality Act 1981 (c. 61) (acquisition of British citizenship by birth or adoption) is amended as follows.
(2) After subsection (1) insert—
"(1A) A person born in the United Kingdom or a qualifying territory on or after the relevant day shall be a British citizen if at the time of the birth his father or mother is a member of the armed forces."
(3) In subsection (3), after "subsection (1)" insert ", (1A)".
(4) After subsection (3) insert—
"(3A) A person born in the United Kingdom on or after the relevant day who is not a British citizen by virtue of subsection (1), (1A) or (2) shall be entitled to be registered as a British citizen if, while he is a minor—
(a) his father or mother becomes a member of the armed forces; and
(b) an application is made for his registration as a British citizen".
(5) In subsection (4), after "subsection (1)" insert ", (1A)".
(6) After subsection (8) insert—
"(9) The relevant day for the purposes of subsection (1A) or (3A) is the day appointed for the commencement of section 42 of the Borders, Citizenship and Immigration Act 2009 (which inserted those subsections)."

Acquisition of British citizenship etc. by registration

43 Minors

(1) Section 3 of the British Nationality Act 1981 (c. 61) (acquisition by registration: minors) is amended as follows.
(2) In subsection (2), for "within the period of twelve months from the date of the birth" substitute "while he is a minor".
(3) Omit subsection (4).

44 British Nationals (Overseas) without other citizenship

(1) Section 4B of the British Nationality Act 1981 (acquisition by registration: certain persons without other citizenship) is amended as follows.
(2) In subsection (1)—
(a) omit "or" immediately before paragraph (c), and
(b) after that paragraph insert ", or
(d) British National (Overseas)".
(3) In subsection (2)(c), for "4th July 2002" substitute "the relevant day".
(4) After subsection (2), insert—
"(3) For the purposes of subsection (2)(c), the "relevant day" means—
(a) in the case of a person to whom this section applies by virtue of subsection (1)(d) only, 19th March 2009, and
(b) in any other case, 4th July 2002."

45 Descent through the female line

(1) Section 4C of the British Nationality Act 1981 (the title to which becomes "Acquisition by registration: certain persons born before 1983") is amended as follows.

(2) In subsection (2), omit "after 7th February 1961 and".

(3) For subsection (3) substitute—

"(3) The second condition is that the applicant would at some time before 1st January 1983 have become a citizen of the United Kingdom and Colonies—

(a) under section 5 of, or paragraph 3 of Schedule 3 to, the 1948 Act if assumption A had applied,

(b) under section 12(3), (4) or (5) of that Act if assumption B had applied and as a result of its application the applicant would have been a British subject immediately before 1st January 1949, or

(c) under section 12(2) of that Act if one or both of the following had applied—

(i) assumption A had applied;

(ii) assumption B had applied and as a result of its application the applicant would have been a British subject immediately before 1st January 1949.

(3A) Assumption A is that—

(a) section 5 or 12(2) of, or paragraph 3 of Schedule 3 to, the 1948 Act (as the case may be) provided for citizenship by descent from a mother in the same terms as it provided for citizenship by descent from a father, and

(b) references in that provision to a father were references to the applicant's mother.

(3B) Assumption B is that—

(a) a provision of the law at some time before 1st January 1949 which provided for a nationality status to be acquired by descent from a father provided in the same terms for its acquisition by descent from a mother, and

(b) references in that provision to a father were references to the applicant's mother.

(3C) For the purposes of subsection (3B), a nationality status is acquired by a person ("P") by descent where its acquisition—

(a) depends, amongst other things, on the nationality status of one or both of P's parents, and

(b) does not depend upon an application being made for P's registration as a person who has the status in question.

(3D) For the purposes of subsection (3), it is not to be assumed that any registration or other requirements of the provisions mentioned in that subsection or in subsection (3B) were met."

(4) After subsection (4) insert—

"(5) For the purposes of the interpretation of section 5 of the 1948 Act in its application in the case of assumption A to a case of descent from a mother, the reference in the proviso to subsection (1) of that section to "a citizen of the United Kingdom and Colonies by descent only" includes a reference to a female person who became a citizen of the United Kingdom and Colonies by virtue of—

(a) section 12(2), (4) or (6) only of the 1948 Act,

(b) section 13(2) of that Act,

(c) paragraph 3 of Schedule 3 to that Act, or

(d) section 1(1)(a) or (c) of the British Nationality (No. 2) Act 1964."

46 Children born outside UK etc. to members of the armed forces

After section 4C of the British Nationality Act 1981 (c. 61) insert—

"**4D Acquisition by registration: children of members of the armed forces**

(1) A person ("P") born outside the United Kingdom and the qualifying territories on or after the relevant day is entitled to be registered as a British citizen if—
   (a) an application is made for P's registration under this section; and
   (b) each of the following conditions is satisfied.

(2) The first condition is that, at the time of P's birth, P's father or mother was—
   (a) a member of the armed forces; and
   (b) serving outside the United Kingdom and the qualifying territories.

(3) The second condition is that, if P is a minor on the date of the application, the consent of P's father and mother to P's registration as a British citizen has been signified in the prescribed manner.

(4) But if P's father or mother has died on or before the date of the application, the reference in subsection (3) to P's father and mother is to be read as a reference to either of them.

(5) The Secretary of State may, in the special circumstances of a particular case, waive the need for the second condition to be satisfied.

(6) The relevant day for the purposes of this section is the day appointed for the commencement of section 46 of the Borders, Citizenship and Immigration Act 2009 (which inserted this section)."

47 Good character requirement

(1) After section 41 of the British Nationality Act 1981 insert—

"**41A Registration: requirement to be of good character**

(1) An application for registration of an adult or young person as a British citizen under section 1(3), (3A) or (4), 3(1), (2) or (5), 4(2) or (5), 4A, 4C, 4D, 5, 10(1) or (2) or 13(1) or (3) must not be granted unless the Secretary of State is satisfied that the adult or young person is of good character.

(2) An application for registration of an adult or young person as a British overseas territories citizen under section 15(3) or (4), 17(1) or (5), 22(1) or (2) or 24 must not be granted unless the Secretary of State is satisfied that the adult or young person is of good character.

(3) An application for registration of an adult or young person as a British Overseas citizen under section 27(1) must not be granted unless the Secretary of State is satisfied that the adult or young person is of good character.

(4) An application for registration of an adult or young person as a British subject under section 32 must not be granted unless the Secretary of State is satisfied that the adult or young person is of good character.

(5) In this section, "adult or young person" means a person who has attained the age of 10 years at the time when the application is made."

(2) In section 1 of the Hong Kong (War Wives and Widows) Act 1996 (c. 41) (acquisition of British citizenship), in subsection (1)—
   (a) omit "and" immediately before paragraph (b), and
   (b) after that paragraph insert "; and
   (c) the Secretary of State is satisfied that she is of good character".

(3) In section 1 of the British Nationality (Hong Kong) Act 1997 (c. 20) (acquisition of British citizenship), after subsection (5) insert—

"(5A) An adult or young person shall not be registered under subsection (1) unless the Secretary of State is satisfied that the adult or young person is of good character.

(5B) In subsection (5A), "adult or young person" means a person who has attained the age of 10 years at the time when the application for registration is made."

(4) In section 131 of the Nationality, Immigration and Asylum Act 2002 (c. 41) (supply of police information), for paragraph (b) substitute—

"(b) determining whether, for the purposes of an application referred to in section 41A of the British Nationality Act 1981, the person for whose registration the application is made is of good character;

(ba) determining whether, for the purposes of an application under section 1 of the Hong Kong (War Wives and Widows) Act 1996, the woman for whose registration the application is made is of good character;

(bb) determining whether, for the purposes of an application under section 1 of the British Nationality (Hong Kong) Act 1997 for the registration of an adult or young person within the meaning of subsection (5A) of that section, the person is of good character;".

(5) In section 40 of the UK Borders Act 2007 (c. 30) (supply of Revenue and Customs information), in subsection (1), for paragraph (h) substitute—

"(h) determining whether, for the purposes of an application referred to in section 41A of the British Nationality Act 1981, the person for whose registration the application is made is of good character;

(ha) determining whether, for the purposes of an application under section 1 of the Hong Kong (War Wives and Widows) Act 1996, the woman for whose registration the application is made is of good character;

(hb) determining whether, for the purposes of an application under section 1 of the British Nationality (Hong Kong) Act 1997 for the registration of an adult or young person within the meaning of subsection (5A) of that section, the person is of good character;".

Interpretation etc.

48 Meaning of references to being in breach of immigration laws

(1) After section 50 of the British Nationality Act 1981 (c. 61) insert—

"50A Meaning of references to being in breach of immigration laws

(1) This section applies for the construction of a reference to being in the United Kingdom "in breach of the immigration laws" in—

(a) section 4(2) or (4);

(b) section 50(5); or

(c) Schedule 1.

(2) It applies only for the purpose of determining on or after the relevant day—

(a) whether a person born on or after the relevant day is a British citizen under section 1(1),

(b) whether, on an application under section 1(3) or 4(2) made on or after the relevant day, a person is entitled to be registered as a British citizen, or

(c) whether, on an application under section 6(1) or (2) made on or after the relevant day, the applicant fulfils the requirements of Schedule 1 for naturalisation as a British citizen under section 6(1) or (2).

(3) But that is subject to section 48(3)(d) and (4) of the Borders, Citizenship and Immigration Act 2009 (saving in relation to section 11 of the Nationality, Immigration and Asylum Act 2002).

(4) A person is in the United Kingdom in breach of the immigration laws if (and only if) the person—

(a) is in the United Kingdom;

(b) does not have the right of abode in the United Kingdom within the meaning of section 2 of the Immigration Act 1971;

(c) does not have leave to enter or remain in the United Kingdom (whether or not the person previously had leave);

(d) does not have a qualifying CTA entitlement;

(e) is not entitled to reside in the United Kingdom by virtue of any provision made under section 2(2) of the European Communities Act 1972 (whether or not the person was previously entitled);

(f) is not entitled to enter and remain in the United Kingdom by virtue of section 8(1) of the Immigration Act 1971 (crew) (whether or not the person was previously entitled); and

(g) does not have the benefit of an exemption under section 8(2) to (4) of that Act (diplomats, soldiers and other special cases) (whether or not the person previously had the benefit of an exemption).

(5) For the purposes of subsection (4)(d), a person has a qualifying CTA entitlement if the person—

(a) is a citizen of the Republic of Ireland,

(b) last arrived in the United Kingdom on a local journey (within the meaning of the Immigration Act 1971) from the Republic of Ireland, and

(c) on that arrival, was a citizen of the Republic of Ireland and was entitled to enter without leave by virtue of section 1(3) of the Immigration Act 1971 (entry from the common travel area).

(6) Section 11(1) of the Immigration Act 1971 (person deemed not to be in the United Kingdom before disembarkation, while in controlled area or while under immigration control) applies for the purposes of this section as it applies for the purposes of that Act.

(7) This section is without prejudice to the generality of—

(a) a reference to being in a place outside the United Kingdom in breach of immigration laws, and

(b) a reference in a provision other than one specified in subsection (1) to being in the United Kingdom in breach of immigration laws.

(8) The relevant day for the purposes of subsection (2) is the day appointed for the commencement of section 48 of the Borders, Citizenship and Immigration Act 2009 (which inserted this section)."

(2) Section 11 of the Nationality, Immigration and Asylum Act 2002 (c. 41) ("the 2002 Act") (unlawful presence in the United Kingdom) ceases to have effect.

(3) Notwithstanding its repeal, section 11 of the 2002 Act is to continue to have effect for the purpose of determining on or after the relevant day—
 (a) whether a person born before the relevant day is a British citizen under section 1(1) of the British Nationality Act 1981 (c. 61),
 (b) whether, on an application under section 1(3) or 4(2) of that Act made but not determined before the relevant day, a person is entitled to be registered as a British citizen,
 (c) whether, on an application under section 6(1) or (2) of that Act made but not determined before the relevant day, the applicant fulfils the requirements of Schedule 1 for naturalisation as a British citizen under section 6(1) or (2) of that Act, or
 (d) whether, in relation to an application under section 1(3) or 6(1) or (2) of that Act made on or after the relevant day, a person was in the United Kingdom "in breach of the immigration laws" at a time before 7 November 2002 (the date of commencement of section 11 of the 2002 Act).

(4) Where section 11 of the 2002 Act continues to have effect by virtue of paragraph (d) of subsection (3) for the purpose of determining on or after the relevant day the matter mentioned in that paragraph, section 50A of the British Nationality Act 1981 is not to apply for the purpose of determining that matter.

(5) The relevant day for the purposes of subsection (3) is the day appointed for the commencement of this section.

(6) In paragraph 7(a) of Schedule 3 to the 2002 Act (definition of persons unlawfully in the UK who are ineligible for support), for "section 11" substitute "section 50A of the British Nationality Act 1981".

49 Other interpretation etc.

(1) In section 50 of the British Nationality Act 1981 (c. 61) (interpretation), after subsection (1), insert—
 "(1A) Subject to subsection (1B), references in this Act to being a member of the armed forces are references to being—
  (a) a member of the regular forces within the meaning of the Armed Forces Act 2006, or
  (b) a member of the reserve forces within the meaning of that Act subject to service law by virtue of paragraph (a), (b) or (c) of section 367(2) of that Act.
 (1B) A person is not to be regarded as a member of the armed forces by virtue of subsection (1A) if the person is treated as a member of a regular or reserve force by virtue of—
  (a) section 369 of the Armed Forces Act 2006, or
  (b) section 4(3) of the Visiting Forces (British Commonwealth) Act 1933."

(2) In Schedule 1 to that Act (requirements for naturalisation as a British citizen), in paragraph 9(1), for "paragraph 2(b)" substitute "paragraph 2(1)(b) or 4(b)".

(3) After paragraph 10 of that Schedule insert—
 "11 (1) This paragraph applies for the purposes of this Schedule.
 (2) A person has qualifying temporary residence leave if—
  (a) the person has limited leave to enter or remain in the United Kingdom, and
  (b) the leave is granted for a purpose by reference to which a grant of probationary citizenship leave may be made.

(3) A person has probationary citizenship leave if—
(a) the person has limited leave to enter or remain in the United Kingdom, and
(b) the leave is of a description identified in rules under section 3 of the Immigration Act 1971 as "probationary citizenship leave",
and the reference in sub paragraph (2) to a grant of probationary citizenship leave is to be construed accordingly.
(4) A person has permanent residence leave if the person has indefinite leave to enter or remain in the United Kingdom.
(5) A person has a qualifying CTA entitlement if the person—
(a) is a citizen of the Republic of Ireland,
(b) last arrived in the United Kingdom on a local journey (within the meaning of the Immigration Act 1971) from the Republic of Ireland, and
(c) on that arrival, was a citizen of the Republic of Ireland and was entitled to enter without leave by virtue of section 1(3) of the Immigration Act 1971 (entry from the common travel area).
(6) A person has a Commonwealth right of abode if the person has the right of abode in the United Kingdom by virtue of section 2(1)(b) of the Immigration Act 1971.
(7) A person has a permanent EEA entitlement if the person is entitled to reside in the United Kingdom permanently by virtue of any provision made under section 2(2) of the European Communities Act 1972.
(8) A person has a temporary EEA entitlement if the person does not have a permanent EEA entitlement but is entitled to reside in the United Kingdom by virtue of any provision made under section 2(2) of the European Communities Act 1972.
(9) A reference in this paragraph to having leave to enter or remain in the United Kingdom is to be construed in accordance with the Immigration Act 1971."

PART 3
IMMIGRATION

Studies

50 Restriction on studies

(1) In section 3(1)(c) of the Immigration Act 1971 (c. 77) (conditions that may be imposed on limited leave to enter or remain in the United Kingdom), after subparagraph (i) insert—
"(ia) a condition restricting his studies in the United Kingdom;".
(2) A condition under section 3(1)(c)(ia) of that Act may be added as a condition to leave given before the passing of this Act (as well as to leave given on or after its passing).

Fingerprinting

51 Fingerprinting of foreign criminals liable to automatic deportation

(1) Section 141 of the Immigration and Asylum Act 1999 (c. 33) (persons from whom fingerprints may be taken) is amended as follows.
(2) In subsection (7)(f), after "persons" insert ", other than a dependant of a person who falls within paragraph (c) by reason of a relevant immigration decision within subsection (16)(b) having been made in respect of that person".

(3) In subsection (16)—
(a) after "means" insert "—",
(b) the words from "a decision" to the end become paragraph (a), and
(c) after that paragraph insert ", or
(b) a decision that section 32(5) of the UK Borders Act 2007 applies (whether made before, or on or after, the day appointed for the commencement of section 51 of the Borders, Citizenship and Immigration Act 2009 which inserted this paragraph)".

Detention at ports in Scotland

52 Extension of sections 1 to 4 of the UK Borders Act 2007 to Scotland

(1) In section 2 of the UK Borders Act 2007 (c. 30) (detention at ports), after subsection (1), insert—
"(1A) A designated immigration officer at a port in Scotland may detain an individual if the immigration officer thinks that the individual is subject to a warrant for arrest."
(2) In section 3 of that Act (enforcement of detention at ports), after subsection (4), insert—
"(4A) In the application of this section to Scotland, the references in subsections (2)(a) and (3)(a) to 51 weeks shall be treated as references to 12 months."
(3) In section 60(1) of that Act (provisions which do not extend to Scotland), omit "1 to 4,".

PART 4
MISCELLANEOUS AND GENERAL

Judicial review

53 Transfer of certain immigration judicial review applications

(1) In section 31A of the Supreme Court Act 1981 (c. 54) (England and Wales: transfer from the High Court to the Upper Tribunal)—
(a) after subsection (2) insert—
"(2A) If Conditions 1, 2, 3 and 5 are met, but Condition 4 is not, the High Court must by order transfer the application to the Upper Tribunal.", and
(b) after subsection (7) insert—
"(8) Condition 5 is that the application calls into question a decision of the Secretary of State not to treat submissions as an asylum claim or a human rights claim within the meaning of Part 5 of the Nationality, Immigration and Asylum Act 2002 wholly or partly on the basis that they are not significantly different from material that has previously been considered (whether or not it calls into question any other decision)."
(2) In section 25A of the Judicature (Northern Ireland) Act 1978 (c. 23) (Northern Ireland: transfer from the High Court to the Upper Tribunal)—
(a) after subsection (2) insert—
"(2A) If Conditions 1, 2, 3 and 5 are met, but Condition 4 is not, the High Court must by order transfer the application to the Upper Tribunal.", and

(b) after subsection (7) insert—

"(8) Condition 5 is that the application calls into question a decision of the Secretary of State not to treat submissions as an asylum claim or a human rights claim within the meaning of Part 5 of the Nationality, Immigration and Asylum Act 2002 wholly or partly on the basis that they are not significantly different from material that has previously been considered (whether or not it calls into question any other decision)."

(3) In section 20 of the Tribunals, Courts and Enforcement Act 2007 (c. 15) (Scotland: transfer from the Court of Session to the Upper Tribunal)—

(a) in subsection (1), for the "and" at the end of paragraph (a) substitute—

"(aa) must, if Conditions 1, 2 and 5 are met, but Condition 4 is not, and", and

(b) after subsection (5) insert—

"(5A) Condition 5 is that the application calls into question a decision of the Secretary of State not to treat submissions as an asylum claim or a human rights claim within the meaning of Part 5 of the Nationality, Immigration and Asylum Act 2002 wholly or partly on the basis that they are not significantly different from material that has previously been considered (whether or not it calls into question any other decision)."

Trafficking people for exploitation

54 Trafficking people for exploitation

In section 4(4) of the Asylum and Immigration (Treatment of Claimants, etc.) Act 2004 (c. 19) (trafficking people for exploitation: meaning of exploitation), for paragraph (d) substitute—

"(d) a person uses or attempts to use him for any purpose within sub paragraph (i), (ii) or (iii) of paragraph (c), having chosen him for that purpose on the grounds that—

(i) he is mentally or physically ill or disabled, he is young or he has a family relationship with a person, and

(ii) a person without the illness, disability, youth or family relationship would be likely to refuse to be used for that purpose."

Children

55 Duty regarding the welfare of children

(1) The Secretary of State must make arrangements for ensuring that—

(a) the functions mentioned in subsection (2) are discharged having regard to the need to safeguard and promote the welfare of children who are in the United Kingdom, and

(b) any services provided by another person pursuant to arrangements which are made by the Secretary of State and relate to the discharge of a function mentioned in subsection (2) are provided having regard to that need.

(2) The functions referred to in subsection (1) are—

(a) any function of the Secretary of State in relation to immigration, asylum or nationality;

(b) any function conferred by or by virtue of the Immigration Acts on an immigration officer;

(c) any general customs function of the Secretary of State;
(d) any customs function conferred on a designated customs official.

(3) A person exercising any of those functions must, in exercising the function, have regard to any guidance given to the person by the Secretary of State for the purpose of subsection (1).

(4) The Director of Border Revenue must make arrangements for ensuring that—
(a) the Director's functions are discharged having regard to the need to safeguard and promote the welfare of children who are in the United Kingdom, and
(b) any services provided by another person pursuant to arrangements made by the Director in the discharge of such a function are provided having regard to that need.

(5) A person exercising a function of the Director of Border Revenue must, in exercising the function, have regard to any guidance given to the person by the Secretary of State for the purpose of subsection (4).

(6) In this section—
"children" means persons who are under the age of 18;
"customs function", "designated customs official" and "general customs function" have the meanings given by Part 1.

(7) A reference in an enactment (other than this Act) to the Immigration Acts includes a reference to this section.

(8) Section 21 of the UK Borders Act 2007 (c. 30) (children) ceases to have effect.

General

56 Repeals

The Schedule contains repeals.

57 Extent

(1) Subject to the following provisions of this section, this Act extends to—
(a) England and Wales,
(b) Scotland, and
(c) Northern Ireland.

(2) Sections 22 (application of the PACE orders) and 23 (investigations and detention: England and Wales and Northern Ireland) extend to England and Wales and Northern Ireland only.

(3) An amendment, modification or repeal by this Act has the same extent as the enactment or relevant part of the enactment to which it relates (ignoring extent by virtue of an Order in Council under any of the Immigration Acts).

(4) Subsection (3) does not apply to—
(a) the amendments made by section 52 (detention at ports in Scotland);
(b) the amendment made by section 54 (trafficking people for exploitation), = which extends to England and Wales and Northern Ireland only.

(5) Her Majesty may by Order in Council provide for any of the provisions of this Act, other than any provision of Part 1 (border functions) or section 53 (transfer of certain immigration judicial review applications), to extend, with or without modifications, to any of the Channel Islands or the Isle of Man.

(6) Subsection (5) does not apply in relation to the extension to a place of a provision which extends there by virtue of subsection (3).

58 Commencement

(1) Part 1 (border functions) comes into force on the day this Act is passed.

(2) The provisions of Part 2 (citizenship) come into force on such day as the Secretary of State may by order appoint.

(3) In Part 3 (immigration)—

(a) section 50 (restriction on studies) comes into force on the day this Act is passed;

(b) sections 51 (fingerprinting of foreign criminals) and 52 (detention at ports in Scotland) come into force on such day as the Secretary of State may by order appoint.

(4) In this Part—

(a) section 53 (transfer of certain immigration judicial review applications) comes into force on such day as the Lord Chancellor may by order appoint;

(b) sections 54 (trafficking people for exploitation) and 55 (duty regarding the welfare of children) come into force on such day as the Secretary of State may by order appoint.

(5) Any repeal in the Schedule (and section 56 so far as relating to the repeal) comes into force in the same way as the provisions of this Act to which the repeal relates.

(6) The other provisions of this Part come into force on the day this Act is passed.

(7) An order under this section must be made by statutory instrument.

(8) An order under this section—

(a) may appoint different days for different purposes;

(b) may include transitional or incidental provision or savings.

(9) An order commencing sections 39 to 41 (acquisition of British citizenship by naturalisation) must include provision that the amendments made by those sections do not have effect in relation to an application for naturalisation as a British citizen if—

(a) the date of the application is before the date on which those sections come into force in accordance with the order ("the date of commencement"), or

(b) the date of the application is before the end of the period of 24 months beginning with the date of commencement and the application is made by a person who falls within subsection (10) or (11).

(10) A person falls within this subsection if on the date of commencement the person has indefinite leave to remain in the United Kingdom.

(11) A person falls within this subsection if the person is given indefinite leave to remain in the United Kingdom on an application—

(a) the date of which is before the date of commencement, and

(b) which is decided after the date of commencement.

(12) The reference in subsection (9) to an order commencing sections 39 to 41 does not include an order commencing those sections for the purpose only of enabling regulations to be made under the British Nationality Act 1981 (c. 61).

(13) In the case of an order commencing sections 39 to 41, transitional provision may, in particular—

(a) provide that the qualifying period for the purposes of paragraph 1 or 3 of Schedule 1 to the British Nationality Act 1981 includes time before that commencement;

(b) provide for leave to enter or remain in the United Kingdom granted before that commencement to be treated as qualifying temporary residence leave or probationary citizenship leave for the purposes of that Schedule.

(14) In the case of an order commencing section 45 (acquisition of British citizenship through the female line), transitional provision may, in particular, provide that section 45 is to apply to an application made, but not determined, under section 4C of the British Nationality Act 1981 before that commencement.

(15) No order may be made commencing section 52 (detention at ports in Scotland) unless the Secretary of State has consulted the Scottish Ministers.

(16) No order may be made commencing section 53 (transfer of certain immigration judicial review applications) unless the functions of the Asylum and Immigration Tribunal in relation to appeals under Part 5 of the Nationality, Immigration and Asylum Act 2002 (c. 41) have been transferred under section 30(1) of the Tribunals, Courts and Enforcement Act 2007 (c. 15).

59 Short title

This Act may be cited as the Borders, Citizenship and Immigration Act 2009.

SCHEDULE
REPEALS

Section 56

PART 1
BORDER FUNCTIONS

Reference	Extent of repeal
UK Borders Act 2007 (c. 30)	Section 21(5)(a). In section 48— (a) in subsection (2), the words from the beginning to "Agency;", and (b) subsection (3).

PART 2
CITIZENSHIP

Reference	Extent of repeal
British Nationality Act 1981 (c. 61)	Section 3(4). In section 4B(1), the word "or" immediately before paragraph (c). In section 4C(2), the words "after 7th February 1961 and". In Schedule 1— (a) in paragraph 1(1)(a), the words from ", or the" to "this paragraph", (b) paragraph 1(3), and (c) paragraph 2(1)(c).
Hong Kong (War Wives and Widows) Act 1996 (c. 41)	In section 1(1), the word "and" immediately before paragraph (b).
Nationality, Immigration and Asylum Act 2002 (c. 41)	Section 11.
Immigration, Asylum and Nationality Act 2006 (c. 13)	Section 58.

PART 3
IMMIGRATION

Reference	Extent of repeal
UK Borders Act 2007 (c. 30)	In section 60(1), the words "1 to 4,".

PART 4
MISCELLANEOUS

Reference	Extent of repeal
UK Borders Act 2007 (c. 30)	Section 21.

APPENDIX 2

Immigration Act 1971, s 2, as in force prior to 1 January 1983

Immediately prior to commencement of the BNA 1981 on 1 January 1983, the Immigration Act 1971, s 2 provided that:

2. (l) A person is under this Act to have the right of abode, in the United Kingdom if—
   (a) he is a citizen of the United Kingdom and Colonies who has that citizenship by his birth, adoption, naturalisation or (except as mentioned below) registration in the United Kingdom or in any of the Islands; or
   (b) he is a citizen of the United Kingdom and Colonies born to or legally adopted by a parent who had that citizenship at the time of the birth or adoption, and the parent either-
      (i) then had that citizenship by his birth, adoption, naturalisation or (except as mentioned below) registration in the United Kingdom or in any of the Islands; or
      (ii) had been born to or legally adopted by a parent who at the time of that birth or adoption so had it; or
   (c) he is a citizen of the United Kingdom and Colonies who has at any time been settled in the United Kingdom and Islands and had at that time (and while such a citizen) been ordinarily resident there for the last five years or more; or
   (d) he is a Commonwealth citizen born to or legally adopted by a parent who at the time of the birth or adoption had citizenship of the United Kingdom and Colonies by his birth in the United Kingdom or in any of the Islands.

(2) A woman is under this Act also to have the right of abode in the United Kingdom if she is a Commonwealth citizen and either-
   (a) is the wife of any such citizen of the United Kingdom and Colonies as is mentioned in subsection (1)(a), (b) or (c) above or any such Commonwealth citizen as is mentioned in subsection (1)(d); or
   (b) has at any time been the wife-
      (i) of a person then being such a citizen of the United Kingdom and Colonies or Commonwealth citizen; or
      (ii) of a British subject who but for his death would 1948 on the date of commencement of the British Nationality Act 1948 have been such a citizen of the United Kingdom and Colonies as is mentioned in subsection (1)(a) or (b);

but in subsection (1)(a) and (b) above references to registration as a citizen of the United Kingdom and Colonies shall not, in the case of a woman, include registration after the passing of this Act under or by virtue of section 6(2) (wives) of the British

Nationality Act 1948 unless she is so registered by virtue of her marriage to a citizen of the United Kingdom and Colonies before the passing of this Act.

(3) In relation to the parent of a child born after the parent's death, references in subsection (1) above to the time of the child's birth shall be replaced by references to the time of the parent's death; and for purposes of that subsection-

(a) "parent" includes the mother of an illegitimate child; and

(b) references to birth in the United Kingdom shall include birth on a ship or aircraft registered in the United Kingdom, or on an unregistered ship or aircraft of the Government of the United. Kingdom, and similarly with references to birth in any of the Islands; and

(c) references to citizenship of the United Kingdom and Colonies shall, in relation to a time before the year 1949, be construed as references to British nationality and, in relation to British nationality and to a time before the 31st March 1922, "the United Kingdom" shall mean Great Britain and Ireland; and

(d) subject to section 8(5) below, references to a person being settled in the United Kingdom and Islands are references to his being ordinarily resident there without being subject under the immigration laws to any restriction on the period for which he may remain.

(4) In subsection (1) above, any reference to registration in the United Kingdom shall extend also to registration under arrangements made by virtue of section 8(2) of the British Nationality Act 1948 (registration in independent Commonwealth country by United Kingdom High Commissioner), but, in the case of a registration by virtue of section 7 (children) of that Act, only if the registration was effected before the passing of this Act.

(5) The law with respect to registration as a citizen of the United Kingdom and Colonies shall be modified as provided by Schedule to this Act.

(6) In the following provisions of this Act the word "patrial" is used of persons having the right of abode in the United Kingdom.

Index